Charles MacCarthy Collins

Celtic Irish Songs And Song-Writers

A Selection -With an Introduction And Memoirs

Charles MacCarthy Collins

Celtic Irish Songs And Song-Writers
A Selection -With an Introduction And Memoirs

ISBN/EAN: 9783744725446

Printed in Europe, USA, Canada, Australia, Japan

Cover: Foto ©Thomas Meinert / pixelio.de

More available books at **www.hansebooks.com**

CELTIC IRISH

SONGS AND SONG-WRITERS.

A Selection.

WITH AN

INTRODUCTION AND MEMOIRS.

BY

CHARLES MACCARTHY COLLINS, M.R.I.A.
BARRISTER-AT-LAW.

LONDON: JAMES CORNISH & SONS.
DUBLIN: COMBRIDGE & CO., 18, GRAFTON STREET.
1885.

PREFACE.

THE native Irish song-writers of the period embraced in this volume have left compositions having an interest to their countrymen, beyond that evoked by their peculiar and undoubted merit.

The following is a selection from their writings, and is confined to authors of undoubted Celtic descent.

Biographical notices, necessarily brief and condensed, of the principal writers from whom selections have been made are included in the volume. The arrangement of the songs into Love Songs, Convivial Songs, and Patriotic Songs, will be found advantageous to the reader.

The collection contains songs of various degrees of merit, but, while the majority are fairly worth reproducing, some specimens not altogether of the highest order are included. The names of a few of the authors have not an Irish sound, but I have assured myself that these are but Anglicised forms of Celtic cognomens.

I have included no living author in this present series.

I hope to publish a further series treating of the Anglo-Irish song-writers, such as Goldsmith, Davis, Lover, Léfanu, Ferguson, etc.

To those who have generously given me permission to publish copyright selections I tender my most sincere thanks; to Messrs. J. Duffy and Sons, for the poems of J. Clarence Mangan; to Messrs. Cameron and Ferguson, for J. Keegan Casey's ballads; to Messrs. Chappell, for the poems of the Hon. Mrs. Norton; and to Mr. Aubrey de Vere for his translations.

If I have unwittingly appropriated any copyright poems without permission, I hope it may be attributed to ignorance of the claim of the owners, and forgiven.

With great pleasure I acknowledge my gratitude to the late Mr. A. M. Sullivan, and to Mr. T. D. Sullivan, M.P., for their courteous kindness in so readily supplying information on several matters.

C. M. C.

CONTENTS.

PAGE

THE IRISH BARDS AND SONG-WRITERS:
  The Celtic Irish Song-writers, 1600-1870 . . . 1
BIOGRAPHICAL AND CRITICAL:
  Keating 27
  Macward 30
  O'Dugan 31
  Duffet 32
  O'Naghten 33
  Carolan 34
  Concanen 41
  MacDonnell 43
  Cunningham 45
  Kane O'Hara 47
  Magrath 48
  Dermody 50
  Lysaght 56
  Sheridan 59
  Milliken 68
  Curran 69
  Callanan 75
  Kenney 77
  Moore 78
  Griffin 84
  Mangan 87
  'Father Prout' 91
  Banim 94
  Keegan 96
  Fraser 96
  Walsh 97

CONTENTS.

BIOGRAPHICAL AND CRITICAL—*continued:*

	PAGE
Lady Dufferin	100
Mrs. Norton	101
M'Gee	103
Williams	106
Casey	108

DRINKING SONGS:

O'Rourke's Feast	110
Song in Praise of Drinking	113
My Grand Recreation	114
Maggy Laidir	115
Liquor of Life	117
October Ale	119
Newcastle Beer	120
Push about the Jorum	123
Love *versus* the Bottle	123
Here's to the Maiden	124
Let's drink like Honest Men	125
'Let us be merry before we go'	125
The Monks of the Screw	126
The Wine-bibber's Glory	127
'I filled to Thee'	129
Send round the Bowl	130
Come, send round the Wine	131
One Bumper at Parting	131
Fill the Bumper Fair	133
Oh! the days when I was Young	134

PATRIOTIC SONGS:

The Sorrows of Innisfail	136
Keating to his Letter	138
Ode written on leaving Ireland	139
Lament (for the Tyronian and Tyrconnellian Princes buried at Rome)	141
Claragh's Lament	148
Old Erin in the Sea	150
Claragh's Dream	154
The Coming of Prince Charlie	157
Our Island	158
To Henry Grattan	160
The Green little Shamrock of Ireland	161
Cushla Ma Chree	162
The Irishman	163
Song of an Exile	164
John O'Dwyer of the Glen	166

CONTENTS.

PATRIOTIC SONGS—*continued*:

	PAGE
On Cleada's Hill the Moon is bright	168
Dark Rosaleen	170
Duhallow	173
Cáhal Mór of the Wine-red Hand	175
Lament for Banba	177
The Brightest of the Bright	179
The Fair Hills of Eire, O!	180
O Eire, my Soul, what a Woe is thine!	182
A Welcome for 'King' Charles	184
Mayo	185
Soul and Country	186
The Poet's Prophecy	188
The Poet's Grief	189
Gougane Barra	191
The Virgin Mary's Bank	192
O say, my Brown Drimin!	194
Lament for Ireland	195
Adare	197
Orange and Green	198
O Bay of Dublin!	200
The Bells of Shandon	201
Dirge of Rory O'More	203
Am I remembered in Erin?	204
The Death of O'Carolan	205
Adieu to Innisfail	206
Erin! the Tear and the Smile in thine Eyes	208
The Harp that once through Tara's Halls	208
Rich and Rare were the Gems she wore	209
The Meeting of the Waters	209
Let Erin remember the Days of Old	210
Oh, the Shamrock!	211
The Minstrel Boy	212
Oh for the Swords of Former Time!	213
The Boyne's Ill-fated River	214
The Prayer of Eman Oge	215
The Heart's Resting-place	215
Orange and Green	216
The Homeward Bound	221
Feagh M'Hugh	222
The Exile's Devotion	224
Ben-Heder (the Hill of Howth)	225
St. Kevin and Kathleen	227

CONTENTS

LOVE-SONGS AND SONGS OF THE AFFECTIONS:

	PAGE
The Coolin	231
Since Cœlia's my Foe	232
Come all you Pale Lovers	233
Peggy Browne	234
Gentle Brideen	235
Bridget Cruise	236
Carolan on his Wife's Death	237
A Song for Mabel Kelly	239
How to manage a Man	241
I hate a Long Courtship	242
Cupid's Revenge	242
'I'd wed if I were not too Young'	245
A Love Pastoral	246
Friendship	247
Love and Gold	248
The Sylph Lover	248
On Songs	249
When I sat by my Fair	250
The Linnet	251
My Burial-place	252
Kate of Garnavilla	253
The Sprig of Shillelah	254
Kitty of Coleraine	255
By Cœlia's Arbour	255
Had I a Heart for Falsehood framed	256
If I had thought Thou could'st have died	256
Mary Maguire	258
Oh, Mary Dear!	259
Sleep, my Child! (Cusheen Loo!)	260
Think no more on Me	261
Why are you wandering here?	262
The Green Leaves all turn Yellow	263
I was the Boy for bewitching them	263
My Life is like the Summer Rose	265
Gille ma Chree	266
I love my Love in the Morning	268
The Tie is broke, my Irish Girl	269
My Mary of the Curling Hair	270
The Blind Piper	272
The Dying Mother's Lament	275
The Holly and Ivy Girl	276
Brideen Ban mo Store	278
Over the Hills and Far Away	279

CONTENTS.

LOVE-SONGS AND SONGS OF THE AFFECTIONS—*continued:*

	PAGE
My Cluster of Nuts (Mo Craoibhin Cno)	280
The Irish Emigrant	281
Terence's Farewell	283
My own Darling Katey	284
The Blind Man to his Bride	286
My Irish Wife	287
If Will had Wings, how fast I'd flee	288
The Man of the North Countrie	289
None remember Thee, save Me!	290
Song of the Peasant Wife	291
The Dying Girl	292
Kathleen	294
The Sister of Charity	296
My Colleen Rue	298
Donal Kenny	299
Mary Donn Asthore	301
The Wreath you wove	302
Woman	302
Oh, still remember Me	303
Constancy	304
Inconstancy	305
Lesbia *versus* Nora	306
The Time I've lost in Wooing	307
Love	308
An Elysium on Earth	309
The Flower of all Maidens	310
White's Daughter of the Dell	312
My Connor	313
The 'Dark Girl' by the 'Holy Well'	314
The Last Reproach	316
Ellen Bawn	318
Love Ballad	319
Give Isaac the Nymph who no Beauty can boast	322
Oh, had my Love ne'er smiled on Me!	323
Thou can'st not boast of Fortune's Store	323
Air	324
Dry be that Tear	325
Soggarth Aroon	325
The Reconciliation	327
Ailleen	328

IRISH SONGS AND SONG-WRITERS.

THE IRISH BARDS AND SONG-WRITERS.

THAT Ireland possessed a literature of its own in very remote ages, and that in it poetry, as then understood, occupied a foremost place, are facts which have been abundantly proved. Hardiman, Walker, and Miss Brooke —names well known in connection with the literature of the early poetry of the nation—have done much by researches and translations towards enabling us to form an estimate of these ancient singers, and to encourage us to believe that, in spite of the hyperbole and weary iteration and commonplace which mark many of their effusions, they were somewhat more and better than mere rhapsodists and extemporisers. Hardiman gives examples of compositions of a date about 1000 B.C.—compositions which he can praise. Yet, however much at fault the chronology may be, and however ordinary the compositions may be, there is satisfactory evidence that in most ancient times the chief bards of the nation, called *Ollamhs*, held a position inferior only to the king. Walker's book on the subject points out that, in compliance with a law that each class should distinguish itself by a certain number of coloured stripes on their garments, these *Ollamhs* wore the greatest, next after the regal, number; and that this law is supposed to be anterior to the time of the Druids, a race by the way now being debated out of any real existence. The person of an *Ollamh* was sacred—more sacred even than royalty; for kings were killed and plotted against, but the *Ollamhs* lived unmolested, feared, and worshipped.

At some subsequent period of Irish history, the bardic functions were divided and distributed amongst four classes: the chief bards (*Fileas*); the law-makers and law-givers (*Brehons*); the historians and genealogists (*Seanachies*); and the instrumental musicians (*Orfidigh*). The duties of the chief bard were honourable, and his recompense was substantial. Each king or chief had a principal poet, and a score or so of inferior poets. The chief poet was the confidant and trusty counsellor of his prince; he cheered his master's drinking hours with feast-songs, he soothed his repose with love-stories, he animated him and his warriors on the field of battle with his war-songs: 'marching,' remarks Walker, 'at the head of the army, arrayed in white flowing robes, harps glittering (*sic*) in their hands, and their persons surrounded with instrumental musicians.' The rewards for these distinguished and imposing services were grants of castles and lands—of which Mr. Joyce finds evidence in the present names of places,—gifts of valuable personal adornment, and the highest consideration and intimate friendship of royalty. The illustrious monarch Ollamh Fodhla—the King Alfred of Irish history—who instituted the Great National Convention, founded, it is said, seminaries for poetry and learning at Tara, the historic hill whose very name is suggestive, being 'so-called from Tea-mur, the wall of music and melody.'

All of these Tara bards were doubtless great in their day, but are not now worth a serious thought; and we fear, notwithstanding Mr. Hardiman and Mr. Walker, that to the nineteenth century, the Irish bards and poets of the first are altogether an uninteresting race very much of the Windbag type. There are, of course, some strokes of nature—some simple sentiment—some heartfelt sorrows expressed here and there; but the chaff is in abundance, the wheat-grains occasional and sparse. Ossian or Oisin is said to have lived about 250—300 A.D., and though nothing authentic of his survives, MacPherson's forgeries are perhaps fairly illustrative of what Ossian may have written, and they may be reasonably regarded as representative of the best bardic work of the time. And what is Ossian as we have him? Grattan acknowledged that the Ossianic poems are calculated to inspire 'valour, wisdom, and virtue;' but the opinion was in response to a dedication of the Baron de Harold's composition of so-called Ossianic fragments. But one cannot to-day read MacPherson's Ossian—we never tried the Baron's—from cover to cover; tumid, stilted, bombastic,—insipidities and absurdities abound on every page, and the passages worth reading can be counted on the fingers of one hand. Miss Brooke discovered in an anonymous chant of this period (*circa* A.D. 300), a work of one Fergus, an 'Ode to Gaul, the Son of Morni,' and found it full of excellences; but even in Miss Brooke's stirring and sympathetic translation there is nothing remarkably brilliant. In another, by the same author, assumedly a 'War Ode to Osgur, the Son of Oisin,' she finds a sentence which elicits from her the following comment: 'It is impossible that the utmost stretch of human imagination and genius could start an image of greater sublimity than this'! This wonderful image which drove the talented translator into ecstasies is as follows:

> 'As the proud wave on whose broad back
> The storm its burden heaves,' etc.

And she further says, 'Had Fergus never given any further proof of his talents than what is exhibited in the ode now before us, this stanza alone would have been sufficient to have rendered his name immortal.' Immortality was cheaply earned in Miss Brooke's opinion. It is to be regretted that the general tone of comment by Irish exponents on Irish subjects is one of enthusiastic gush. Enthusiasm has done much for the world, and it is a quality always admirable and oftentimes appropriate. But the indiscriminate ecstasy that fondles and gushes over a subject, not because of its abstract worth or intrinsic merit, but because it is Irish and old— is a species of enthusiasm that tends to defeat the object it would advance. It invites hostile criticism, and is open wide to it. Walker even lets his enthusiasm run riot till one is not impressed or converted, but amused into a smile. For example, in reference to Carolan, he writes: 'The spot on which his cabin stood will be visited at a future day with as much true devotion by the lovers of natural music, as Stratford-on-Avon and Binfield are by the admirers of Shakespeare and Pope.' This is too extreme: it is altogether out of proportion to Carolan's place in song, high as it is, or to his merits, great as they are, to compare him to Shakespeare and Pope. If Walker's or Miss Brooke's judgment is so extravagant on these points, critics will say that it is not to be relied on at all—they will be esteemed as blind guides whom it were a vanity to follow.

In the translations accessible to us of sundry Odes and Laments, attributed, with sufficient evidence, to the fifth, sixth, and seventh centuries, there is sometimes something to be admired, though very little worth remembering. The scope and standard of the bards' abilities continued almost unvaried—perhaps indeed they deteriorated—until the Danish incursions, and the consequent ravages, burnings, and slaughterings ruined the peaceful pursuit of the 'arts of peace,' and poetry languished and poets fell from their high estate. About the time of the English invasion, there seem to have been three or four notable poets; but after that, the profession was apparently entirely neglected. Giraldus Cambrensis discovered no poets, but even his hostile soul admired the native Irish music. 'The skill of the Irish in music,' he wrote, 'is incomparably superior to that of any other nation. For their modulations are not slow and morose, as in the instruments of Britain, to which we are habituated; but the sounds are rapid and precipitate, yet sweet and pleasing .... Such agreeable swiftness, such unequal parity, such discordant concord .... so delicately pleasing, so softly soothing, that it is manifest the perfection of their art lies in concealing art.' From this almost unwilling testimony we may assume that if the spirit and art of Poetry were moribund, those of Music were in full vitality and vigour. The minstrelsy did not then—nor for centuries later—lapse into desuetude. '*Musica peritissime*,' says Higden of it in the thirteenth century. Bacon heard the Irish harp and praised it: its music was 'melting' to him. Evelyn said it was superior 'to whatever speaks with strings.' Fuller, in his 'Holy War,' has a kindly word to say of it.

It was but natural that this minstrelsy and consummate playing on the harp should resuscitate the art of Poetry. Music and Poetry are mutual handmaidens—and so, after a blank lapse of a couple of centuries, we find bards and bardism reviving. The O'Dalys are the most conspicuous of the race; one Donough More O'Daly, Abbot of Boyle about 1230, was called the Irish Ovid. His brother, Carrol O'Daly, was, it is asserted, the author of the music and words of the beautiful and unsurpassed melody, 'Eileen-a-roon.' The history of this composition is a romance in itself; the lyric is of the tenderest, and the melody so affected Handel that he said he would rather have created that simple air than be the author of the most elaborate composition he had published. Carrol O'Daly deserves immortality far better than Miss Brooke's friend, the ancient Fergus.

It was, however, but a brief revival of bardism. The perpetual internecine struggles extinguished again the poetic spirit. The bards also had used their position to stir up strife and encourage feuds and factions: they became political agitators under the guise of musicians. They were proscribed; and by the statute of Kilkenny (Edward III.) it was made penal to shelter one of them. They—such as they were—led a fugitive life, and sunk to a very low level: became village satirists or perambulating versifiers; lost their natural power and place—the very poetry was harassed out of them. Edmund Spenser, in his 'View of the State of Ireland,' advocated their abolition. He had, it is true, 'caused divers of their poems to be translated unto me, and surely they savoured of sweet wit and good invention . . . .

sprinkled with some pretty flowers of their natural device which gave grace and comeliness unto them.' But, notwithstanding, he found that they 'seldom choose the sayings and doings of good men for the argument of their poems; but whomsoever they found lawless in life, most dangerous and desperate in his disobedience, him they set up and glorify, and make an example to the young men to follow.' Hence, argued the gentle Spenser, it were expedient the race of bards should be exterminated.

The race, however, though proscribed, lingered on, and were represented by men of varying ability in each succeeding century. Some translations from the songs of the better-known of these in later times are given herein, but, with few conspicuous exceptions, there is nothing very brilliant or remarkable in the poems, odes, and songs of the transition period—that is, the period when the English language was superseding the native. The old system of hereditary bardship was maintained down to the Elizabethan wars—a system which, though sanctioned and hallowed by antiquity, was, from a poetic point of view, open to the objection that the divine afflatus is not hereditary, and that a very eloquent bard and poet might be the ancestor of a race of most unpoetic and altogether worthless bards. The bardic productions of this long transition period run in one trite groove: denunciation of invaders and settlers—Cromwell and his men—and attachment to the Young Pretender and hope of his restoration. In fact, the songs of this time are political in a great measure, and with political minstrelsy the ancient race of hereditary bards in Ireland happily became extinct. And a new and better style of composition—more true to nature, more simple, more homely—is to be found in the humble poets who, amongst a nation of voiceless singers, found voice for the hopes, and joys, and loves that lay round their hearts. The spirit and tone of the songs of these later writers are peculiar to Ireland, and are characteristic of the race. Before, however, we endeavour to explain the peculiarities of this branch of Irish literature, and briefly consider the condition of Irish poetry at this period, we shall inquire what the bards have done for Irish literature.

To the bards, no matter how poorly we esteem them now, the credit is due of having nurtured and perpetuated the poetic instincts of the Irish race. For nearly a thousand years they were a power in the land second only to the kings and chiefs. They elevated their patron chiefs into heroes; invented for them elaborate genealogies to show a descent from royal and remote ancestors; manufactured history and magnified tradition; and preached a standard of excellence toward which all should strive. They composed and sung their martial songs to incite the warriors to battle, and to assure them of immortal renown when they 'fell fighting fearful odds, for the ashes of their fathers and the temples of their gods.' They made heroes of men and gods of heroes. The eulogiums on kings and heroes were, in Ireland as in ancient Greece, cast into a verse shape by the bards—as were the laws of the country and the actions of the great men. These versifying records or monodies or historical cadences were recited or sung, and though they were very unpoetic, they satisfied the ear of a people who, dwelling in a pastoral country, had not only the leisure to learn and to sing, but also an artless and frank spirit fitted to admire heroes, and a nature suited for the appreciation of the simple dignity of the warlike odes chanted to them. The war-songs and all the compositions are rather ordinary, judging by a nineteenth-century standard; but they were designed for no more than to animate the vulgar, and were only of an ephemeral character. They were composed for a sympathetic audience with whom military ardour, glory and fame were summits of ambition, and as such they served their aim; but as poems, the writers of them never shook themselves free of exaggeration or emancipated themselves from myth. Magnified exploits of mythical ancestors were considered by the bards as creating the noblest emulation to heroism and bravery. But however stirring they may have been as incentives to uphold the renown of ancient intrepid heroism, they are so abundant in trivialities and absurdities as to be tiresome to the last degree.

But though the bards perpetuated the poetic instincts of the nation, and kept alive and intensified the fervour of national feeling which still is strong in the Celtic character, it cannot be said that they or their works have had any effect whatsoever on the later poetic literature of the country. Indeed, notwithstanding Hardiman and Walker and Miss Brooke, it is a small loss, and one little to be regretted, that the majority of their 'poems' have gone irrevocably and irretrievably down the stream of Time into the great ocean of Oblivion. The so-called historical poems of which they were the fathers, were no more than metrical records, which to judge from the remains were mere prose of a very ordinary, not to say bald, character. This seems somewhat anomalous in a nation that had earned a reputation for an epigrammatic style and that was early renowned for its poetic powers, and in a race to which so unfriendly a critic as Mommsen allows a most decided talent for poetry. Yet, though the annals of the country are full of events which could have supplied all the elements for historical epics, full of dramatic action, of love and war, of feasting and mourning, of fidelity and treachery, of moving incidents of all descriptions, still the bardic literature is singularly deficient in this respect. Later song-writers have indeed caught the spirit of some of the early historical incidents; but whether it is because of the want of the power of sustained effort, or from some other cause, these events are subjects for songs only—are condensed into a few verses, whereas they are large and wide enough for an epic or a drama. In regard to immortalising the salient episodes of the history of the land, a Maclise has served us better even than a Moore.

The bards and their works are altogether disappointing, and they possess no human interest to any of this generation, except antiquaries and the like—not even to the most patriotic. Place the work of the best of the early bards in comparison with such early poetry as that of the entire book of Job, and see how insignificant and jejune the literary remains of these royally-honoured poets are. They themselves, high as their estate was and great the honours paid to them, were unable to maintain a pre-eminence and dignity which were primarily based on their poetic powers. They became degraded and even hateful occasionally. Old Keating in his wonderful 'History of Ireland' says once of them, while yet they were an institution: 'These professors were become very chargeable to the inhabitants, and being of a covetous disposition were a grievance insupportable to the people; and upon account of the privileges and immunities enjoyed by these versifiers from the indulgence of former kings, a third part of the whole kingdom passed under the notion of poets, and professed themselves regular members of that society: for it was a plausible cover to idleness and ease, it being ordained by law that they should be supported by other men's labours, and billeted upon the people throughout the island from All Hallowtide till May.' It was worth one's while to be a poet in Ireland in those days. On the whole, then, it is perhaps best that the works of these 'professors' are to a large extent lost, and themselves forgotten. What of theirs we have, does not make us desirous for more. The copious, bold, and expressive language of old Ireland was admirably adapted for poetry—was even in itself a poetry—and it was used for inflated nothings, and not for undying words. The country's literature owes little to the bards, and to them the song-writers owe nothing whatsoever.

Bardism proper—that is, when the bard held his office by hereditary right, and was of the chief's household—in its decline produced a poor literature. It had lost its eloquence, its fire was quenched; there was little of heroism in it—it had reached a very low estate. As an illustration of the latest bardic effusions, and as an argument for our confining ourselves to the songs and song-writers, to the exclusion of the bards, we will give a specimen of the poetry of Bard Teige MacDaire MacBrody, one who was in his day (*circa* 1570—1640) an eminent person in his profession. He was chief bard to Donough O'Brien, fourth Earl of Thomond, from whom, after the ancient custom, he held as his appanage the castle and lands of Dunogan in Clare. To him is due the 'Contention of the Bards,' which is a series of so-called poems, the sequel of a debate between him and

Bard O'Clery, on a subject of vital interest then, we suppose, but of none now, except to the archæologian and historian. He—determined to elevate the house of O'Brien, whom he served, above the tribes descended from the great Niall of the Nine Hostages, to wit, the O'Neills, O'Donnells, etc.—'attacked the works of Torna Eigeas, the last of the *heathen* bards.' The method of vindication may seem to us peculiar, but O'Clery, the hereditary bard of the disparaged septs, took up the battle on behalf of Torna. MacDaire replied and O'Clery rejoined; and soon, in genuine Irish fashion, the fray became general, and almost all the bards within the four seas of Ireland got into the poetic scrimmage. The contest ran to seed—wore itself out, leaving no conclusion or judgment on Torna to solve the anxious perplexity of future ages. We may mention that MacDaire perished, in his old age, rather ingloriously for an hereditary bard who had been counsellor to the kingly O'Brien. He was flung over a precipice during the Cromwellian wars by one who, with brutal and unpoetic malice, accompanied the murderous act with a cruel taunt, 'Go say your verses now, my little man;' a sad fate truly. In his capacity as Laureate to Thomond he was in duty bound to greet his chieftain upon election with a bardic poem—that is, one full of the praise and glory of the chief's ancestors, and with some advice, half didactic and half flattering, to rule so as to maintain that glory undimmed and undiminished. From one of these odes the following lines are selected as a sample of the poetry of the latest hereditary bards, the remnants of an institution that had flourished with various degrees of pride and honour for its thousand years. Having pointed out the responsibilities of kingship and the power of a king for good and ill (though

Thomond was not a king); having inculcated pious exercises and daily prayers 'to Him whom glory veils above the skies;' having assured O'Brien that from God alone redress for anxious cares was to be sought; having animadverted on the immorality and scandal of corrupt and unjust judgments, and the advantage and honour of 'pious decisions;' having given instruction (hardly needed) on the chief's bearing and conduct in war, MacDaire MacBrody goes on to say :

> 'Though numerous precepts still I could unfold
> For thy sure guidance, yet will I withhold,
> Reserved my further counsel—for imprest
> Be this just maxim deep upon thy breast,
> *Instruction briefly given is the best.*
> I will not, till my footsteps you pursue,
> Praise thy fair limbs, or frame of fulgent hue ;
> Nor round, strong knee, and limbs well formed and fair ;
> Nor tapering active foot, alert as air ;
> Nor liberal soul, majestic, great and good,
> Prompt, fearless, brave, impetuous as the flood,
> Undaunted, firm, with native valour fired,
> For prowess, might, and steadiness admired ;
> Facetious—mild as zephyr's gentle flow—
> Nor ever furious but against the foe.
> Yet will I praise—nor will my voice alone
> Be raised to celebrate thy great renown.
> If thou fulfil the purport of my lays
> From lettered source derived of wisdom's ways,
> The glorious sun shall spread thy praises round,
> And feathered songsters warble the sweet sound ;
> Each element beneath high heaven's expanse,
> Earth, water, air, will in full choir advance
> To sing in strain sublime that ne'er will die,
> Thy beaming sprightly animated eye.'

This must have been a peculiar eye indeed that required the sun, and the birds, with earth, water, and air, in full chorus, to sing it. He goes on :

> 'The hum of bees will murmur o'er the woods,
> And sportive trouts will wanton through the floods ;
> And e'en the sea-calves their deep tones will raise
> At once with me, to celebrate thy praise.'

On the occasion of this ode it is to be presumed that the bard was in too solemn a frame to joke, but it is difficult to suppress a smile at his hope that the sea-calves will join him in a bass chorus in praise of his master and patron. MacDaire was in parts of this ode practical enough, and he is pious all throughout. But is it not sorry stuff? Is it not as unpoetic an ode as ever bard or no bard sung? Its wisdom is most heavy and commonplace—its tediousness is superlative and intolerable, though with ingenuous candour he confesses that 'Instruction briefly given is the best.' Could it be imagined that this style of thing could have stimulated an O'Brien or anyone else to the extent the fond bard hoped? There is much of this at hand in Irish bardic literature of those days. This is a mere instance, and is inserted here as a warning to latter-day readers to avoid the bards, and as an argument for leaving them buried in the centuries with their Odes and 'Contentions' heaped high and solid above them.

There are however, happily, interesting compositions in the records of the country's literature, but it is not to the hereditary bards we look for them. There are songs sprinkled over a period of about four hundred years which are not commonplace or tedious, maudlin or intolerable, and most of which are as fresh and full of interest to-day as when they were sung. The song-composers began to write in English between two and three centuries ago; but there are many written before this time in the native language, which have been translated during the present century; and of these songs, original and in translations, of dead Celtic Irish singers, the best lie between the years embraced in this volume, 1600—1870. It has been remarked that the tone and spirit of these songs are peculiar to Ireland, and are characteristic of the Celtic race; and it is worth a brief while to examine the peculiar and exceptional traits, and show what condition, poetically, Ireland was in at this period.

Though there have been some true poets of Irish descent and birth, there has not been one great one. There is not in the entire literature of the country a great epic like the 'Æneid' or the 'Divina Commedia,' a great tragedy like 'Hamlet' or 'Lear;' not even an ethic poem. The reasons for these facts are not difficult to determine. One of the characteristics of the Celt is an incapacity for sustained effort and continuous application—two elements essential to the production of a great work of either description. The conditions of existence in Ireland in the earlier years of what we may call its modern literature have been adverse to the fostering of those qualities which make for a great poet or great dramatist, even had the disposition of the race rendered it capable of striving and attaining to such eminences: legislative oppression and repression from abroad; perpetual crusades of spoliation and extermination; increasing and incurable turmoil, turbulence, and bloodshed; an education, if it did exist, of the most meagre, narrow, and restricted description, stunted by prohibitions and insane enactments—all contributed to the annihilation of a poetic spirit and the quenching of a poetic fire. Yet, under all these difficult conditions, the spirit survived though it languished, and the fire did not die though it paled. The Celtic nature, prone to that melancholy which is the true root of pure sentiment, found solace throughout in poetic outpourings of a pathetic patriotism. The nation cherished a love of their country for its natural beauty, for the kindly hospitality of its children, for the tenderness of its domestic relations, for its simple homely legends, for its ancient clannish fidelities, for its old sweet melodies, for its faith-full pious deeds. The melancholy spirit found food in the contemplation of its ruined abbeys and churches, consecrated by the pious memories of countless ages, yet transformed by the ravages of Time and the brutal profanity of war into dreary howling Golgothas. This love of country is a chief trait of Irish songs. Love itself—human love for the Kathleens and Brideens, the 'colleens' and 'Gal machrees,' frequently humorous, always tender and true—is the foremost characteristic, as it should be, amongst a people of whom Grattan said, 'Their genius is affection.' The jovial rollicking qualities of the race are displayed in drinking and feast songs; and then the Irish poetry, properly so-called, of the period we have chosen, is exhausted. No epics with a trace of the fire of Homer, of the grandeur of Dante, of the majesty of Milton, are to be found ; no descriptive poems like 'Childe Harold ;' no satires like the Dunciad. The Irish poets were song-writers, and were poets of the human passions. That all might appreciate they sung in songs that all could learn, to the old melodies that all could sing, and had sung from their childhood. Cynicism, satire, and sarcasm are almost entirely absent. These are complex arts, and the Irish song-writers had mastered only the elementary arts of simplicity and fidelity to nature. Thus the songs go straight to the heart, in a homely fashion, with a kindly tenderness.

Their stock subject was poor, oppressed Erin, so loveable, withal her robes of sorrow and mourning; to her they never forgot to manifest and declare their fidelity, as they do to her dark-eyed maidens and her brave sons. The love of country is not of the heroic and warlike, but of the pathetic and sentimental type; and therefore the songs are chiefly marked by a melancholy repining retrospectiveness, which hugs past glories and cherishes the renown and remembrance of past greatness and happiness. The future is not a subject for song so much as the past; and when the poet does project himself into the future, he but lights it up with a faint and faltering ray of hope. As Fate had brought Erin down from her high estate, and caused her to sit in the dust, discrowned amongst the nations, begirt in sackcloth, so in Fate was reposed the hope and trust of regeneration, and of a return to the bright happiness of the old legendary life. The independent energy and aggressive boldness essential to a patriotism of action had been crushed out of the Irish soul by harassing, cruel oppression, and the feelings that should have culminated in action found vent in dispiriting but sweet lamentations. Perhaps the 'melancholy ocean' was the *causa causans* of this sinking under oppression; but the people sunk, broken-spirited. There are no heroic songs with the warlike ring of arms to awaken, as in old days, the sons of the oppressed to deeds of prowess; and if there were, they would have been sung in vain. A Davis in later years, and no Celtic Irish poet, awoke the martial lyre from its long sleep.

The love of country is with the song-writers like a human endearment, an affection that is for ever casting 'longing, lingering looks behind' into the past days when their kings were conquerors, and Malachi wore the collar of gold that he won from the proud invader. The patriotism may be a poor patriotism, but from its very helplessness and fidelity it deserves more than mere esteem or praise. Patriotism was proscribed, but love was left to them; and so the rebellious hopings and dark complainings are woven round the name of a loved one. Thus we have the personification of Ireland under the name of a woman, and the inculcation of nationality under the guise of a love-song,—a frequent device of the song-writers. The singers *will* idealise and magnify the glory of the past, and ruminate and realise it in its exaggeration, and sit down in the dust and weep. The dark and doleful side is always upturned, as in hard truth it well may be. What Davis said of the music applies to the patriotic songs also—'they are too full of tears.' The regrets are admittedly futile, the longings admittedly vain; and although bitter, almost savage, hatred of the devastator Saxon is unforgotten, it still is impotent. It is but clanking the iron that has entered into the soul; it is but furious fuming against the irresistible and irremediable. There is no sharpening of spears and brightening of swords; no incitement to a grand tempest-rush to freedom or death. The anger is confined to lamentations and imprecations. The spirit may be willing, but the flesh is weak. Yet it is to be observed that there is no inculcation of treachery; no counselling to conspire in deceit. Broken and wounded, helpless and inert, they in their songs raged and sighed, dreamed dreams 'that did not wait for sleep.' The Celtic race, as far as Ireland was concerned, was now in hard reality 'one of the beaten nations of the earth.' This patriotism, such as it is, was and is the paramount sentiment in the Irish breast. It dominates over the religious sentiment. Thus it is with Emmet, Fitzgerald, Tone, Grattan, Smith O'Brien, Butt, Mr. Parnell, and others; though they belonged to an alien and hated creed, nevertheless the masses rose with almost one accord to flock to their standard, because upon it was inscribed, vaguely but comprehensively, the one word 'Ireland.' This word was at once a confession of doctrine and an appeal, to which even religion itself was subordinate. The people did not pause to consider who it was assumed the patriotic apostleship: the stripling or the veteran, the wise or wild, the novice or the adept, the Celt or the settler—of the old faith or the alien creed—it was immaterial. They were fain to follow anyone who, qualified or unqualified, proclaimed himself a leader, and stood forth with a project, practicable or impracticable, to clothe with some reality the intangible and cloudlike sentiment which was ever supreme within them. This sentimental fidelity is the ruling characteristic of the Celtic Irish.

The love-songs and songs of the affections were during this period what they ever were in Irish literature, full of simplicity, tenderness, and elegance, full of the true language of the true heart. Even in bardic times these were frequently of unusual excellence. The turgid bombast and preposterous exaggeration of the odes and war-songs were absent from the love-songs. Then, as in later times, these were marked by a peculiar, tender melancholy, a genuine pathos, a suppressed humour, that we seek in vain in the love-songs of other nations. In them virtue is extolled, as valour is extolled in the war-songs; the poets deal with the human passions which were their everyday observations; they wrote of true feelings which many should experience and all could comprehend; and their excellence lies in the fact that truth and nature were the well-springs of their muse. There is no striving after effect, no adherence to fashion-codes, no hypocrisies. There is no mawkish sentimentality. All is of the heart, hearty, and of the home, homely. They are the best portion of the country's literature. They are the charm of Irish poetry. They 'dwell in reality,' and thus, according to Mr. Carlyle, contain the essence of permanence. There is nothing foreign or impossible in them, nothing untrue to nature or humanity. The 'boys' are the same, and the 'colleens' the same in the nineteenth century as they were in the seventeenth. Those songs written a few centuries ago are as fresh and as real as those written to-day. They are full of goodness and beauty, are bright and abiding. The ineffable tenderness, the gentle reproachings, or the irresistible coaxings; the utter freedom from immodesty or indecorum; the familiar but respectful sentiment; the sympathetic melodies—these and the eternal qualities of truth and reality will preserve them to literature and humanity as long as the sun and moon endure.

The convivial songs differ from others of a similar description, in that though they are wholly in praise of the bowl, not for any sentimentality, but because it affords the very material delight of getting drunk, they are never coarse or indecent. If it be true that the songs of a people are the truest indication and surest test of the nature and disposition of the people, the songs of Ireland will demonstrate that the Irish were a convivial race, with hearts always susceptible to the tender passion, and minds ever full of a love of country and hatred of the invader. But the conviviality is never half-hearted—no sentiment of depression or disappointment can attach to the bottle. The festal songs are full of enjoyment of the present, and—undisturbed by care or thought of the morrow—they insist on joviality. Reckless, hilarious profusion is enforced—no stint, no half measures, no approach to temperance is tolerated. But the drink is indulged in, not for base motives, but because it is good, it makes friendship stronger and life altogether pleasanter; not for brutal gluttony, but because it exhilarates and cheers. Comical excuses for excess are ever ready, but the grosser motives and the consequences of over-indulgence are never dwelt on.

Though, therefore, from a political point of view the Celtic nations may have, in a critic's words, 'proved themselves useless,' from a poetical point of view the Irish branch of the race is by no means so. The qualities that endowed them with a poetic disposition, the extreme susceptibility, the impetuosity and fervour, the vividness of fancy and sympathetic imagination, rendered them incapable of being great poets, for these qualities were over-compensated by a want of perseverance, the incapacity to maintain a steady self-reliance, the unenduring nature of their impressions and resolutions, the lack of industry, the tendency to melancholy inaction. Thus we have sweet airs, but no oratorios; thrilling lyrics, but no epic; tender songs, but few dramas.

The assertion, therefore, that the Irish were at all times a poetic nation is but half true. They were poetical in that they possessed the deep poetic glow; that is to say, the mental ingredients that go to make a poet. But they possessed it mostly in silence, and sought not for the lesser glory of poetic fame. Poets, in the sense of creators or seers, they were not. In vain we seek distinctive periods with distinguishing characteristics in their poetic literature. The Celtic mind in its songs and poetry, as in most things, has ever been conservative. The poetry of to-day has the same features, the same methods of thought, is urged by the same influences that marked it in days gone by. It has also, at all events in later times, a fugitive, half-furtive tone about it. It has not by a new departure shaped or influenced the coming literature, however much it had an influence in maintaining the character and traits of the people. The poets and song-writers of the period we have chosen—which in another country and under other conditions would have been a Renaissance period—were, for the most part, obscure persons, of whom little is recorded and little known. Of many of them, of the place and time of birth, of the mode of life, of the manner and date of death—absolutely nothing is known of a certainty; much is conjectural, much apocryphal. The materials for the construction of their biographies are either non-existent or of the scantiest. The singers emerge from obscurity, sing their songs—one or more of which by chance, or because of real merit, are snatched from oblivion—and pass on into the eternities, unwept, unhonoured, and unsung. Many may have deserved immortality, but they never attained it; they may have followed after Fame, but they never, in their lifetime, overtook her. But with all these disadvantages, notwithstanding all the oppression and hunting-down of which they were the victims, though they themselves are wrapt in gloom and darkness, the songs shine out brightly. These heart-outpourings were a consolation and a solace to them and their little world in their affliction; and because of their artlessness and naturalness they have not lost their power to please the generations that come after them. They have none of the melodious lusciousness of a Swinburne, none of the etherialism of a Shelley, none of the dignity of a Tennyson, none of the majesty of a Byron, but they have a sweetness and tender eloquence, a coyness and a pathos, a pureness and unaffectedness, a light-hearted sentimentality, which are not found so constantly, or not found at all, in the songs of other peoples. The songs, whether of love, or patriotic, or convivial, come from the heart, appeal to the heart, and dwell in the heart; they are intensely human. It is because of these qualities, rather than because of literary merit, that they are ever fresh and that they deserve to be known, remembered and sung by the sons of the people for whom they first were sung.

The deficiency in literary merit is easily accounted for. Not only is it to be remembered that there were no facilities or means of literary education, but, even if there had been, the majority of these poets made their songs for their own time and their own people. The chief aim was to gain and maintain a contemporary popularity and fame, and not a fame amongst posterity. The preservation of many of their compositions is accidental, and due, not to the composer's industry and care, but to the care of friends and admirers and to tradition. The songs may remain, but, as we have said, the writers are mere shadows, nonentities to us. Their names are strange and unfamiliar; their lives are deep in the dark. They are obscurities on the whole, and on the whole they did not rise to a high literary level. Because of these circumstances, and because of the entire paucity of poets who might be esteemed as great poets, we find a Thomas Moore unduly magnified and belauded until he is made to seem as great as his poet-contemporaries. We also find that compilers and collectors of Irish literature claim as Irish writers numbers who have no title whatsoever to be so regarded. The exigencies of an editor perhaps compel him to this course; for Celtic-Irish literature cannot provide a very brilliant collection of writings, and therefore Anglo-Irish writers, and writers who were in no sense Irish or part Irish, are pressed into the service. Perhaps it is a pardonable vanity to claim such as Irish, and to make boast of them; it is hero-worship, though of a distorted and selfish description. Thus we find Swift and Sterne, Congreve and Farquhar, 'Cooper Hill Denham' and Steele, and a multitude of minor *literati*, set down in our collections of Irish authors. For this there is no other reason than that the mothers of these happened to be on Irish soil when they gave birth to them. These names may be surrendered with reluctance, but Ireland has no claim on them. Goldsmith, Davis, Lover, Lever, and numerous others, are not Celtic-Irish, but Anglo-Irish; and they and their songs will form a second series of this work. This volume deals only with song-writers of the Celtic-Irish race; for we are satisfied that their songs, be they forgotten or famous, are sufficiently interesting to be collected, sufficiently meritorious and characteristic to be read and studied, sufficiently gay and humorous to be remembered, and sufficiently melodious, pure, tender, and pathetic to touch the hearts and affections of all readers, even in this commercial and 'costermonger age.'

There are a few considerations to be noted in regard to those whose biographies are here briefly given. With the exception of the Sheridan family, all the Celtic-Irish song-writers are of immediately humble birth. We say 'immediately humble,' for possibly they were all descendants of ancestors who, in remote mythical ages, or even later, were kings, or chiefs, or hereditary bards. But in Irish poet-biographies there are no Surreys, or Buckhursts, or Byrons, or Swinburnes—no aristocratic writers, in fact. From the peasant class, or a social grade but one degree above it,

Irish song-writers are taken. Nor is this to be wondered at, when it is remembered that the Irish nobles and chiefs, before they were plundered, exiled, or exterminated, filled their days with sterner pursuits than the study and fosterage of polite literature. As long as bards were an institution, it was their office to make and recite poetry; and harpers were in permanent service to play and sing. The extinction of bardism was simultaneous with the extinction of the Irish aristocracy. There was not either a middle class in Ireland. After the Elizabethan settlement the native Irish were, on the whole, reduced to a condition of serfdom, were made 'hewers of wood and drawers of water;' in fact, the Irish nation became, between Elizabeth and Cromwell, a nation of peasants. Their own language was proscribed, and the conditions attached to learning the English language were intolerable to them. The wonder, therefore, is, not that these singers should have been peasants, but that there were any singers at all: and having sung, that they should have sung so well and truly. In the ancient days the bards were of the kin of princes, were rewarded with lands and castles, were circled with privileges, were regarded with a sacred awe. But in the later days those who made songs enjoyed no privileges, but struggled through countless difficulties, and emancipated themselves from disheartening drawbacks; they received no rewards, were humble and poor. Of the song-writers whose lives are briefly recorded in this volume, the majority were directly the sons of peasants, or a little better; which fact considering, and considering also the wretched means for a fugitive and, at best, elementary education which were alone accessible to them, the productions of these Irish song-writers are marvellous for their poetic power, their purity, and truth. The long neglect in which they have been held is a proof of the truth of Johnson's opinion—'Slow rises worth by poverty depressed.'

There is another consideration that will force itself upon any who take the trouble of perusing the biographies, such as they are, of these singers. That is, the uniform sadness, unhappiness, and wretchedness of the lives of almost all of them. We are oppressed with the feeling that the times were always out of joint with them. Most of them died young, after a life-struggle of penury and hardship, counting death, doubtless, as 'kind Nature's signal for retreat.' Many of them could not shake off the demon of intemperance. In disease and poverty, ill in mind and body, the majority of them existed; without honour in their own country; their talents unrecognised and unrewarded. There is not over the mortal remains of several of them even a stone to mark who rests beneath. Posthumous fame is no consolation to those who, in their life-time, struggled and hungered; but if they have left to their country songs that give pleasure, and that show them to have been something above the common herd, their country might preserve their names, make familiar their songs, and endeavour to bestow on them a little fame, faltering and feeble though it be.

THE CELTIC IRISH SONG-WRITERS,
1600—1870.
Biographical and Critical.

KEATING.

Geoffry Keating is in these days better remembered as an historian than as a poet, though, to do him justice, his poetry is somewhat more readable than his 'History of Ireland.' Both are patriotic; but whereas in the songs transcribed in this volume we discover the usual subjects, the usual tone of lamentation, the usual sorrowful love for the motherland—characteristics fully intelligible and appreciable—in the 'History of Ireland' each page is full of absurd traditions, impossible legends, preposterous chronologies, ridiculous genealogies, ludicrous miracles, extraordinary wars. 'An extravagantly mad performance,' it has been truly called. Even Keating himself was aware of the incredulity of some of his records, for he naïvely confesses that he inserts his narrative of the settlement of Ireland, *previous to the Flood*, 'not with any desire that it should be believed, but only for the sake of order and out of respect to some records that make mention of it.' The 'History' proves, nevertheless, that Keating was a person of exhaustless credulity in matters historical, or quasi-historical, relating to his native land. But in his poetry he is human and rational. His epitaph records that he was 'a poet, a prophet, and a priest,' from which it would appear that his fame as an historian was left for later ages to discover. Very little is known of his earlier years. It is generally accepted that he was born at Tybrud, or Tubbrid, near Clogheen, in the county Tipperary, sometime about 1570. In his youth he was sent to Spain, and, at the college of Salamanca, studied for the priesthood for twenty-three years. He was, on his return in 1610, appointed priest of his native parish of Tybrud. He was a man of varied attainments, and, as a divine, was distinguished for his fervent zeal, his blameless life, and his fervid eloquence. That he must have been benevolent, amiable, and tolerant, is made manifest by the recorded circumstance that the Protestants of the neighbourhood contributed towards the expenses of the building of his church; and that he was a fearless pastor is proven by the event that drove him into exile, a fugitive and a recluse. In discharge of his sacred functions he excommunicated, some say, others say he merely preached against, a lady, 'a gentleman's wife,' who was believed to be too familiar with the Lord-President of Munster. In all times, but especially in those times in Ireland, the recompence of such temerity as this act of excommunicating the favourite of the ruler of the province, was persecution, and thus Keating's life was endangered to such a degree, that, to avoid apprehension and punishment, he fled from his parish and hid himself in the glen of Aherlow, which lies between the town of Tipperary and the Galtee Mountains. There his 'History' was begun, and perhaps his poems and songs written; and there he remained till 1633, the year that Sir George Carew, the offended Lord-

President, had been recalled to England. He returned to Tybrud, and, with one Father Eugene Duhy as coadjutor, he there spent the remainder of his useful and laborious life. There he died, in 1644, and there, over the porch of the church that he built, and where he and Duhy ministered, in rather eccentric lettering, is the following inscription :

'Ora.te, proaebq. P. Eugenij : Duhy vic. de Tybrud : et D. Doct. Galf. keating huiq sacelli Funda-Toru : necno et-prooibq alijs Ta sacerd. Quam Laicis quoru corpa. in eod. jacet sa. Ao. Doni 1644.'

The foregoing inscription is thus plainly expressed :

'*Orate pro animabus Parochi Eugenii Duhy, Vicarii de Tubrud, et Divinitatis Doctoris Galfridii Keating, hujus Sacelli Fundatorum; necnon et pro omnibus aliis, tam Sacerdotibus quam Laicis, quorum Corpora in eodem jacent Sacello. Anno Domini* 1644.'

In English :

'Pray for the souls of the Priest Eugenius Duhy, Vicar of Tybrud, and of Jeoffry Keating, D.D., Founders of this chapel; and also for all others, both Priests and Laity, whose Bodies lie in the same chapel. In the year of our Lord 1644.'

> In one urn in Tybrud, hid from mortal eye,
> A poet, prophet, and a priest doth lie ;
> All these, and more than in one man could be,
> Concentred were in famous Jeoffry.'

In addition to his 'Thoughts on Innisfail,' which, as translated by Mr. Read, will be found, together with his 'Song to his Letter,' on a subsequent page, he wrote ' An Elegy on the Death of Lord Decies,' 'A Farewell to

Ireland' (an ode addressed to his harper), and a prose treatise called the 'Three Shafts of Death.'

MACWARD.

OF Owen MacWard, or Owen Roe MacBhaird, nothing is known beyond that he was the bard of the O'Donnells, and was the descendant of a long line of bards, attached from a remote period to that sept.* He fled with O'Donnell and O'Neil, the Earls of Tyrowen and Tyrconnell, from Ireland in 1607, and his chief poem is his 'Lament' for them, at their decease. They died and were buried in Rome, and the elegy was addressed to Nuala, the sister of O'Donnell of Tyrconnell. It is a poem entirely charged with the national spirit and sentiment of the time—a record of the great deeds of the noble princes, a wail of grief for poor Erin, a pathetic appeal to God to 'sustain us in these doleful days, and render light the chain that binds our fallen land.' We give the translation of this noble ode, by Mangan, and it will be readily conceded that it is a poem that merits the encomiums passed on it by modern critics. It is a mournful song of triumph, a proud, heroic elegy, soaked through and through with the languishment of a hopeless hope, an utter and incurable grief for the 'hapless fate' of Ireland. Entirely spirit-broken, there is no whisper of revenge, no anticipation of recovery. The only consolation he can offer to the bereaved Nuala is painfully hopeless:

> 'Thou daughter of O'Donnell! dry
> Thine overflowing eyes, and *turn*
> *Thy heart aside;*
> *For Adam's race is born to die,*
> *And sternly the sepulchral urn*
> *Mocks human pride.'*

---

* MacBhaird means the Son of the Bard, and has been Anglicised into MacWard and Ward.

This is no sentimentalism, no unreal woe, assumed for effect; it is the drops wrung from a crushed and broken heart, an utterly sad and hopeless grief. The power is sustained throughout—the power to grieve and the power to glorify. 'Ichabod' is the text—an appropriate one, when it is remembered that in the flight of Tyrconnell he was accompanied by nearly all who were noble and illustrious in Ireland, of Irish birth and descent. There are other poems extant in the native language, by Owen Ward, but none can approach in melancholy magnificence this 'Lament for Tyrowen and Tyrconnell.' When the poet died, or where, is unknown, is even unconjectured. His history is smothered up in gloom; but this one work, the elegiac wail, will preserve his name, illustrious as a faithful servant and a true poet.

O'DUGAN.

MAURICE O'DUGAN, or Dugan, is remembered because he wrote 'The Coolin,' setting the words to an air 'the finest in the whole circle of Irish music,' which, like almost all the Irish melodies, dates from such a remote period that the composer is unknown; and which is familiar to everyone in this nineteenth century. O'Dugan, it is asserted, upon what evidence we know not, was descended, like Ward, from a race of hereditary bards (there was a John O'Dugan, chief bard of The O'Kelly in Connaught, who wrote a topograpical poem, and died about 1370); but of himself and his other writings nothing is known except that they were and are not. He appears to have lived near historic Benburb, sometime about 1640, but where and whence he came, and when and whither he departed, are in the blackest darkness.

In this respect he is not worse than many of his fellows, than many greater than he. But his love-song, 'The Coolin,' has rescued his name from the gloom, and should preserve it.

DUFFET.

THOMAS DUFFET was a writer of burlesques and of songs. Of his half-dozen dramatic burlesques, it is acknowledged that they were favourably received and somewhat successful in his own day, though no one except readers of extinct literature know or care about them now. He burlesqued Dryden and Shadwell, and others of minor note—presumption which was attended with general denunciation. 'Mr. Duffet,' say his biographers, 'stood more indebted to the great names of those authors whose works *he attempted to burlesque and ridicule*, than to any merit of his own.' But the originals, like the burlesques, are little thought of now; and a Renaissance, when Dryden and Settle and Shadwell will as dramatists be too great and high to be burlesqued, has yet to dawn. Whatever his abilities and powers of ridicule may have been, his talent for song-writing will at all times be acknowledged. 'Come all you pale Lovers,' and 'Since Cœlia's my Foe,' are excellent in their way, and, like all he wrote, bear evidence of the influence of the English literature of the time, and are without the distinguishing spirit of Celtic poetry. Of his birth or death nothing is known. All that is recorded of him is that he was an Irishman who originally owned a milliner's shop in the New Exchange, London, and subsequently devoted his talents to literature. Possibly he was a Duffy in his native land, who in London Anglicised his name and forgot his country, as others have done. He is generally supposed to have lived about 1650—1700, but his biographers were so zealous to extinguish him for his daring in ridiculing the then literary gods, that they refused to honour him with a record of his birth or parentage.

O'NAGHTEN.

JOHN O'NAGHTEN, or O'Neachtan, holds, according to Hardiman in his 'Irish Minstrelsy,' 'the same rank in Irish literature that Young, the author of "Night Thoughts," occupies in English. With equal genius and learning the Irish bard's compositions are more equal (*sic*) and correct, and his style less diffuse, than those of the favoured English author.' Hardiman had more materials for forming a judgment than we have, for he had in his possession a copious treatise in Irish, by the bard, on geography, 'extending to nearly five hundred closely-written pages, and containing many interesting particulars;' and also O'Naghten's 'Collection of Curious Annals of Ireland, from A.D. 1167 to the beginning of the seventeenth century.' But from the remains of O'Naghten's works now accessible to the English reader—from his 'Maggy Laidir' and his 'Lament on Queen Mary' (D'Este), we think a more complimentary judgment might, without injustice, be passed on the poet. Of his 'Maggy Laidir,' Hardiman says:

'This inimitable description of an Irish feast was written in the seventeenth century by John O'Neachtan, and is now printed from a transcript made in the year 1706 . . . . In point of composition, "Maggy Laidir" is superior to "O'Rorke's Feast," so humorously translated by Dean Swift. Here the chairman only speaks throughout. His first toast is old Ireland, under the name of "Maggy Laidir"; then the beauteous daughters of Erin; the ancient families of the four provinces, Leinster, Munster, Ulster, and Connaught; the clergy who have been always dear to the Irish; and finally he wishes disappointment to the foes, and success to the friends of the country. After these libations he becomes a little gay, and must have music. He calls on the harpers to strike up. Finally a quarrel, *more* Thracian, ensues, which our elevated chairman, in the true Irish style of commanding peace, orders to be quelled by knocking down the combatants; and he concludes by alluding to his noble ancestry and kindred to enforce his claim to respect and obedience. The air, as well as the words of "Maggy Laidir," though long naturalised in North Britain, is Irish. . . . . The name signifies, in the original, strong or powerful Maggy, and by it was meant Ireland, also designated by our bards under the names of Granua Weale, Roisin Dubh, Sheelah na Guira, etc. By an easy change the adjective "laidir," strong, was converted into Lauder, the patronymic of a Scotch family, and the air was employed to celebrate a famous courtesan of Crail.'

As usual, of the personal history of the bard, next to nothing has been ascertained. He lived in the later part of the seventeenth century, and was a native of Meath. These two facts exhaust his biography. He was an industrious collector and compiler, and is supposed to have died young.

CAROLAN.

THE name of Turlough O'Carolan, 'the last of the Irish bards,' stands out pre-eminent in the annals of Irish song as that of a man the record of whose life is worth reading; as a composer whose music is fresh, vigorous, and appropriate to to-day; and as a songster whose love-poems and drinking-songs command as great a pleasure and satisfaction now as they did nearly two centuries ago, when, a blind itinerant harper, he roamed from place to place, delighting and enthralling the high and low, the rich and poor, with his own songs, sung to his own music, played by himself on his Irish harp. Pathetic and humorous, sad and facetious, melancholy and rollicking— a Celtic genius—he sang himself through a long life, enjoying the friendship, hospitality, and protection of the great; and drank himself out of it, having practised what he preached, and manifested, in word and deed, a faithful love for the native and national drink.

Carolan, though his father was a cottier and his mother the daughter of a peasant, was descended from an ancient family of Meath, in which county there is a place still called Carolan's Town, a partial evidence that the family was once of some importance—were at all events of a better class than peasantry. He was born, according to some biographers, at Nobber, in the county Westmeath; but the better opinion is that his birthplace was the village of Baile-nusah, since Anglicised to Newtown, in the same county. He was born about the year 1670, and, as a lad, attended the school at Cruisetown, in county Longford; when and where he formed the acquaintance of Miss Bridget Cruise, and fell in love with her after the manner of a boy. Bridget Cruise, and his love and remembrance of her, ran through his harp-strings all his life. When sixteen or eighteen years of age, he lost his sight through an attack of small-pox, and remained utterly blind. 'My eyes,' said he, on his affliction, 'are transplanted to my ears.' About the same time his father moved to Carrick-on-Shannon, and possibly entered into the service of the MacDermott Roe, because we find that Madame MacDermott, attracted by the lad's intelligence, undertook Turlough's education, procured his instruction in English as well as Irish, and had him taught the harp. The old music of his country set his genius in a flame, and 'suddenly, in his twenty-second year, he resolved to become a harper.' 'He became,' says Hardiman, 'a minstrel through accident, and continued it more through choice than necessity.' During his tutelage at Alderford, MacDermott Roe's residence, he developed into an accomplished harpist; his playing and singing were the pleasure of his patroness and the delight of her visitors; and when his sudden resolve to live the life of an itinerant bard was announced, Madame MacDermott provided him with horses for his journeyings and with a boy attendant to carry his harp. Equipped also with genius and reputation, he went forth after the fashion of his antetypes, on a round of visits to the neighbouring Irish gentry, to whom he was already known, and by whom he was already esteemed and appreciated. He did not play for hire; he was received as a friend and honoured as a welcome guest at the houses he visited in his itinerary; and, in return for the profuse hospitality of the time and country, he played his own music and sang his own songs of love and of drink, to those who were in sympathy with music, who knew what love and drink were—and enjoyed all three.

> ' 'Twas his in their mirth to entrance the throng,
> Or soothe the lone heart of sorrow,'

as an eminent rival brother bard sang of him.

In his peregrinations, either impelled by a pardonable vanity to return as a person of some fame and honour to the place where as a youth he moved an insignificant school-lad, or attracted by her upon whose beauty, while yet light dwelt in his eyes, he had looked lovingly, he journeyed to Cruisetown in Longford, and visited his child-love, Bridget Cruise. Judging by his poems, it must have been love rather than vanity that directed his steps thither. She, like himself, could sing to her harp-playing. In fervid song and earnest prose he spoke his love, but was rejected. To her he says now or subsequently:

> ' Look on those eyes whence sleep hath flown,'

and whence light had flown too. Poor eyes, punished by Providence, they might be spared punishment by her whose indifference drove sleep from them!

> 'My hopes, my thoughts, my destiny,
> All dwell, all rest, sweet girl, on thee.'

And again, with blessings on his lips for her, he says:

> 'Life is not life without thee.'

He wandered away, and then, in truth, gave his whole heart and soul to his minstrelsy. He did not die, however, and though Bridget Cruise was always a fond memory with him, he found solace for the bitterness of his disappointment in dying poetically for others. For one, Peggy Browne, said to be an ancestress of the Sligo family, he is in equal love-throes, his heart-misery is equally ruinous and intense.

> 'Oh, dark are my days doomed to be
> While my heart bleeds in silence and sorrow for thee;
> In the green spring of life to the grave I go down,
> Oh, shield me, and save me, my loved Peggy Browne!'

But Peggy was as obdurate to the amorous blind bard as Bridget; and yet he did not die—and other girls exercise as potent a charm over him. But he pours out his songs and his 'liquor of life,' and at length marries Mary Maguire, a well-descended lady whom he loves tenderly in spite of her wilfulness, haughtiness, and extravagance; gave up his wandering life for her; built a house at Mosshill, and became what is now described as a gentleman-farmer; lived gaily, and begot a numerous progeny; and, having spent all his possessions in lavish and promiscuous hospitality, thriftlessness, and extravagance, he lapsed into poverty, and took again to his harp and his wanderings. His wife remained at Mosshill with the offspring until her death in 1733; an event that cast him into a profound melancholy, which beset him during the few years he survived her. The Lament, or Elegy, which he composed upon her death is sorrowful and pathetic in the extreme—even in a translation, which cannot be made to convey the pathos and plaintiveness of the original Irish. His after-life proves the sincerity of his grief.

> 'Alone I'll wander, and alone endure,
>   Till death restore me to my dear one's side;
> And ceaseless anguish shall her loss deplore,
>   Till age and sorrow join me to the dead.'

He continued to roam from castle to castle, and having in 1738, five years after the death of his wife, visited Alderford, the home of his early patrons, he fell ill from excessive drinking and died there. He was buried amongst the MacDermotts, and his grave was in after years rifled, and his skull, which was carried away, found its way into the museum of Sir John Caldwell, of Castle Caldwell, in Fermanagh. His harp is now in the possession of The O'Conor Don—another, said also to have been his, is in the Royal Irish Academy—and the large chair, in which he was wont to sit at Alderford and play and sing and drink, still occupies its old position unremoved. He left six daughters and one son, who was subsequently a teacher of the harp in London.

There is a rough but sincere elegy on Carolan by one McCabe, a contemporary and friend, 'a wit but no poet.' Hearing that Carolan was at the MacDermott's, McCabe made haste to visit him, not having seen him for some years; and having arrived at Alderford, in passing through the churchyard, he accosted a peasant, and inquired after Carolan. The man replied by pointing to his grave. McCabe, shocked and overwhelmed, tottered to the mound and wept forth his sorrow. He wrote the following elegy, detailing the circumstances, a tribute sad and sincere to the old blind bard:

> 'I came, with friendship's face, to glad my heart,
> But sad and sorrowful my steps depart:
> In my friend's stead a spot of earth was shown,
> And on his grave my woe-struck eyes were thrown.
> No more to their distracted sight remained
> But the cold clay that all they loved contained;
> And there his last and narrow bed was made,
> And the drear tombstone for its covering laid.
> Alas! for this my aged heart is wrung,
> Grief chokes my voice, and trembles on my tongue;
> Lonely and desolate I mourn the dead,
> The friend with whom my every comfort fled!
> There is no anguish can with this compare;
> No pains, diseases, suffering, or despair,
> Like that I feel, while such a loss I mourn,
> My heart's companion from its fondness torn.
> Oh, insupportable, distracting grief!
> Woe, that through life can never hope relief!
> Sweet-singing harp—thy melody is o'er!
> Sweet friendship's voice—I hear thy sound no more!
> My bliss, my wealth of poetry is fled,
> And every joy, with him I loved, is dead.
> Alas! what wonder (while my heart drops blood
> Upon the woes that drain its vital flood)
> If maddening grief no longer can be borne,
> And frenzy fill the breast with anguish torn!'

A memorial tablet has been erected in St. Patrick's Cathedral, Dublin, to Carolan's memory, on which is the following inscription, underneath a bas-relief representing in marble the old man playing on his harp:

> 'BY THE DESIRE OF LADY MORGAN.
> TO THE MEMORY OF
> CAROLAN,
> The Last of the Irish Bards.
> Obiit A.D. MDCCXXXVIII.;
> Ætatis Suæ An. LXVIII.'

The scanty remnants of the life-work of Carolan, as a

poet and composer, which remain to us, extort a regret that so much, and possibly the best, of his songs and poems, and of his music, should be lost. His love-songs, born of a passion strong and sincere for the time, even if fleeting, and his monody on his wife's death, prove him to have been a true poet. His 'Ode to Whisky' will immortalise him as a humourist of the true Celtic type; while his musical compositions, of which a representative one is that to which the song 'Bumper Squire Jones' is written and sung, will convince that he was entitled to the praise bestowed on him *il genio vero della musica.*' Goldsmith, capable to estimate and appreciate, was unstinted in his praise; he says that of all the bards Ireland had produced, 'the last and the greatest was Carolan the blind. His songs in general may be compared to those of Pindar, as they have frequently the same flight of imagination.' The few examples of his genius which are extant are the survivals of over two hundred songs—all of which, except one, were written in his native language, and sung to his own minstrelsy. He himself, too, is more than a shadow on the page of Time; he is a reality, and there is something to record in a biographical notice. His lowly birth; his school; the patronage, interest, and encouragement of Madame MacDermott; his blindness; his harpings; his pious pilgrimage to Patrick's Purgatory; his marriage; his convivial and extravagant hospitality; his house and home; his bankruptcy; his dear Mary's death—are all facts that we grasp and realise in this genius's life. Through all appears a heart large with a love for the girls and the whisky, which could extrude all doleful patriotic repinings.

The two ruling passions of his life—the passion for

Music and the passion for Whisky — were, perhaps, at their strongest in his death. He was always a magnificent drinker. He composed his music with a bottle and cup at his elbow. He would drink 'whole pints of usquebaugh' at a sitting. Not long before his death his physician frighted him into sobriety; but the abstinence produced a melancholy, to relieve which he returned to the bottle. But his 'Liquor of Life' was a liquor of death to him. When on his deathbed, with a knowledge of the near approach of the end, he called for his harp, and crowned a life of song with a wild and touching 'Farewell to Music,' which, it is said, drew tears from the listeners. It is further narrated by Goldsmith that in his last moments he called for a bowl of usquebaugh, or whisky — essayed to drink and failed; but he kissed the bowl lovingly, saying, 'It is hard that two such good old friends should part without a kiss,' and fell back and expired. A death-scene thoroughly characteristic! A subject for a painting! Somehow, notwithstanding the drunkenness (which was the only fault of this genial genius), one must like the old man, and leave him with kindly feelings, with perhaps a tender regret. He was an Irishman of the traditional type, who for his age and country, and with his opportunities, deserves to be regarded as a star in Irish literature, and to be seated in no mean seat amongst the immortals.

CONCANEN.

OF Matthew Concanen's parentage, of the time or place of his birth, of his earlier years, absolutely nothing is known. It is conjectured that he was of the province of Connaught; and as he afterwards became Attorney-

General of Jamaica, it is apparent that he was educated for the law and called to the Bar. It is certain that he was an Irishman of Irish descent. The name means, we are told, 'the head of a hound'—a nickname which became a surname. He went to London early in life, and lived by political writings which appeared in the *London Journal*, the *British Journal*, and the *Speculatist;* he wrote against Pope and Pope's friend Bolingbroke not only in journalistic papers, but published a pamphlet, 'A Supplement to the Profound,' in which he vilified the poet, retailing all the malicious gossip concerning him, and imputing to him conduct most dishonourable and disgraceful.

For his latter adventures in literature he was installed in a niche in the 'Dunciad,' and 'damned to everlasting fame.' Amongst those who entered on the 'Dunciad' diving contest where the reward was to be obtained by him who 'the most in love of dirt excelled,' and 'who flings most filth and wide pollutes the stream,' Concanen, 'author of several dull and dead scurrilities,' had a prominent place and a fair chance of a prize :

> 'True to the bottom, see Concanen creep,
> A cold, long-winded native of the deep.'

His abilities as a political writer obtained for him, from the Duke of Newcastle, the Attorney-Generalship of Jamaica, whither he went in 1731 ; and for seventeen years he discharged the duties of the office with credit and integrity. Here he realised a large fortune, upon which it was his intention to live out his days in his native country. To this end he returned from Jamaica and arrived in London, *en route* to Ireland, in January, 1749, where after a few weeks' illness he died of consumption on the 22nd of January, 1749.

The immortality conferred on him by the 'Dunciad,' and by Warburton's letter upon him, would never have been his on account of his own political and dramatic writings. Some of his songs, however, have the elements of popularity in them, and deserve to be reprinted. His play of 'Wexford Wells' can still be read, and his ballad-opera 'The Jovial Crew,' adapted from Broome's play, enjoyed a considerable success in his day. When he was still a very young man, apparently, he wrote a large number of songs, of various degrees of merit, which were published in 1724, with poems by others, in a volume entitled 'Miscellaneous Poems by Several Hands.' He is humorous and satirical, witty and boisterous, with little pathos, and less grace. He is hardly Celtic in the quality of his attributes, but worse songs than his are unforgotten.

MACDONNELL.

HARDIMAN pronounces John MacDonnell, called Claragh, as a poet to be the equal of Pope—a verdict as unjust and derogatory to MacDonnell as it well could be. Pope was at best a cold-blooded philosopher, moralist, and satirist in verse; MacDonnell was full of the pathos and fancy and fire of impetuous poetic genius. In him all the distinguishing characteristics of the Celtic genius abound. He loves his 'Old Erin' with melancholy, passionate affection, because Fate has oppressed her, and she is beautiful. He says:

> ' The very waves that kiss the caves
>   Clap their huge hands in glee,
> That they should guard so fair a sward
>   As Erin by the sea.'

He was a Jacobite, not so much because the Pretender

claimed or deserved his homage, but rather because the Pretender and himself were objects of the relentless hate of the common persecutor: a common sorrow begot sympathy. Thus his lament for 'My Hero! my Cæsar! my Chevalier!' though it represents in rich hyperbole a whole nation's grief for the 'youth of their love,' the keynote of the lament is 'that he should be banished by a rightless foe.' In the Pretender there were some faint hopes of a possible freedom. He was against the rightless foe, and so were all the children of 'Old Erin by the sea.' With him they were ready to make common cause against the common oppressor; partly from an exaggerated idea of his prowess as a military leader and his personal lovableness, but chiefly because in him lay the sole hope of Erin's return to a state of happiness and content, such as she enjoyed ere her warlike sons betrayed her, when she knew not the yoke of the foreign tyrant. An ardent Jacobite, a bard inspiring a dispirited race in whom the down-trodden fire of rebellion was ever ready to blaze out, he was an object for exceptional suppression by the English, and had frequently to fly for his life, and roam amongst his native mountains.

He was born near Charleville, in the county Cork, in 1691, and he died in 1754, and was buried in the churchyard of Ballyslough, near where he was born. He was known as MacDonnell Claragh (because, according to some, this was the name of his ancestor's homestead, but rather from the broad cast of his features, for which peculiarity 'claragh' is the Irish expression), and he is, after Carolan, one of the most eminent names amongst the later Irish minstrels. He commenced a translation into Irish of Homer's 'Iliad,' but did not live to finish it; he amassed materials for a 'History of Ireland,' and began the work, but never completed it; he was 'a man of great erudition, and a profound Irish antiquarian.' He was most popular throughout Munster, and to this day is not forgotten there. He was the last, or one of the last, who maintained the ancient practice of holding Bardic Conventions. He sung more than patriotic wails and Jacobite laments. He looked back at what his country was in old days, and saw what she was in his day, and his heart took fire, and he cried out for the sword, and called on his countrymen to 'unite in valorous fight for the land that gave them birth.' But their spirit is cold, and they have not in their veins the blood of their fathers, who 'were men.' And so MacDonnell Claragh, with the language and fervour of a poet, and the soul of a warrior, would fain have made a stroke for Freedom with the 'soldier lad,' young James, with his depressed and degraded fellow-bondsmen, with anyone, under any conditions—but all in vain; and himself, hunted and oppressed, goes down to the grave with his works unfinished, his hopes unfulfilled.

CUNNINGHAM.

JOHN CUNNINGHAM is one of the many whom Fame has treated hardly, and rewarded niggardly. His epitaph records that 'his works will remain a monument for ages' —a prediction as yet unfulfilled, though his ballads, it is said, are even at present, after a lapse of more than a century, sung in the streets of Dublin, and his name is never heard as the author. A farce, written while he still was in his teens, gave Garrick matter for the 'Lying Valet;' but the 'Lying Valet' is remembered, and Cunningham and his 'Love in a Mist' are forgotten. A

Cowley in precocity, a Shenstone in style, he enjoyed a fair reputation during his brief lifetime, and had a more successful career, in all its vicissitudes, than many of his contemporaries.

Dr. Johnson praised him: 'Although Cunningham cannot be admitted to a very high rank among poets, he may be allowed to possess a considerable share of genius. His poems have peculiar sweetness and elegance; his sentiments are generally natural; his language simple, and appropriate to his subject.' This was said of his volume of 'Pastoral Poems,' in the composition of which he was a disciple and imitator of Shenstone. His 'Day: a Pastoral,' is in every respect excellent, and is one of the best poems of that description in the English language. But notwithstanding contemporary praise and appreciation, his name is to-day strange—almost unknown.

John Cunningham was the son of a Dublin wine merchant, and was born in that city in 1729. He wrote verses and ballads at twelve years of age which found refuge in 'Poets' Corners' in the newspapers, and eventually sunk to street-singers—presumably their fit destination. At seventeen he wrote 'Love in a Mist;' a farce which was not unsuccessful in Dublin. At twenty he was a strolling player, and made a name in the English provinces. At thirty-four he retired from the stage, settled in Newcastle-on-Tyne, wrote his 'Pastorals' and 'Poems;' and after a long and painful illness died in 1773. He rewarded the kindness of the Newcastle folk, with whom as a player he had been ever a favourite, by immortalising the beer manufactured in the town; and, although the versification betrays his nationality—rhyming 'placed' with 'feast,' and 'diseases' with 'raises'—his song, 'Newcastle Beer,' is, of its kind, a good drinking-song, full of jollity and humour, and without a touch of coarseness. The 'Holiday Gown; or, I'd Wed if I were not too Young,' is a song of surpassing excellence; and these two compositions alone entitle Cunningham to no mean place in Irish anthology.

KANE O'HARA.

KANE O'HARA is, in the biographical notices, said to have been a younger son of a gentleman whose children moved in the fashionable circles of Dublin, in the middle of the last century. So little, however is known of his parentage and early life that the date of his birth is variously assigned to any year between 1715 and 1733. That he died on the 17th June, 1782, is an ascertained fact, and that during his lifetime he enjoyed a great and deserved popularity, and earned a fame which lasted long after his death, are matters of history. He made his reputation by his burlesques—to which he exclusively devoted himself—and his knowledge of music, the vivacity of his style, the humour of his songs, situations and dialogues, insured in almost every instance an immediate success and popularity to his writings. His 'Tom Thumb' was produced at Covent Garden in 1780. It is based on Fielding's 'Tom Thumb,' of which work it is recorded of Dean Swift that he never laughed but twice in his life, once at a trick performed by a conjurer, and once at the scene where Tom Thumb kills the ghost. To have caused the great grim Dean to laugh is a superlative tribute to Fielding's mirth-moving qualities, and yet it is generally allowed that O'Hara's version excels Fielding's, in humour as in every other respect. His first burlesque, the well-known 'Midas,' is unquestionably almost, if not altogether, his best. It was meant to throw ridicule on the Italian operas, and was produced in the old Dublin Theatre in Crow Street in January, 1764; was reproduced in Covent Garden in the following month in a condensed form, and was repeated nine times during the season—no small distinction in those days. In 1773 'The Golden Pippin' was brought out, also at Covent Garden Theatre, and the success that attended its production was considerably enhanced by the acting and singing of Nan Catley. In 1775 the 'Two Misers' was performed; and in 1777, at the Haymarket Theatre, 'April Day' was produced.

Of Kane O'Hara's personal history some meagre particulars have been preserved. His conversation, as is the case with many witty and humorous writers, gave no indication of the wit and humour of his burlesques. Indeed, he is generally spoken of as dull and tiresome in the manner and style of his talk. He was a remarkably tall man—'cruel tall' in the words of a contemporary joke —'with the appearance of an old fop with spectacles and an antiquated wig.' He lived and probably died in Molesworth Street, Dublin, and it was through his influence and exertions the Musical Academy of Ireland, of which he became vice-president, was founded in 1758.

MAGRATH.

THE usual uncertainty and haziness envelops the life of Andrew Magrath, the last Irish poet who wrote in his native language. Hardiman in his 'Minstrelsy,' in language of doubtful eulogy, says: 'As a poet he not only excelled the mob of English gentlemen who wrote with ease, but also many of those whom Dr. Johnson has designated

English poets. His habits and writings closely resembled those of Prior. Like him, Magrath delighted in mean company. His life was irregular, negligent, and sensual. He has tried all styles from the grotesque to the solemn, and has not so failed in any as to incur derision or disgrace.'

He was a prolific writer of songs 'of a jovial, amatory, and political nature;' and in Munster, more especially in his own county of Limerick, he was known in his lifetime and is even still remembered, because of his wit and eccentricity, by an Irish nickname which means 'Mixture of Drollery,' or 'Merry-dealer.' He was a friend of contemporary poetasters. He was born in Limerick 'by the banks of the Maig' sometime about 1720—1725, and was alive in 1790; but he seems to have melted, mist-like, out of the world, for the time and circumstances of his death —beyond that it is traditionally said he died at the house of one O'Donnell, near Kilmallock, and to him bequeathed his voluminous and versatile manuscripts—are known no better than the time of his birth. He seems to have become a kind of schoolmaster occasionally, and to have been a drunkard and licentiate always. He was migratory in his habits, 'a roving blade' who lampooned and ridiculed those obnoxious to him with a free spirit, and had to rove further to escape the vengeance he invoked. He was a sot amongst sots, but always seems to have been esteemed as a personage even by the most degraded; and notwithstanding his mode of life he lived to a ripe old age, 'an eccentric genius, but true poet.' He was buried in Kilmallock churchyard, near which it is said he breathed his last; but we are informed there is no stone to mark his grave, and no inscription therefore to supply us with the dates of his birth and death.

DERMODY.

THOMAS DERMODY is one of the most remarkable figures in Irish literature. With a brilliant and extraordinary genius, and all the mental qualities to make a great and wonderful writer, he led a life of such utter depravity, and died so young and so miserable, that the mind alternates between feelings of loathing at the degraded tastes and bestial life, and of compassion on him for the splendid abilities and the many accomplishments wrecked and misapplied. Of him, Raymond, his biographer, wrote: 'His poetical powers may be said to have been intuitive, for some of his best pieces were composed before he had reached twelve years of age. His language was nervous, polished, and fluent. His wonderful classical knowledge, added to a memory uncommonly powerful and comprehensive, furnished him with allusions that were appropriate, combinations that were pleasing, and sentiments that were dignified. He had an inquisitive mind, but could never resist the temptations which offered to seduce him from his studies. No one ever wrote with greater facility; his mind was stored with such a fund of observation, such an accumulation of knowledge gathered from science and from nature, that his thoughts, when wanted, rushed upon him like a torrent, and he could compose with the rapidity with which another could transcribe. There is scarcely a style of composition in which he did not in some degree excel. The descriptive, the ludicrous, the didactic, the sublime, each, when occasion required, he treated with skill, with acute remark, imposing humour, profound reflection, and lofty magnificence.' And on the whole, this is not an exaggerated description of Dermody's character as a poet, though it may seem so. 'With sense to know the right and choose the wrong,' he dragged on a life in which mean beggary and dissipation alternated with literary work marked by much beauty, learning, humour, pathos and genius—and at the early age of twenty-seven, disgraced, dishonoured, but yet immortalised, he was buried in Lewisham graveyard.

In the entire record of literary genius we find no such character as Dermody. Some one has called him the Chatterton of Ireland—a comparison surely not to Chatterton's advantage. It can scarcely be credited—would have scarcely been credited by Mr. Shandy, who made researches into the history of precociousness, and quoted some peculiar examples thereof—that this Dermody was as an infant an accomplished wine-bibber, a deliberate drunkard. It is said he inherited this taste from his father, a schoolmaster in Ennis; but hereditary theories will not sufficiently explain the recorded fact that at the age of ten Dermody was a confirmed and seasoned whisky-drinker.

He was born in 1775 at Ennis, the son of a schoolmaster there, who afterwards moved to Galway; and we read that in 1785 he abandoned or pretended to abandon the bottle—a temporary awakening and repentance caused by the death of an elder brother. We are more surprised at this than to hear that at this age he had written much, for Cowley and Pope and others are standing examples of juvenile powers. Soon after the death of this elder brother, Dermody, animated by the 'History of Tom Jones' to a life of adventure, secretly started for Dublin with two shillings in his pocket, and there commenced a career full of vicissitude, but more full of wretchedness and sickening depravity. No youth of his class ever had such opportunities; no one abused such opportunities as he did. Had he led a life of industry, rectitude, and sobriety, his name might to-day have been that of the National Poet of Ireland—a far greater than Moore. As it was, though rescued time after time out of the mire, he always turned again to it, till at length disgusted Patronage and exhausted Friendship cast him adrift to die in the gutter he loved.

When he arrived in Dublin, yet a mere child, he spent his time hovering around bookstalls. The owner of such a stall, fearful of a theft, and watching the boy, discovered him one day, not thieving, but reading a Greek author; whereupon he employed the furtive student to teach his son 'the classics.' The engagement was cut short by Dermody's drunkenness. The bookseller compassionately procured him a new employment, which was soon lost through the same cause. He managed to make friends with several gentlemen studying at Trinity College, who befriended him, to be imposed on by him. Mr. Owenson, the actor, Lady Morgan's father, took an interest in him and introduced him to a Dr. Young, who volunteered to advance his studies and support him. But studies were neglected, and Dermody, possessed of his old devil, dismissed to destitution once more. But Fortune befriended the prodigy. A clergyman—a Mr. Austen, rector of Maynooth—noticed him, took him to his house, raised a subscription amongst his friends for the maintenance and education of the young genius. But to no avail; Dermody, after repeated offences, was again expelled.

Mr. Owenson for the second time obtained for him a patron—a Mr. Atkinson, on whose advice and recommendation the Dowager Countess of Moira adopted the boy-poet, sending him to the Rev. Mr. Boyd, of Killeigh, under whom, at her expense, he was to be perfected in his studies. Here for a time he was steady and made progress in learning. He added knowledge of French and Italian to his acquaintance with the dead languages; he delighted Lady Moira, who was proud of her *protégé*; but the old habit again conquered him, and again he is out on the world, not entirely friendless, for Lady Moira is ready with her purse for his destitution. He wrote afterwards of her the lines commencing:

'Ah! deeds of tenderness to earth unknown,
Felt by her keener sense and heaven alone.'

But her forbearance is soon exhausted, and, sunk to the lowest depths of debauchery and wretchedness, friendless and destitute, he tries to gain a living by writing political pamphlets. He would walk sixteen miles to solicit a subscriber's name, and, disappointed and penniless, pledge his very shoe-buckles for a drink. This was in 1793, when he was eighteen years of age. Pamphlets and politics did not pay, and he essayed a new and facile composition, begging letters. At this point of his career he was saved from death by starvation by Mr. Attorney-General Wolfe (afterwards the ill-fated Chief Justice Lord Kilwarden), who placed him in Trinity College, undertaking to pay the expenses of his education and contribute thirty pounds a year towards his maintenance. Another splendid opportunity thrown away!

The next we hear of Dermody is serving as a private soldier—somewhat reformed, for he is promoted to be a sergeant. He goes to England with his regiment, gains Lord Moira's favour, and by it obtains a lieutenancy of some kind. While a soldier, and when in his nineteenth year, he wrote a poem called 'The Retrospect.' He retired from the army on half-pay; and the next scene is a relapse to the old vicious course, and Dermody starving in a cobbler's garret. He is rescued this time by Mr. Raymond, afterwards his biographer, who induces him to collect his poems and to have them published. This is done; the collection is dedicated to the Lady Moira whose patronage and protection he thrice forfeited; it is a success, and on its proceeds he lives respectable for a while—for a little while. Back he sinks to debauchery and misery. But he has made a name as a poet and satirist, and Laureate Pye procures for him money-grants from the Benevolent Royal Literary Fund. These minister not to his mind, but to his vices; his constitution is broken down, and to retrieve wasted and lost health he is advised to seek change of air. Another volume is issued, full of merit and power, but no patronage is present to secure purchasers. Friends are all alienated; and neglected, in utter poverty and friendlessness, he finds refuge in a hovel in a purlieu of Sydenham. Raymond discovers him and again succours him; but he is past succour, and after lingering for a day or two he dies, aged twenty-seven years and six months.

His life was of such persistent depravity that it is repulsive; his character was unredeemed by a single virtue; yet when we turn to his poetry we must feel regret that such noble talents were unfostered, were stained with vice and soaked in drink. The song 'The Sensitive Linnet,' written before he was ten years of age, is worthy of the Elizabethan age. His 'Contentment in Adversity' is full of humour:

> 'In a cold empty garret contented I sit,
> With no spark to warm me but sparks of old wit.

*   *   *   *   *   *

> Here's a health then to Fate, and to Fortune her daughter
> (Misfortune I mean), though I'm sorry 'tis water;
> Yet water itself, sirs, may toast such a madam,
> For 'twas wine, beer, and rum, in the fair days of Adam.
> So why may not I, then, imagine it claret?
> For his taste was as fine as his son's in a garret.'

What can be finer or purer than those lines in 'Patronage,' where he speaks of the consolations he discerns through the sable shroud of sorrow which wraps him? Friendship solaces him:

> 'And fair Devotion, brightly fleeting by,
> Unbars new portals to a purer sky;
> Whence seraphs, leaning from th' angelic quire,
> Invite to sweep a more immortal lyre.'

We have alluded to the comparison which some one has instituted between Dermody and Chatterton. There is one similitude that will occur to everyone. Chatterton's 'Farewell to Bristol' is suggested by Dermody's 'Farewell to Ireland.' Chatterton wrote:

> 'Farewell Bristolia's dingy piles of brick,
> Lovers of mammon, worshippers of trick;
> You scorned the boy that gave you antique lays,
> And gave him in reward some empty praise.'

And so on in this strain. Chatterton's contempt and wrath were perhaps due to a real cause. Dermody's 'Farewell to Ireland,' written in 1794, is masterly in invective, but is a monument of ingratitude and callousness. We may quote it here, as it cannot find place in the subsequent pages; it will show what a versatile genius the boy was dowered with, and justify our regrets at his misspent, wretched, brief life:

> 'Rank nurse of nonsense, on whose thankless coast
> The base weed thrives, the nobler bloom is lost;
> Parent of pride and poverty, where dwell
> Dulness and brogue and calumny—farewell.
> Lo! from thy land the tuneful prophet flies,
> And spurns the dust behind in Folly's eyes.

* * * * * *

In vain thy children tuned the lofty strain—
Thy children propped the sinking isle in vain:
Vice is well pensioned, virtue seeks the shades,
And all the muse, and all the patriot fades.
No Moira comes to clear thy circling fogs,
But Westmorland still rules congenial bogs.

* * * * * *

Oh, pause on ruin's steepy cliff profound!
Oh, raise thy pale, thy drooping sons around;
Exalt the poor, the lordly proud oppress,
Thy tyrants humble, but thy soldiers bless,
Worn by long toil, as if foredoom'd by fate
To glut some pampered reprobate of state;
Thy artists cherish, bid the mighty soul
Of wisdom range beyond cold want's control;
And haply when some native gem you see
Unknown, unfriended, lost—oh, think on me!'

LYSAGHT.

THE man who wrote such songs as 'The Sprig of Shillelagh' and 'Kitty of Coleraine,' and that one addressed to Henry Grattan, 'The Gallant Man who led the Van of Irish Volunteers,' to say nothing of countless others which charmed and delighted at the time, but which are now lost or dispersed or without their father's name, would be sure of being remembered, even had he no further title to fame. But 'Pleasant Ned Lysaght,' as he was known by his contemporaries, was a well-known barrister, an accomplished wit, a notable *bon vivant*, an uncorrupted politician in days when corruption, naked and not ashamed, swayed the politics of Irishmen.* He was the son of John Lysaght, of the county Clare, and descended from an ancient Irish family, an offshoot of the royal house of O'Brien. It is said the name is derived from the Irish *Lae sacht* ('seven days'), a surname conferred on an

* Sir Jonah Barrington says, however, that Lysaght was employed and paid by Lord Castlereagh to write up the Union.

O'Brien who most valorously defended his castle for seven days against an enemy's attack. He was born on 21st December, 1763, and was educated in Cashel, at a Catholic school, though he was a Protestant, and entered Trinity College, Dublin, in 1779, where he graduated B.A. in 1782. He afterwards was at Oxford, where he graduated M.A. in 1784, and he was called to the English Bar at the Middle Temple, and to the Irish Bar, in the year 1798—being then thirty-five years of age. His intention was to live and practise in England, but he had to leave that country owing to monetary difficulties. He therefore returned to Ireland, and attained to a very successful practice at the Bar, from which he retired on being appointed a Divisional Police Magistrate of Dublin, in 1809. He died in 1810, and the best evidence of his worth and popularity is in the fact that the members of his profession, the judges and barristers of Ireland, contributed over £2,500 to a fund for his widow and children.

Lysaght was a bright particular star in the midst of a literary constellation. The Munster Bar, with which he went circuit, was in his time 'the most brilliant, eloquent, and gifted body of barristers that any circuit has ever assembled together;' and in a company composed of such men as Curran, O'Connell, Deane Grady, Keller, Quin, McCarthy, etc., Lysaght occupied a pre-eminent position. Mr. Owen Madden, in his 'Revelations of Ireland,' speaking from a personal acquaintance with him, says : ' A man of more varied talents it was impossible to meet. In his personal character he was a thorough Irishman—brave, brilliant, witty, eloquent, and devil-may-care.' His bravery was shown in his attitude in respect to the Volunteer movement, and his vigorous opposition to the proposed Act of Union. His brilliance and wit were the talk of his contemporaries. His eloquence was notable amongst an eloquent bar. His devil-may-careness is seen in the many anecdotes preserved of him. He is the reputed author of the 'Rakes of Mallow,' and, whether he wrote it or not, he was worthy to be the author:

> 'Spending faster than it comes,
> Beating waiters, bailiffs, duns,
> Bacchus' true-begotten sons,
> Live the Rakes of Mallow.'

He was, Mr. Owen Madden tells us, 'a very decided rake.' People esteemed it a privilege to be in his company, and yet he lived in constant fear of arrest for debt. 'He used only to skulk out at night; he lived in Trinity College in order to be out of the reach of bailiffs and duns.' 'He was short in stature, with a very long nose;' and withal preferred his bottle and his pleasure, his jokes and his songs, to his briefs and law-books. 'Poetry and pistols, wine and women,' were, in his own words, all he lived for. He earned a happy name, 'Pleasant Ned Lysaght,' and left a happy memory amongst his friends and acquaintances; but life was never a serious matter with him. He was acting as second, on one occasion, to Deane Grady, in a duel between the latter and Counsellor O'Maher. O'Maher's second, during the preliminaries, drew Lysaght's attention to the fact that his pistol was cocked. 'Take care, Mr. Lysaght, your pistol is cocked.' 'Well, then,' says Pleasant Ned, '*cock yours, and let me take a slap at you, as we are idle.*'

He married, and Sir Jonah Barrington records that he discovered his father-in-law, whom he believed to be a wealthy Jew, to be only a bankrupt Christian; yet the disappointment had little or no effect; his exuberant spirits, his irrepressible gaiety and wit, were superior to greater misfortunes. In his private life he was irreproachable—'a nobly-spent life,' says Madden; and there is throughout his songs a healthy tone of feeling and lofty sentiment that, notwithstanding his debts and difficulties, and dodges and devil-may-careness, show that he was a pure-minded and good man.

SHERIDAN.

THE concluding lines of Byron's rather heavy monody on the death of Sheridan,

> 'Nature made but one such man,
> And broke the die in moulding Sheridan,'

convey a true idea of the estimation in which the great Irishman was held by his contemporaries, and in which he will ever be held—for another Sheridan is as impossible as another Shakespeare. To our thinking he was far and away the greatest Irishman whose name is on the roll of Irish literature; not the greatest song-writer, but greatest in the combination of brilliant qualities, varied accomplishments, extraordinary characteristics. A wonderful genius; his life is itself a comedy, his death a pitiable tragedy. He wrote 'The Rivals'; he delivered the Begum oration; he said more witty things than would have sufficed to give a reputation to a dozen men. The boon companion of princes of the blood; the cynosure of London society, to which his presence was life and laughter; the applauded of the populace, the schools, and the senate, he yet was drunk in the gutters one day, in the spunging-house another, and again sleeping-off the previous night's debauch to rise at midday to booze and gamble with Fox. He died heart-broken and harassed, neglected and forsaken by those whom he was wont to delight. He enjoyed political offices, and was a privy councillor; his life was a succession of intellectual triumphs, one of which would suffice for an immortality; and side by side with these we find a life of dissipation, debts, difficulties, duns, through which his extraordinary wit, his powers for raillery and persuasion, carried him almost unharmed. A human anomaly; profligate and profuse, yet he never had a shilling of his own; lazy, careless, and indolent—he was offered £1,000 by a publisher if he would write out for the press the Begum speech, accepted the terms, but never performed the easy task, though at the time a thousand pence would have been a sum of consequence to him—yet at times industrious, careful, and energetic.

The dialogues in his plays were altered and polished and elaborated with scrupulous care, and his great orations were prepared for days beforehand. Nevertheless, in almost every incident of his life he seems to have acted on the principle that what could be done to-morrow should never be done to-day. The Begum speech was the crowning effort of his genius. Pitt, Burke, and Fox, themselves Parliamentary orators of the highest distinction, adjudged it to be the most splendid speech ever delivered to mankind. Pitt said 'that it surpassed all the eloquence of ancient or modern times, and possessed all that genius and art could furnish to agitate and control the human mind;' Burke declared it to be 'the most astonishing effort of eloquence, argument, and wit united, of which there was any record or tradition;' and Fox said, 'all that he had ever heard or read when compared with it dwindled into nothing, and vanished like vapour before the sun.' As to his wit, Fox pronounced him to be 'the wittiest man he had ever known.' His wit was great even in his cups. The Wilberforce anecdote is superb. He was found drunk in the channel, and when asked by the watchman where he lived and what was his name, he in a whispered hiccup replied: 'Wilberforce.'—Wilberforce drunk and incapable in the gutter! 'Sherry all over,' says Byron.

'The Rivals' was written in two months, and though the first representation was a failure, the play, when pruned and improved, was a conspicuous success. 'The School for Scandal' was an immediate and pronounced success, and is even a greater favourite now than it was in his own day. 'The Critic' is the best of his plays and the best play of its kind—a success in a line where others had failed. Of his comedies, however, Macaulay —who declared the Begum speech to be 'the finest which had been delivered within the memory of man'— recorded his opinion that Sheridan was not the equal of Wycherley, and that 'no writers have injured the comedy of England so much as Congreve and Sheridan,' and supports it by arguments to be found in his 'Essay on Machiavelli.' But though the wit and humour of 'The Rivals' is artificial and laboured, and the plot meagre, and the characters, excepting Sir Anthony Absolute, disappointing and unnatural, yet it is to be borne in mind that it holds the stage at present, and shows no decline in public favour.

Dr. Johnson, between whom and Sheridan's father there was ill-feeling sufficient to cause a rupture in an old friendship, said that 'the man who has written the two best comedies of his age is surely a considerable man'—no weak praise from Johnson. Byron's commendation is superlative likewise: 'He has written the best comedy, the best drama, the best farce, and the best address; and, to crown all, delivered the very best oration ever conceived or heard in this country.'

He softened the hearts of hostile attorneys and averted ruinous suits. He was a huge and notorious fraud in money matters, yet he was idolised and his unprincipled conduct condoned. He could joke with and at the Prince Regent and the Duke of York, and charm Madame de Staël. Contrast all this with his tears when declaring 'he never knew what it was to have a shilling of his own,' and his 'passionate weeping' at the profanation his person suffered in the spunging-house in Tooke's Court, near Chancery Lane, and with that wretched, saddest, and most pathetic last letter of his to Rogers, written when the bailiffs were in possession a few days before his death: 'I am absolutely undone and broken-hearted. They are going to put the carpets out of the windows and break into the room and take me.' The laughter and admiration that are evoked by his life-story are turned into the utmost pity by the record of his death.

The incidents of his life are well-known, and we have space only to summarise them chronologically.

1751.—Born at 12, Dorset Street, Dublin, Sept. Baptized in St. Mary's Church, 4th October, by the names Richard Brinsley Butler Sheridan.

1758.—Sent to Whyte's celebrated school in Grafton Street. Pronounced to be 'a hopeless dunce.'

1762.—Sent to Harrow, parents having moved to England.

1769.—Left Harrow, where he was 'idle and careless,' and went to reside in London and Bath.

1771.—Published, in conjunction with Mr. Halked, a 'Translation of Aristænetus,' 'Jupiter, a farce,' etc., both total failures. Meets Miss Linley, 'The Maid of Bath.'

1772.—Miss Linley flies with Sheridan to London, thence to Dunkirk and Lisle. Married in March. Returns to Bath. Sheridan's duel with Captain Mathews, who traduced Miss Linley. Second duel on 4th July between Sheridan and Mathews—'they hacked at each other with their broken swords, rolling upon the ground;' both wounded.

1773.—13th April. Marriage by licence of Sheridan and Miss Linley. Writes occasionally for Woodfall's *Public Advertiser.*

1774.—'The Rivals' written. Residing in Orchard Street, Portman Square, London.

1775.—17th January. 'The Rivals' produced at Covent Garden—a failure. 2nd May. 'St. Patrick's Day' acted. 21st November. 'The Duenna' performed—a great success; ran for seventy-five nights, a longer period than that of the first run of 'The Beggar's Opera.'

1776.—June. Becomes patentee and manager of Drury Lane Theatre in succession to Garrick. The following were the payments made for half the property:

Sheridan $\frac{7}{14}$ths	-	-	£10,000
Linley $\frac{2}{14}$ths	-	-	10,000
Dr. Ford $\frac{3}{14}$ths	-	-	15,000

1777.—'The School for Scandal' written and performed.

1778.—Purchases for £45,000 the moiety of Drury Lane Theatre, held by Mr. Lacy. How or where he got the money is a mystery. Appoints his father, from whom he had been estranged for years, manager of the theatre.

1779.—Produces 'The Critic.'

1780.—Oct. Returned as M.P. for Stafford through Fox's influence. 20th November. Makes his first speech, upon which Woodfall told him 'it was not in his line.' Sheridan rejoined, 'It is in me, however; and by God it *shall* come out.'

1782.—Appointed an Under-Secretary of State in the Rockingham Administration.

1783.—Made Secretary of the Treasury under the Shelburne Ministry.

1787.—7th Feb. Great speech on Impeachment of Warren Hastings. 3rd June. Begum speech.

1788.—His father dies.

1792.—His wife dies. Five months after he offered his hand to Pamela, afterwards the wife of Lord Edward Fitzgerald.

1795.—Married again, a daughter of Dr. Ogle, Dean of Winchester; receives £5,000 fortune.

1798.—'The Stranger' and 'Pizarro' produced.

1804.—Appointed by the Prince of Wales Receiver of the Duchy of Cornwall.

1806.—Elected M.P. for Westminster.

1807.—Loses his seat for Westminster. Returned for Ilchester.

1809.—24th Feb. Drury Lane Theatre burned. While watching the destruction of all his property from the Piazza coffee-house, where he was drinking, a friend reproached him for his calmness. 'A man may surely be allowed to take a glass of wine *at his own fireside*,' he answered.

1812.—Speaks in House of Commons in favour of Catholic Emancipation: 'Be just to Ireland as you value your own honour. Be just to Ireland as you value your own peace.' Sept. Defeated at Stafford. Political career ended.

1813.—Frequently arrested for debt. Pictures, books, presents, etc., sold. Hopes to be returned for Westminster.

1816.—7th July. Dies at the house of Mr. Peter Moore, in Great George's Street, Westminster (his own residence, 17, Saville Place, being in the hands of bailiffs), and buried in the Abbey.

This is a succinct relation of the incidents of Sheridan's life, to which we need add little beyond drawing attention to the early development of his genius. He was but twenty-three when 'The Rivals' was written, and twenty-six when 'The School for Scandal' was produced.

He absolutely died in penury and misery. Writs and executions thick as autumn leaves in Vallombrosa showered upon him, and with bailiffs in the house and a sheriff's officer arresting him on his death-bed, and threatening to carry him to the spunging-house, blankets and all, he learned that a public appeal on his behalf had been made in the *Morning Post*, and heard the too-late inquiries of dukes and earls at his door. He was borne to his grave by the highest nobility, he who a week before was at the mercy of a brutal sheriff's officer. Thomas Moore wrote the following noble and just lines on the sad and disgraceful circumstances attending poor Sheridan's death and burial:

> 'Oh! it sickens the heart to see bosoms so hollow,
>   And friendship so false in the great and high born;
> To think what a long line of titles may follow
>   The relics of him who died friendless and lorn.
> How proud they can press to the funeral array
>   Of him who they shunned in his sickness and sorrow;
> How bailiffs may seize his last blanket to-day,
>   Whose pall shall be held up by nobles to-morrow.'

Sheridan was a remarkable instance of hereditary genius. His father, Thomas Sheridan (who was born at Quilca, in Cavan, in 1721, the descendant of the sept of O'Sheridan of Cavan), was the author of the well-known 'Dictionary,' and of the 'Life of Swift,' whose collected works he edited. He was an M.A. of Trinity College, Dublin; took to the stage, making his first appearance at the theatre in Smock Alley, Dublin; taught elocution; became manager of Drury Lane; obtained a pension of £200 a year from Lord Bute. He married Frances, the authoress of 'Sidney Biddulph'—a novel much admired by Dr. Johnson—and other less known works. Thomas Sheridan was the son of Dr. Thomas Sheridan, who forfeited his appointment of Vice-regal Chaplain by preaching on the day of the anniversary of the succession of the House of Hanover from the text 'Sufficient unto the day is the evil thereof.' He once had a great school in Dublin; was the intimate friend of Dean Swift; was slovenly, indigent, cheerful, good-natured, improvident; a punster, and a fiddler—a parson and schoolmaster by turns—a joker and fiddler always. He died in great poverty in Dublin, in 1738. The descendants of Richard Brinsley Sheridan—two of whom, Lady Dufferin and Hon. Mrs. Norton, we refer to subsequently—are living proofs of hereditary genius.

Sheridan's songs are full of beauty and tenderness, of gaiety and *élan*. Some of them are unsurpassed in lyric literature. The celebrated song—in 'The School for Scandal'—'Here's to the Maiden of Bashful Fifteen,' is evidently suggested by and framed on the song 'A Health to the Nut-brown Lass,' in Suckling's play of 'The Goblins.' But all he touched he adorned in a manner solely his own. 'He ran through each mode of the lyre, and was master of all.' A just and delicate estimate of his genius will be found in Hazlitt; his songs speak for themselves.

There is one episode in Sheridan's life which his biographers overlook—his nomination as joint candidate with Mr. Colclough, of Tintern Abbey, for the representation of the county Wexford, at the general election of 1808. The facts of that contest, the mortal duel between Colclough and Alcock the rival candidate, are to be found in Barrington's 'Sketches.' Needless to say that Colclough being killed, Sheridan was not elected.

One final word: whatever the opinions may be of Sheridan's character, founded on his imprudence, extravagance, embarrassments, and unprincipledness, there can be but one opinion of his magnificent genius, and of the works that he has left as the perpetual delight of every generation. Yet Ireland has never done anything for his memory—no statue in a street, not even a tablet in a church. During his lifetime Ireland did something for him. 'My old friend,' said Dr. Johnson, speaking of him, 'had been honoured with extraordinary attention in his own country by having had an exception made in his favour in an Irish Act of Parliament concerning Insolvent Debtors. Thus to be singled out by the Legislature as an object of public consideration and kindness is a proof of no common merit.' We will not dispute the attention, the consideration and kindness thus once shown him by his countrymen : we will merely observe that public money is yearly spent in Ireland on objects and projects far less creditable and honourable than that of erecting a public memorial to the greatest and most versatile Irishman of his day—the man of most varied, brilliant, and manifold gifts which Ireland has yet produced.

MILLIKEN.

RICHARD ALFRED MILLIKEN, attorney-at-law, painter and musician—from all of which pursuits he derived neither profit nor fame—wrote 'The Groves of Blarney,' and brought to himself renown. The genesis of this celebrated and popular song is worth recording. At a gathering at a country seat, Castlehyde, in county Cork, an ambitious production of a local 'poet'—one of those strolling versifiers and ballad-singers who were peculiar to Ireland a century or so ago—was read and talked over after dinner. It was absurd in its expressions, confused in its ideas, and floundering in its facts; and Milliken undertook to write a song equal to it or excelling it in absurdity; and he wrote the famous 'Groves of Blarney.' He was a genial, jovial soul. Lysaght was 'Pleasant Ned Lysaght' with his companions: Milliken was 'Honest Dick Milliken.' He was born in 1767 at Castle Martyr, in Cork; was an attorney, and tried to practise, but the business was not congenial, and so he spent his life in rhyming and painting and playing music, and delighting the social circles of Cork. He tried blank verse with indifferent success, and edited a monthly journal—*The Casket*—which disappeared in the troubles of 1798. He died the 16th of December, 1815, was buried at Douglas, near Cork, and was justly lamented as one of the many brilliant men that Cork has contributed to the wit and literature of the kingdom.

CURRAN.

CURRAN is remembered as the greatest forensic orator of a day when eloquent advocates were more plentiful than at present; and as a great wit, amongst great wits, rather than as a song-writer. He was Master of the Rolls in Ireland, but was no lawyer; he was a conspicuous member of the Irish Parliament, but no statesman. He was the most brilliant ornament in Irish society, the most popular man at the Irish Bar; a fearless advocate, a true patriot; and his last years were overclouded with domestic sorrow; his great genius drooped into a melancholy, and, hopeless and depressed, he saw his beloved Ireland 'like a bastinadoed elephant kneeling to receive the paltry rider.' Before he was forty years of age he was offered a judgeship and a peerage if he would take the Government side in the Regency Debate in the Irish Parliament, but resolutely refused to sell himself, his principles, and his honour. Throughout his life he was honest and uncorruptible amongst the corrupt and dishonest, and his last speech in Parliament, in 1797, was devoted to an endeavour to effect some reform in the Administration, and to stay the flood of venality, intrigue, and jobbery that so soon debauched the Irish Legislature. His speeches at the Bar are familiar to most readers; his jokes and witticisms are daily recounted, as fresh at present as when they were uttered. We have already quoted Byron's opinion of Sheridan; his opinion of Curran is likewise superlative in its laudation: 'Curran's the man who struck me most. Such imagination! There never was anything like it that ever I saw or heard of. His *published* life, his published speeches, give you *no* idea of the man—none at all. He was wonderful even to me, who had seen many remarkable men of the time. The riches of his Irish imagination were exhaustless. I heard him speak more poetry than I have ever seen written. I saw him presented to Madame de Staël, and they were both so ugly that I could not help wondering how the best intellects of France and Ireland could have taken up respectively such residences.' 'His imagination was infinite, his fancy boundless, his wit indefatigable,' says one who had a long and close intimacy with him, 'and his person was mean and decrepit, very slight, very shapeless—spindle limbs, a shambling gait, one hand imperfect, and a face yellow and furrowed, rather flat, and thoroughly ordinary; yet,' continues the writer, Sir Jonah Barrington, 'I never was so happy in the company of any man as in Curran's for many years.'

Personal defects amounting to deformity were no depreciation to the meteoric eloquence and marvellous wit. The flat yellow face was redeemed by his wondrous dark lustrous eyes.

But it is not as a master of eloquence or wit—as barrister or politician—that he here finds a place, but as a song-writer. He was not much of a poet, though his eloquence was all poetic, and though he wrote a most tender song, 'Let us be merry before we go'—'The Deserter's Meditation,' as he styled it—one that gave Byron the cue for one of his best songs. He once asked Godwin what he thought of a certain jury-speech, not a brilliant one, he had made at the Carlow Assizes, and Godwin said, 'I never did hear anything so bad as your prose, Curran, except your poetry;' a harsh misjudgment of both. He was not a splendid success in every species of literary and intellectual labour he engaged in: his songs are not extraordinarily good, but they are good; and the same can be said of his music, for he was also a musician.

We shall be as succinct as possible in our biography of this great man. The Currans, we are told, were, in the old semi-legendary history of Ireland, 'eminent as poets and men of learning. They filled the positions of bards and historians in Leitrim, and poets in Breffni.' His father was 'seneschal of the Manor Court' (a species of town-bailiff) of Newmarket, a small village now, of 1,000 inhabitants, in the county Cork; and here John Philpot Curran was born on the 24th July, 1750. He was educated out of charity by the rector of the town (who discerned in the lad a mental capacity and power beyond the ordinary youth), and was subsequently sent to a school under a foundation of Lady Elizabeth Villiers (1709), in Midleton, a town not far distant. He matriculated at Trinity College, Dublin, in 1769, with the intention of entering the Church. His college career was rather distinguished—he obtained his scholarship in 1770—and in 1773, the intention to join the Church having been relinquished, he was admitted at the Middle Temple; and, while a student there, married his cousin, a Miss Creagh. 'Stuttering Jack Curran'—'Orator Mum'—these were the nicknames bestowed upon him, and prove that he had many natural difficulties to overcome before he could earn fame. He was called to the Irish Bar in 1775, and though in his earlier years at the profession his abilities were unacknowledged and unrecompensed, chiefly because he had had no opportunity of displaying them, yet, having once been heard, he rapidly earned the reputation that grew with each succeeding year of practice. His progress is exhibited by his changes of residence: Redmond's Hill, Fade Street, St. Andrew Street, Ely

Place (now No. 4), and 80, Stephen's Green, were his successive dwellings. He rapidly also became popular in society, and a favourite amongst the members of his own profession. He was one of the 'Order of St. Patrick,' or 'The Monks of the Screw,' whose charter-song he wrote. This was a convivial and intellectual club which met weekly, on Saturdays, at a house in Kevin Street, Dublin, when Curran lived in Redmond's Hill; and subsequently at his country house at Rathfarnham, when he was 'Prior' of the 'Monks.' The club, or 'society,' was composed of the brilliant men at the Bar and in Parliament, and came to an end in 1795. Curran was returned to the Irish Parliament as member for Kilbeggan in 1783, Flood being his colleague in the representation of that village borough; and he joined the opposition, his politics being the liberalism of Grattan. He was also (1786—1797) M.P. for Rathcormac, another village borough. He retired from Parliament in May, 1797.

His greatest fame was earned by his defence of those charged with complicity in the rebellion of 1798. Of his speech on behalf of Hamilton Rowan, Lord Brougham said it was 'the greatest speech of an advocate in ancient or modern times.' His undaunted advocacy of the rebels led, on one occasion, to Lord Carleton, the Chief Justice, threatening to deprive him of his silk gown. He was appointed Master of the Rolls in Ireland, and made a Privy Councillor by Pitt, in 1806, and from that time he seems to have declined mentally and physically. He contested Newry for a seat in the Imperial Parliament in 1812, and was defeated by two votes; and in the following year he resigned the Mastership of the Rolls, and went into retirement on a pension.

Most of his time while he held the judicial office, and after his retirement, was spent in travelling, in the endeavour to regain his old vigour of mind and body, and to shake off the melancholy and depression that were overwhelming him. He died in Brompton, London, on the 14th October, 1817—the effects of a paralytic stroke with which he had been attacked at Moore's dinner-table —and was buried in the vaults of Paddington Church, whence, in 1837, his remains were removed to Glasnevin. There they repose under a magnificent tomb, a fac-simile of that of Scipio Barbatus opposite the Baths of Caracalla in Rome—a fitting and enduring monument. In St. Patrick's Cathedral, Dublin, there is, surmounted by a life-like bust by C. Moore, also a monument to his memory, which was erected in 1842 by a public subscription, and which bears the following inscription:

'PRÆ HONORABILIS JOHANNIS PHILPOT CURRAN,
Rotulorum Magistri;
Obinter Hiberniæ oratores eximii,
Cujus reliquiæ sepultæ sunt apud Glasnevin.
Hoc monumentum erectum fuit A.D. 1842,
Ex dono publico et amore.
Obiit 1817. Æt. 67.

The kaleidoscopic view of Curran's life is varying and attractive. A rough Irish-speaking poor country lad who rose to be the welcome guest of princes; a wit whose presence charged the atmosphere with gaiety, and in whose train followed laughter loud and hearty, wearing out a weary life in peevish, dismal melancholy. He, it is narrated, left the severe paths of respectability on one occasion, disguised as a tinker, and threw in his lot with a band of tramps—abandoned himself to the careless freedom of tinker life, and left it not till it became his lot to go on tramp, and not till he had a month's experience of low life in the Coombe in Dublin. Contrast this episode with that where we see an enthusiastic populace cheering him to the echo, carrying him in triumph to his home, because he was the dauntless champion of freedom, the eloquent advocate of the oppressed. His great intellect overcame great obstacles. He was at the outset without influential friends, and a poor man—the only furniture of his rooms was his offspring; —he was endowed with a contemptible personal appearance, a stuttering tongue, an enfeebling nervousness, yet he was the greatest and most successful and most popular orator at the Irish Bar, in the early days of the century when the Irish Bar was renowned for its eloquence.

A feeling of sadness at the decline of a great spirit, somewhat similar to that evoked by a consideration of the final scene of Sheridan's life, is present also in regard to the final days of Curran. How brilliant and celebrated he was in the Senate and at the Bar, for his wit and eloquence, is well known. Courted and flattered he was, like Sheridan, in his heyday while he could amuse; and yet he died in obscurity, broken down by domestic sorrows, wretched from the depression of settled melancholy—'he burst into tears and hung down his head' upon an allusion to Irish politics a few days before his death;—the eloquence was turned to prosiness, the wit to grossness, the ready repartee and flashing sarcasm to the drowsy inanities of hopeless imbecility—forgotten—neglected! Yet his talents and pure patriotism were alike splendid, and alike creditable to Ireland, and he is fully deserving of Byron's eulogistic sentence—'the best intellect of Ireland' of his time.

CALLANAN.

LIKE most of the Irish song-writers, Jeremiah (or James) Joseph Callanan was sprung from the people, and like many of them, he died while still a very young man. Callanan *was* a poet, and his brief life was yet long enough to earn a fame for his name. He was born in Cork in 1795, and of his early years nothing is known. Of obscure birth, he grew in obscurity, and at the age of nineteen entered the Maynooth Seminary, with the intention of becoming a priest. After a residence here for about two years, he discovered the Church was not his vocation, and in 1816 he went to Dublin, where he managed, through the charitable kindness of a friend, to enter Trinity College. While pursuing his course here, he gained the Vice-Chancellor's prizes for poems on 'Alexander the Great,' and 'The Accession of George IV.' His intentions during his collegiate career as regards a profession oscillated between the Bar and medicine, but he seems now, as throughout his life, to have been the victim of a restlessness and indecision which found an easy prey in his sensitive and nervous organisation. He left Trinity College after a two years' connection, and made his way to Cork. But he found neither parents nor relations nor friends here, and in a fit of dejection he enlisted in the 18th Royal Irish, as the only means open to him to gain a living. He was bought out of the service by some friends in time to prevent his sailing for Malta with his regiment. He next lived in Millstreet, a little town in Cork county, as tutor in the family of a Mr. McCarthy. This employment was soon relinquished, for in 1822 he is back in Cork writing verses, and doing nothing more than write verses, for his livelihood. In the following year he obtained a mastership in the school of the celebrated Dr. Maginn, in Marlborough Street in that city. The young doctor discerned and fostered Callanan's talents, and obtained space in the pages of *Blackwood's Magazine* for some of his translations from the Irish. But the demon of unrest and indecision was ever with him, and he became dissatisfied with Dr. Maginn and with the drudgery of his ushership, and gave up his post after a few months, and took to wandering through the south of Ireland with the ostensible object of collecting materials in the shape of old Irish legends and songs for future literary labours. In this object he was somewhat successful, and his translations are full of beauty, music, and power. He took up his abode on the Island or Islet of Inchidoney, at the mouth of Clonakilty Bay, and here he lived a simple and frugal life, and mused his fill. Here he wrote 'The Recluse of Inchidoney, a Spenserian poem full of a tender simplicity which characterises all his descriptions of nature. Here he wrote his best known poem, 'Gougane Barra'—'the best of all minor Irish poems,' according to one critic. He continued writing and roving in this fashion till 1829, when his health (he was of a naturally delicate constitution) became affected, and the medical advice to try a southern climate disposed him to again become a tutor—this time in an Irish family in Lisbon. The mild and sunny clime of Portugal benefited him for a brief while, but the remedy had been too long deferred. After a residence there of only a few months, he set his foot on a ship to reach Ireland to die in his native land; but he was too prostrate to undergo the sea-journey. He disembarked, and died on the foreign shore, on the 19th September, 1829, aged thirty-four.

His place amongst the Irish poets is high and sure. He is the Irish poet of nature, ever in close and sweet communion with the sea and sky, the verdure, the streams and hills—all the works of God's hands! He is full of grace and feeling, of unaffected piety, of unobtrusive virtue, of love of country—and over all there is a shadow of melancholy, of something unsatisfied, which gives a sorrowful, but not altogether joyless, tinge to his writing. There is no pettiness or frivolity in him. He is a purified and healthy Childe Harold. He has the tenderness without the gaiety, the sigh without the smile, the tear without the fun, of Irish poetry. Romantic and delicate, his poems are with him a means of regaining his old simplicity of mind and life, when

'With soul unsullied, and with heart unseared,
Before he mingled with the herd of men,'

he was 'sweetly lured on to virtue's shrine,' by a contemplation of the glories of that God of Nature to whose service he surrendered the last and best years of his brief life.

KENNEY.

THE creator of 'Jeremy Diddler,' even if he had never written anything but 'Raising the Wind,' would have been sure of being remembered. James Kenney, besides giving the world the great 'Jeremy Diddler,' with half a dozen plays, wrote long didactic poems and sparkling songs. According to a critique written immediately on his death, 'he was, as a farce-writer, one of the happiest and most popular artists of his time. He was a cultivated gentleman, moving in the best literary society, and will be gratefully remembered for his kindness to aspirants in dramatic authorship.' Notwithstanding that his writings enjoyed such a favour and popularity in his lifetime, and that he obtained large remunerations from time to time for them, he drifted into penury in his old age, and the voluntary benefit at Drury Lane, which was organised on his behalf, was of no avail to the veteran, for he died, it is said, on the morning of the performance, the 1st August, 1849. Of Kenney's youth, little or nothing is known. He was born in the county Limerick, in 1780, of respectable parents, and removed at an early age to London, where the chief part of his after-life was spent. Though the *University Magazine*, in an obituary notice, said all his pieces were 'eminently attractive,' Byron's opinion was anything but favourable:

> 'While Kenney's *World*—ah! where is Kenney's wit?—
> Tires the sad gallery, lulls the restless pit.'

Kenney suffered from a painful nervous affection, which gave such an eccentricity to his movements and appearance that he was sometimes taken for an escaped lunatic.

MOORE.

THOMAS MOORE, 'the poet of all circles, and the idol of his own,' is signally and unapproachedly *the* song-writer of Irish song-writers. A modern critic, himself a poet and an Irishman, has spoken of Moore as the 'tomtit amongst poets.' This is not the place to enquire at length into the justice or injustice of this judgment; nor is this the place to write a critical and exegetical essay on his merits and demerits as a poet. Briefly and perfunctorily we shall refer to his productions, prose and poetic; but whatever may now be the opinions of critics, however he may stand in the estimation of this age, when fashion so frequently decides merit and confers applause, there can be no question of this, that, as a song-writer, Moore will never decline from the supreme position he occupies amongst Irish authors. In his national songs, sung all the world over, to-day as half a century ago, to the 'Irish Melodies,' his fame may safely rest confident of immortality.

Thomas Moore, like the majority of the Irish songwriters, was sprung from a humble origin. His father, John Moore, was a small tradesman, a grocer or such— it is said the business was established with the fortune he obtained with his wife, Miss Anastasia Codd—and the illustrious poet was born on the 28th May, 1779, at his shop in Aungier Street, Dublin. The house is at the corner of Little Longford Street, is now occupied by a publican, and has a little bust set in a niche in the wall, and a tablet with an inscrutable inscription, to mark the birthplace of the national poet of Ireland. True, there is another memorial in his native city. In the most public thoroughfare there is a statue, which is the jest of the burlesques, the ridicule of tourists, the shame of the citizens. Moore would be more honoured by the removal and annihilation of that wretched memorial.

As a boy, he was educated at the schools of Mr. Malone and the celebrated Samuel Whyte, in Grafton Street, Dublin, where Richard Brinsley Sheridan had been his predecessor; and at sixteen years of age entered Trinity College, that had been opened in the previous year, 1794, to members of the faith to which Moore belonged. But even before his matriculation, while he was but fourteen years old, he had contributed verses to a Dublin journal called *Anthologia Hibernica*. The *afflatus* was upon him early, and while in college he translated the Odes of Anacreon, in order to win a college prize, which, however, he did not win. He was an assiduous student, languages being his *forte*, and he cultivated with much success his natural talent for music. He was a member of the College Historical Society, where Emmet and Arthur O'Connor were prominent orators, and his friendship for these almost involved him in the revolutionary proceedings of 1798.

He left Trinity College and Ireland for London when he was twenty, and was entered on 28th May, 1798, at the Middle Temple, as Sheridan was before him, with the intention of being called to the Bar. Under the patronage of Lord Moira, who converted his father from a spirit-dealer into a barrack-master and customs officer, he in 1800 published by subscription his 'Odes of Anacreon,' dedicated by permission, and through Lord Moira's kindly influence, to the Prince Regent. Elated with their success, he abandoned the law, resolved to live on his poetry. This first publication under such auspices was the means of introducing him to the fashionable society of London, and he charmed it with his personal accomplishments, and became what is called its darling. In 1802 he published the 'Poetical Works of the late Thomas Little,'—a play on his name and on his insignificant stature. It was because of this volume that Byron in his 'English Bards,' etc., 'grieved to condemn,' called Moore 'the melodious advocate of lust'—a rather strong description of a production which, though immoral and licentious, could hardly corrupt. Like many such productions, it was openly condemned and widely read.

The next incident in his life was an unfortunate one. His steadfast patron Lord Moira, at Lady Donegall's request, obtained for him in 1803 the appointment to a Government post in Bermuda, whither he went, arriving there in January, 1804, and whence he returned very soon, finding the post uncongenial and the climate unhealthy, and having committed his duties to a deputy. This subordinate embezzled large sums of the Government moneys, for which Moore was responsible. The defalcations, amounting to about £6,000, were brought to light in 1818, and Lord Lansdowne, his friend, paid the amount, and Moore repaid it from the proceeds of his literary labours. Soon after his return to England, in 1806, he published his 'Odes and Epistles.' These were so severely criticised in the *Edinburgh Review*—he was called a 'licentious versifier' and 'poetical propagator of immorality'—that he challenged Jeffrey. The celebrated Chalk Farm duel was arranged, the police interfered, the 'bloodless pistol' was discovered, and—a comedy in real life—the combatants embraced and became friends. The incident was ridiculed by Byron, whom, therefore, Moore challenged with bloodthirsty pugnacity, hardly in keeping with his character; the result of the second challenge, though by different means, was also lifelong friendship between the two. In 1807 the 'Irish Melodies' were projected. In 1811 he married Bessie Dykes, a young Irish actress, by whom he had three children, all of whom died in his lifetime. In 1813 he wrote the 'Twopenny Post Bag,' which ran through fourteen editions in one year. The ambition to emulate his contemporary poets, to produce a poem, and not to rely for fame on short fugitive pieces, love-lyrics and political squibs, now possessed him, and in 1817 'Lalla Rookh' appeared. Longman paid 3,000 guineas for it; the whole country joined in a chorus, a very tumult of applause.

Moore was the most popular man of the time. The world of fashion had cast off their former idol, Byron, and with exaggerated praise and superlative demonstration taken Moore to their hearts. In 1818 'The Fudge Family' appeared. In this year also he visited Ireland, and was hailed with great enthusiasm as the National Bard. He subsequently wrote 'The Loves of the Angels,' 'The Epicurean,' biographies of Byron, Sheridan, and Lord Edward Fitzgerald, a 'History of Ireland,' and other works. In 1819 he made a continental tour with Lord John Russell, who afterwards wrote his 'Life and Memoirs,' and who conferred (in 1835) a pension of £300 a year upon him. In 1832 he was solicited to stand for the Parliamentary representation of Limerick, as an O'Connellite, but declined. He died on the 25th January, 1852, having for three years previously been, like his contemporaries Scott and Southey, almost an imbecile by reason of softening of the brain; and the brilliant triumphs of a life of glory are darkened by this closing scene of sad infirmity. He was buried in Bromham Churchyard, near Sloperton Cottage, where he lived; there also on 4th September, 1865, his wife was laid beside him, and to their memory a beautiful window is in the church.

Moore's versatility and his superiority in some, and his proficiency in the majority, of his literary undertakings have gained for him a high place not only in Irish, but in English literature. He was a translator, a musician, a song-writer, a poet, a satirist, a biographer, an historian, a prose story-teller. His prose story is languid and vague; his 'History of Ireland' is not now read. Of his biographies, that of Byron will always be of interest, not because of the biographer's art, but because of the subject and the extracts from his letters and journals. Of another of his biographies the Prince Regent said that he had been guilty of a criminal offence in attempting the life of Sheridan. As regards his love-poems, their merits and demerits are alike great and striking. Perfect rhythm, unexcelled harmony, happiness of phrase, fidelity of description, felicity of epigram, are adorned with a luxuriance that overpowers, a languor and perfumery that is meritricious and artificial, an intensity that is strained, a feeling that is unreal, a gorgeousness that is tiresome and monotonous. Tenderness and sprightly fancy, picturesqueness and vivacity, exquisite finish and delicious gracefulness, lose much of their beauty and power to charm because of the ever-present conviction that all is artificial and unreal—tinselled and spangled and bright only with a lime-light glare which soon dazzles and wearies. In his 'Translations,' the simplicity of the original is concealed or distorted by the clothings and embellishments of the copyist.

It is as a satirist and song-writer Moore will be best remembered. 'The Fudge Family in Paris,' as a social and political sketch, is unsurpassed for humour, irony, and brilliancy. But as an Irish national song-writer, Moore's immortality is, as we have said, certain and secure. Though he is far and away inferior in robust feeling, healthy intensity, and vigorous and profound sensibility to Burns, he approaches nearly to Béranger. Though in the 'Melodies' the loftiness and dignity is sometimes sacrificed to a conceit or a stroke of wit, on the whole they are irreproachable and of the highest excellence. The melody is exquisite and faultless, the language clear and vigorous, tender and even majestic, the pathos is natural and true, the patriotism is purified.

'They are worth all the epics that ever were written,' says Byron. To these songs his country is partially indebted for the early granting of Catholic Emancipation. The whole English-speaking world will for ever lie under an obligation to this son of the Aungier Street grocer for the sweetest and most singable lyrics in our literature. They were prompted by an enlightened and liberal patriotism, and of them and of him Shelley well said that he was the sweetest lyric of Ierne's saddest song, and 'Love taught Grief to fall like music from his tongue.'

He was, as a husband and a son, irreproachable and estimable. He allowed his parents £100 a year when he was poor himself, and "never omitted to write twice a week to his mother." His wife idolised him, as he idolised her, but even her loving solace could not relieve the bitterness occasioned by the loss of all his children in his lifetime.

With many whose biographies are here briefly recorded —Sheridan, Curran, and others—the closing scenes of their lives are a strong and sad contrast to the brilliancy and triumphs of their literary and social careers. Moore is no exception. Though he did not, like Swift, expire 'a driveller and a show,' his life-light perished in pitiable imbecility. Nothing can be sadder than that picture of him weeping over one of his own melodies, which hearing, he did not recognise. It was an altogether mournful and dismal termination to the darling of society, who in his heyday fascinated and enraptured that world of fashion which he so 'dearly loved.'

GRIFFIN.

GERALD GRIFFIN is another on the roll of Irish literature who was of lowly origin, who wrote his name plainly amongst the famous, and who died before his prime. The man who at twenty-two years of age wrote 'Gisippus,' and at twenty three wrote 'The Collegians,' 'the most perfect Irish novel,' was no common person. What he might have been under other circumstances and other conditions is one of those problems which inevitably suggests itself in the perusal of his life. He did great things in a short, laborious, distracted life. He should have done the greatest had he lived on to the threescore years and ten, and had he passed his days in calmness, affluence, and contentment. As it was, his life was marked into successive stages of hope and disappointment, penury and feverish drudgery, success with its attendant praises, and desponding morbid religiousness.

He was born at Limerick on 10th December, 1803, the ninth son of a county Limerick farmer, who afterwards tried brewing as a trade; was intended for the medical profession, but preferred to spend his time in dreaming and poetising. At an early age he wrote a drama, afterwards in later years, perhaps wisely, destroyed by him, and his 'first appearance in public' was in the columns of a local newspaper. His ambition was cabined and cribbed in 'sweet Adare,' where he lived with his uncle after the removal of his parents to Pennsylvania; and before he was twenty years old he betook himself to London with his boyish tragedy in his pocket and his heart full of high hopes. His tragedy was not accepted, and he found it a struggle to eke out his daily bread as a newspaper hack. He toiled on in distress the greatest; 'without food for three days' was not a solitary episode in his life. He wrote poems for the magazines and articles for *The Fashion News,* and completed 'Gisippus,' another tragedy, which was 'written on little slips of paper in coffee-houses.'

In 1827, worn out with the tedious and anxious bread-struggle in London, where John Banim was his only friend, he returned to his kin in Ireland, and within a few months produced his 'Hallowtide Tales' and 'Tales of the Munster Festivals.' The novel of 'The Collegians' was published in 1828 on his return to London, and fame and fortune now smiled hopefully upon him. Nevertheless he relinquished literature for a while, and at the London University entered upon the study of the law. This was soon abandoned in its turn for story-writing again, and then a despondency, which had been intermittent for some years, settled upon him. A religious gloom overshadowed him; melancholy anticipations of an early death—a 'strange feeling' that he had in the days of his childhood—oppressed him; he imagined he discovered that the well-merited fame that had crowned him was a delusion, a mockery, a vanity. The publishers had 'cheated him abominably.' Two guineas was his payment for translating a volume and a half of Prevost's works. He in his melancholy regarded his works as almost pernicious productions, and he destroyed his MSS. And then, 'tired,' as he wrote, 'of a stupid, lonely, wasting, desponding, caterpillar-kind of existence,' he retired from the world, its labours and rewards, its cares and glories, and became one of the Society of Christian Brothers, a body whose aim is to devote their unselfish lives to the education of the poor.

In 1838 he joined their monastery in Dublin, to enter upon a severe and laborious ordeal; from which, however, he derived happiness, we read. In 1839 he was transferred to the Cork establishment. The rigid vigils, the constant fasts, the consuming soul-anxiety wore him away. He contracted a fever, and died at the North Monastery on 12th June, 1840. His resting-place in the cemetery of that institution is marked by a plain slab with the inscription, 'BROTHER GERALD GRIFFIN.'

The best of his many beautiful songs is perhaps 'Gille Machree;' and the following verse from one of his poems, written in his earlier years on the occasion of his sister's death, will afford a fitting insight into the mysterious working of his mind, and a proof of his high poetic power:

> 'If in that land where Hope can cheat no more—
>   Lavish in promise, laggard in fulfilling—
>   Where fearless love on every bosom stealing,
> And boundless knowledge brighten all the shore;
> If in that land, when life's old toils are done,
>   And my heart lies as motionless as thine,
>   I still might hope to press that hand in mine,
> My unoffending—my offended one!
> I would not mourn the health that flies my cheek,
>   I would not mourn my disappointed years,
>   My vain heart mocked and worldly hopes o'erthrown;
> But long to meet thee in that land of rest—
>   Nor deem it joy to breathe in careless ears,
>   A tale of blighted hopes as mournful as thine own.'

MANGAN.

HAD Mangan been an English poet of cleanly life and worldly wisdom, and had his works been given to the world by an eminent London publisher, his fame to-day would have been world-wide. But he was a humble lowly Irishman, who moped through his sober hours, who associated and dissipated with the human dregs of Dublin, who had as much prudence and common sense as the ostrich, who shrank from publicity and avoided notoriety —a bookworm, a dreamer, and a drunkard.

Like Moore, James Clarence Mangan was the son of a grocer. His father had come to Dublin from the county Limerick, from Shanagolden, had married a Dublin girl, and had set up a little struggling grocery business in Fishamble Street, where James Clarence was born, in 1803. The lad went to a school in a quadrangle off Werburgh Street, called Derby Square—a place once respectable, but then, as now, of the dingiest, dismallest dreariness. He left school early, and became an office-boy in a scrivener's, or attorney's—an experience he ever afterwards referred to with loathing and horror—and it is said that out of his paltry wages he maintained a mother and sister and brother. His life, however, about this period is a blank; he was swamped in misery and poverty, from which he never emerged. In 1830 he was contributing translations, from the German and Irish, to a local periodical. He knew not a word of Irish, and, if he had any knowledge of German, how or where he acquired it is a mystery. About this time he became known to Dr. Petrie and Dr. Todd, and was by the latter, who was librarian to the Dublin University, employed to compile a new edition of a catalogue of the college library. From 1833 he was a constant contributor of translations and quasi-translations to the *Penny Journal*, published in Dublin, and to the *University Magazine*, then edited by Isaac Butt. In 1842 he gave his talents to the newly-established *Nation* newspaper, and in 1847 transferred them to the *United Irishman*. Though not ostensibly one of the band of men who, as Young Irelanders, sought to 'redeem, regenerate, and disenthrall' their country, he was with them in so far that their sentiments were his, their aims were his hopes, and his pen was employed in their service. Amongst the literary young men connected with the "'48 movement,' he had many friends; but he was not sympathetic or reciprocal—he was one that scarcely showed that he accepted or appreciated friendly advances. Thus no one seems to have taken much trouble about him; no one knew whence he came or whither he went. He was ghostly, solitary, silent, and mysterious—a man with no intimates. Somehow, in the month of June, 1849, it became known to Mr. O'Daly, a bookseller in Dublin, who had heard of and befriended him, that he was in a wretched condition, grievously ill, in an obscure house in Bride Street, an obscure portion of the city. O'Daly found him, weakened with opium-eating and disease, dying of starvation; had him moved to a hospital, where, after lingering a few days, the unfortunate poet died on the 20th June, 1849. He was buried in Glasnevin Cemetery, where, amongst the abundant grass, his humble grave is hidden away.

It is hard, having read Mangan's poems, to reconcile one's self to the belief that it was the wretched dilapidated figure that glided through his forty-six years of poverty and drink to the disease and starvation that terminated his life, who conceived and wrote them. With his old, shapeless, weather-stained cloak round his odd, shapeless figure; with his long white silken hair unkempt; with his marble, deathly features, and his great blue eyes abstractedly looking into time or eternity; shrinking, rather than walking, through the streets—as such he is still remembered by many. He was to be seen perched on a ladder in the College library, poring over a book for hours, unmoved; he was to be found before the magistrate, fresh from the police-cells, whither he had been brought drunk and helpless from the gutters. He found relief from his earthly miseries in whisky and opium; and despairing and uncomplaining, gentle and affectionate, starving himself to give bread to his womenkind, in quiet, speechless obscurity, he wasted the soul within him.

There is one ballad written by him on himself—'The Nameless One.' It is altogether unlike his other writings. It is a corollary and a supplement to the biography built on the few facts to be ascertained concerning him. It is a cry, a shriek almost, of passionate despair, of utter hopelessness. It is a glance into the soul of him, and a view of the devils tearing to pieces his heart. A few verses of this saddening production will suffice:

> 'Roll forth, my song, like the rushing river,
>   That sweeps along to the mighty sea;
> God will inspire me, while I deliver
>   My soul of thee.
>
> * * * * * *
>
> 'And tell how trampled, derided, hated,
>   And worn by weakness, disease, and wrong,
> He fled for shelter to God, who mated
>   His soul with song.
>
> 'Go on to tell how, with genius wasted,
>   Betrayed in friendship, befooled in love,
> With spirit shipwrecked, and young hopes blasted,
>   He still, still strove.
>
> * * * * * *
>
> 'And he fell far through that pit abysmal,
>   The gulf and grave of Maginn and Burns,
> And pawned his soul for the devil's dismal
>   Stock of returns.
>
> * * * * * *
>
> 'But yet redeemed it in days of darkness,
>   And shapes and signs of the final wrath,
> When death, in hideous and ghastly starkness,
>   Stood in his path.
>
> * * * * * *
>
> 'And tell how now, amid wreck and sorrow,
>   And want, and sickness, and houseless nights,
> He bides in calmness the silent morrow,
>   That no ray lights.'

But, Mangan, as seen in his works, was quite a different mortal. His translations from the German, though not strictly literal, never miss or mar the sentiment, and the language and rhythm are perfect. His pathos is simple and unconstrained; but, when he attempts humour, it is either buffoonery or the unreal laughter of the clown through his mask. We could quote whole songs from his 'Anthologies,' which, in language and natural melodiousness, far excel the renderings of the same songs by Lord Lytton, Brooks, and others. Notwithstanding his mode of life, he was scrupulously pure, even prudish, in his versions and translations. His Irish pieces are well known in his own country, and all he wrote is worthy to be known by all readers of poetry, for they are manifestly the productions of a poet and scholar of refined taste and wide culture.

'FATHER PROUT.'

THE Reverend Francis Sylvester Mahony—or Father Frank Mahony, as his friends called him; or Father Prout, as he is known to readers—is another of the names great in Irish literature which Cork can claim as her own. Of his clerical calling it is enough to say that during his life he did not undertake a cure of souls, and that his later years were clouded by an ever-present remorse at his having obtruded himself into a sacred calling for which he had no vocation. If he had been a lesser man his unclerical life would have entailed on him obloquy, reprehension, censure, from the Catholic Irish people; but, notwithstanding his unreverend life, notwithstanding his contempt for O'Connell, he was regarded with affection by his countrymen; and his townsmen, ever ready to appreciate and applaud literary ability, were proud of him living, and we hope are proud of him dead.

The late Archbishop of Tuam, Dr. MacHale, many years ago reproved one who in his hearing disparaged the unpriestly priest, by saying that 'the Irishman who wrote Father Prout's papers was an honour to his country.' Father Prout did more than this. He sang 'The Bells of Shandon,' a song that everyone has heard; and it is in the fitness of things that, after a wayward, wandering, erratic life, he sleeps near where he was born, beneath the shadow of Shandon Church, beside the bells he made famous.

'Father Frank' was a member of an old and respected Cork family. He was descended, of course, from the first who, in the mythical times, bore the family name (which, we are told, means in Irish 'a calf of the plain'), through the kings O'Mahony, and so forth. But his immediate forefathers were of the middle class, and he himself was designed for the priesthood. He was born in 1804 or 1805, was educated at France and at Rome, took orders, and became a tutor at Clongowes College. He, however, soon discovered that for neither teaching nor preaching was he adapted, and he resigned—in effect —his orders, and embraced literature as his profession. He was a principal writer for *Fraser's* and *Bentley's*—the two chief magazines of the day; and subsequently, in 1846, he became Roman correspondent of the *Daily News*, of which his friend Charles Dickens was editor. In 1858 he became Paris correspondent of the *Globe*, and remained so till his death, which occurred in Paris on the 18th of May, 1866.

'The Reliques of Father Prout,' and 'The Final

Reliques,' have been read by everyone, and the scholarship, wit, humour, and pathos with which they abound have been admired, laughed at, and remembered. His knowledge of numerous languages, his extraordinary powers of versifying in foreign tongues, dead and living, his wonderful versatility, always excite and will continue to excite admiration and applause. He was in all respects an extraordinary character. 'He belonged,' says one biographer, 'to a race of mortals now quite gone out of existence, like the elk and wolf-dog.' His personal appearance was remarkable: 'a short, spare man, stooping as he went, with his right arm clasped in the left hand behind him—a sharp face with piercing grey eyes that looked vacantly upward, a mocking lip, a close-shaven face, an ecclesiastical garb of slovenly appearance.' He was altogether a Bohemian and a profound scholar, brimful of wit, of sarcasm, of comedy.

'The Bells of Shandon' was written when he was quite young, a student at the Irish College in Rome. It is said that the opening lines are still to be seen in a room there, scrawled on the wall just above where his bed used to be. At Clongowes, he had in his class John Sheehan, afterwards a well-known contributor to *Bentley's* under the name of 'The Irish Whisky Drinker.' He had also among his pupils Frank Stack Murphy (afterwards a serjeant-at-law), in conjunction with whom some of the translations into Greek were made and published.

His connection with *Fraser's* brought him into companionship with Thackeray, Coleridge, Carlyle, Southey, Lockhart, Dr. Maginn (also a Cork man), Maclise (another Cork man), and others, then and since notable.

He hated O'Connell, and wrote for the *Times* a bitter sarcasm on him—'The Lay of Lazarus.'

Everywhere a wit, nowhere a cleric, always hilarious—his slovenly, shabby, mendicant garments could not preclude the idea that the bright eyes and 'roguish mouth' and sudden solitary laugh were traits of an uncommon individual. He was classed with Hood and Thackeray into the triumvirate of English humourists by a French critic, and his most recent biographer says, justly, of his works: 'They are as exhilarating as the first runnings of a well-filled wine-press, the grapes heaped together in which have been ripened by laughing suns and grown in classic vineyards.'

BANIM.

JOHN BANIM wrote the song or ballad called 'Soggarth Aroon,' and Lord Jeffrey, in a letter, confessed that of the volume of 'Irish Ballad Poetry' published by Duffy, of all the 'most pathetic and most spirited pieces,' he was 'most struck by "Soggarth Aroon,"' after the two first stanzas. Banim is, however, best known as a novelist; his 'Tales of the O'Hara Family,' written in conjunction with his brother Michael, his 'Boyne Water,' and other prose works, earned for him the distinction of being once described as Ireland's greatest novelist.

He was born on the 3rd of April, 1798, in Kilkenny, where his father was a small shopkeeper, and he manifested at a very early age a tendency to authorship. We are told he composed and wrote a fairy tale when six years old, and at ten wrote 'poems'! The author, however, gave place to the artist, and at eighteen he established himself in Kilkenny, and commenced life with this profession. A romantic and tragic incident terminated his art-career, and at twenty years of age he moved to Dublin, where he procured a precarious subsistence by fugitive contributions to periodicals. He wrote a poem, 'The Celt's Paradise'; and plays, 'The Jest' and 'Damon and Pythias,' which were, through Mr. Lalor Sheil's patronage and influence, brought out at Covent Garden.

'The Tales of the O'Hara Family,' the work which is best known, was next published. He married early and settled in London, and met with some success; so that he could, as we have already mentioned, befriend poor Gerald Griffin in his struggles there. But ill-health and domestic sorrow broke him down, and a charitable subscription was organised to enable him to visit the Continent. The change was of small benefit; in 1835 'he returned to Ireland a complete wreck,' after the burial in France of his only son; and on his way to his native Kilkenny he was detained at Dublin, where he was accorded a benefit at the Theatre Royal, at which he was received with every demonstration of honour. He obtained, on Lord Carlisle's recommendation, a pension of £150 from the Civil List and an allowance for his daughter's education. He died on 1st August, 1842, at Kilkenny, aged forty-four, and was buried in the graveyard of St. John's there.

John Banim has been called the 'Scott of Ireland,' not alone because his novels were founded on national themes, but because he was a palpable imitator of Scott's style. He is sometimes tiresome in his descriptions, and he fails to represent the higher social classes; but his portrayal of the Irish peasantry has never been equalled. He dwells in his novels too much on the horrible; the worst and darkest human passions are too ready to his imagination, but they are the works of a man of genius, and were recognised as such when they were published. As a dramatist, his 'Damon and Pythias' is celebrated; and as a song-writer, 'Soggarth Aroon' and the few others we quote will prove him to be not the least of the tribe.

KEEGAN.

JOHN KEEGAN was the son of a peasant in the Queen's County, and was born about 1809. What his method of teaching himself was, or what opportunities of learning he possessed beyond the local hedge-school, are to be conjectured; but he seems to have somehow acquired a considerable amount of knowledge, of a plain but serviceable character. He was, while yet a young man, a well-known writer of ballads for the *Nation* newspaper, and a contributor of sketches and tales to an Irish journal called *Dolman's Magazine;* and these, with his songs—which are marked by pathetic simplicity, tenderness, and purity, and show a remarkable insight of the feelings and affections of his class—were written in the intervals of his peasant labours. He died in 1849, 'happy,' says Mr. Hayes, 'to die amongst the people whose privations he shared, and the hard realities of whose daily life he illustrated by his prose writings and songs. He was a poor man who wrote for bread—a "peasant poet."'

FRASER.

JOHN FRASER, sometimes called 'The poet of the workshop,' from the circumstance that he was a cabinet-maker, 'a steady and unassuming artisan,' but best known by his *nom de plume* of 'J de Jean'—was born in

Birr, now called Parsonstown, in the King's County, about the year 1809. Considering that throughout his life he worked at his trade diligently, that he was a martyr to ill-health, that he was in straitened circumstances, his writings are numerous, and manifest a power and culture which are remarkable. Had he been affluent, with time to cultivate his talents and tastes, he would have been one of the foremost of Irish verse-writers.

He is best at descriptive poetry, and shows a sympathetic appreciation of rural nature. The songs in which he celebrates the localities familiar to his childhood are marked by a quiet, but vivid beauty. His political verses are powerful and enthusiastic, but generous and tolerant, and his lines on the death of Thomas Davis are of a high order of excellence. He was held in affectionate esteem by his literary acquaintances, led a retired and blameless life—a noble and simple piety is apparent in his writings—and he died in 1849, in Dublin, at the age of forty. His poems were collected and published after his death.

WALSH.

'POOR WALSH! he has a family of young children, he seems broken in health and spirits; ruin has been on his tracks for years, and I think has him in the wind at last. There are more contented galley-slaves moiling at Spike than the schoolmaster. Perhaps the man really does envy me, and most assuredly I do not envy him.' These are the words written by John Mitchell in his *Jail Journal*, upon an interview he had, when a political prisoner in Spike Island, with Edward Walsh, the author of many 'sweet songs and of some very musical translations from Irish ballads,' and the schoolmaster of the juvenile convicts in penal servitude on Spike Island. 'A tall, gentlemanlike person, in black but rather overworn clothes,' with tears in his eyes on the occasion of this interview, Mitchell describes him. 'He stooped down and kissed my hands, and said I was the man in Ireland most to be envied.'

Soon after this episode Walsh was promoted to the schoolmastership of the Cork Workhouse, and after a short interval further promoted to where the inexorable ruin could not overtake him, and where he could rest, for ever released from the moiling worse than that of the convict galley-slave. The sickening drudgery at which death found him was the only means of livelihood given to a man who left two volumes of translations from Irish poetry, who was himself a not insignificant poet, was an accomplished scholar in the Irish language and literature, 'and a man of pure heart and sterling sentiment.'

Edward Walsh's father was a small farmer in the county Cork who had eloped with a girl much above him in social status. He relinquished farming owing to pecuniary straits and enlisted in the militia, and was quartered with his regiment in Londonderry in 1805, when his son was born. When the corps was disbanded the father returned to Cork, and here Edward was educated. His education must have been beyond the average of his class, for he received an appointment as a private tutor while still a young man. He subsequently kept a school in Millstreet, in the county Cork, whence in 1837 he removed to pursue the same occupation in Toureen, in county Waterford. He diligently and resolutely devoted himself to the study of his native language, and perfected the knowledge obtained from books by constant intercourse with the Irish-speaking peasants. He translated the Irish songs and poems accessible to him, and began to publish them in various magazines while at Toureen. These were of such merit, so literal, idiomatic, and characteristic, and withal so melodious, that they attracted the attention, amongst others, of the present Sir Charles Gavan Duffy, and through his friendship and interest Walsh was appointed sub-editor of the *Dublin Monitor*. For some unassigned reason he resigned this post, which, from the advantages it offered—time for literary labour and opportunities for his special study—should have been of superlative value to him. He then published a collection of his own poems and his translations under the title of 'Jacobite Relics of Ireland;' and next he is engaged at the dreary and, to him, degrading task of instructing the juvenile convict criminals at Spike Island. Thence to the Cork Workhouse School, where on the 6th April, 1850, he died, aged forty-five. He was, we are told, 'A shy, sensitive creature,' and the man who wrote his songs spent the best part of his life teaching rogues and paupers their 'Reading made easy.' It is a biographical record of singular sadness and inappropriateness. No wonder he was 'broken in health and spirits,' and that 'ruin had him in the wind at last,' when Mitchell saw him in his wretched office at the convict depôt.

Mr. Hayes says of his writings: 'His contributions to Irish literature have been both considerable and creditable; there is a singular beauty and fascinating melody in his verse which cheers and charms the ear and heart. His translations preserve all the peculiarities of the old tongue, which he knew and spoke with graceful fluency.' The song, 'Mo Craoibhin Cno' ('My cluster of nuts,' 'My nut-brown maid'), is very well known, and in simplicity, pure sentiment, and melody, will compare with any love-lyric in this collection.

LADY DUFFERIN.

It is no exageration to say that Lady Dufferin as a song-writer has not been surpassed by any Irish author, ancient or modern. She is a conspicuous example of the transmission of genius from generation to generation. In her family it has been hereditary. She not only inherited it, but transmitted it. Her son, the present Earl of Dufferin, is a worthy descendant of an illustrious ancestor. The authoress of the song 'I'm sitting on the stile, Mary,' was Helen Selina Blackwood, and though she was at her death the Countess of Gifford, she is best known as Lady Dufferin. She was the eldest daughter of Thomas Sheridan, who was son of Richard Brinsley Sheridan, a brief biography of whom has already appeared in these pages. She was born in 1807, and her earlier years were spent at Hampton Court Palace, where her mother resided after the death of Thomas Sheridan. She, in common with her two sisters, was a noted beauty, and she married on 6th July, 1825, the Honourable Price Blackwood, afterwards Lord Dufferin, an Irish nobleman, and her only son, born in 1826, is the present Earl of Dufferin, well-known in the diplomatic and literary world.

While still very young she, in conjunction with her sister Caroline, afterwards the Hon. Mrs. Norton, published 'The Dandies' Rout,' which was written and illustrated by the two girls.

Her husband died in 1841, and in 1862 Lady Dufferin married the Earl of Gifford, eldest son of the Marquis of Tweeddale, but was left again a widow in two months after her marriage. She died on 13th June, 1867.

If she had written nothing but 'The Irish Emigrant,' 'I'm sitting on the stile, Mary,' her fame as a poet had been established. This, and all her songs and ballads, were prompted not by the ambition for fame, but because of a kindly, hearty, and warm sympathy with the best qualities of the people to which she belonged, and amongst whom she dwelt. She has entered into the ways and thoughts of the Irish, and penetrated into their heart of hearts. The pathos of 'The Emigrant,' and the humour of 'Terence's Farewell' and 'Katie's Letter,' are alike entirely Irish. Most, if not all, of her songs were published anonymously, and no collection of them has yet appeared, an injustice to her memory and a loss to Irish literature. Lady Dufferin was also a composer; she wrote the music for her own song 'Sweet Kilkenny Town:' and she was the author of a prose work, 'The Honourable Impulsia Gushington,' a humorous and light satire on the ways and doings of nineteenth-century fashion. This was written to relieve the weariness and depression of a long sickness of 'a beloved friend.' But it is on her Irish songs her brightest fame rests, and it will remain undimmed as long as songs are sung.

MRS. NORTON.

MRS. NORTON was sister to Lady Dufferin, and had also a large share of the Sheridan heritage of intellectual power; but the life-history of the two is strangely diverse. Helen Selina Sheridan had a happy uneventful life. Caroline Sheridan's was indeed eventful, but calamitous and unhappy.

In 1827, on 30th July, she was married to the Hon. George C. Norton, a brother of the third Lord Grantley—a barrister, and afterwards Recorder of Guildford. She was vivacious, genial, intellectual, enthusiastic: he was a rake who ill-treated her—conceited, without brains—poor, without industry—a very ordinary personage altogether, but the very reverse of what Caroline Sheridan's husband should be. The husband-drone, shameful and shameless, compelled her to write to earn money for him—compelled her to solicit for him an appointment from Lord Melbourne. Her acquaintance with Lord Melbourne, thus originated, was the cause of one of the most unfortunate and the most notorious episodes in her varied life. He had an unsympathetic wife (as Lady Caroline Lamb she is best known), and Mrs. Norton had a contemptible husband; but both had high intellectual tastes and accomplishments, and their dispositions were alike genial and amiable, but vivacious and brilliant. Lord Melbourne granted her request, and appointed her husband a police-magistrate in London. But he was utterly unfit by manner and capacity for such a post; he was quarrelsome and ignorant, and neglected his duty. He was in pecuniary difficulties, and sought loans from Lord Melbourne; and, being refused, he revenged himself by instituting an action for divorce, making the minister co-respondent, and claiming from him £10,000 damages. The suit was scouted out of court; the jury found for the defendants without leaving the box, and Mrs. Norton separated finally from her paltry consort. He died in 1869, and in 1877 she married Sir W. Stirling Maxwell, Bart.—a platonic proceeding resembling her sister Lady Dufferin's marriage to Lord Gifford—and in a few months, in June, 1877, she died, aged seventy.

Mrs. Norton was very industrious with her pen throughout her life. Her earlier poems are her best productions, and her songs are sung in every drawing-room. She wrote novels and tales, a tragedy called 'The Martyr,' and filled up her literary life with numerous and ambitious poems.

Her later writings are didactic, and aimed at effecting some social reforms; some of them are full of references to her own unhappy life. She was one of the most brilliant ornaments of London society before she retired into seclusion. She everywhere commanded the pity and sympathy which should arise in her behalf wherever her husband was known. She occupied and deserved a conspicuous place in contemporary literature; and though there is a staginess about her style, and though she fails in that in which Lady Dufferin excels—the subtle power to be *en rapport* with the heart's best sympathies—yet she has in her poems, and in her songs, maintained with credit the Sheridan mental heritage which devolved upon her.

M'GEE.

THOMAS DARCY M'GEE was, with Sir Charles Gavan Duffy, the only one of all the young Irishmen implicated in the futile movement of 1848 whose after-career gave exercise for a display of the abilities which were, in their own country, unhappily misdirected into the channel of revolution in their youth. The tragic termination of M'Gee's life—his assassination while at the height of his fame and popularity in Canada—is still fresh in the public mind. His maturer years had taught him the folly of his youth. In the Government of Canada he attained to ministerial office; he went over to loyalty; he denounced with eloquent vehemence the aims and ways of those who still adhered to the insurrectionary ideas which ruled his own early years; he poured powerful contempt and derision on the Fenian organisation, and he thus aroused the vengeance of that body against him, and on the night of the 7th April, 1868, he was murdered.

He was a native of the county Monaghan, and was born on the 13th April, 1825; the son of an official in the Irish Coastguard Service, by a Miss Morgan, daughter of a Dublin bookseller. In 1842 he emigrated to America, and having attracted some notice by a speech made by him there, on the occasion of the celebration of the Year of the American Independence, he was employed on the literary staff of the *Boston Pilot*—an influential journal—of which he became editor in 1844, before he had attained his twentieth year. His public speeches, marked by fire and eloquence, carried his name to Ireland; and O'Connell described one of them as an inspired utterance by an exiled Irish boy. He returned to Ireland, and joined the staff of the *Freeman's Journal*, and became editor of it. But his political opinions were, at that time, far in advance of the then moderate and cautious *Freeman*, and he therefore went over to the *Nation*, the newspaper then under the editorship of Gavan Duffy. He entered heartily into the political spirit enunciated so ably by this journal, and he became its sub-editor, and so continued till its suppression in 1848. His ability and energy procured him the secretaryship of the 'Young Ireland Confederation.' He was employed as a public orator throughout Ireland, and despatched to Scotland to awaken public feeling in favour of the movement. He was arrested because of a wild speech on its behalf made in Wicklow, but was released after a brief incarceration; and when the resort to arms took place in 1848, he was in Scotland, promoting the objects of the confederation. He was immediately nominated for arrest, and a reward of £300 offered for his apprehension. Yet he returned to Ireland to see his newly-married wife; and, under the protection of a high ecclesiastic, he contrived, in the disguise of a clergyman, to make good his escape to Philadelphia, where he landed on the 10th October. He established a journal, the *Nation*, in New York, and devoted its pages to blaming the Irish priesthood for the failure of the Young Ireland Movement. He soon abandoned the *New York Nation*, and started the *American Celt* in Boston. Up to this period the sentiments of the revolutionist still animated him; but now they toned down, and he seems to have regarded them as a blunder.

In 1858, still a young man, he left the States and settled in Montreal; was elected to the Canadian Parliament, where his eloquence and administrative ability soon made him a conspicuous member of the Legislature. In 1862 he became President of the Executive Committee, and subsequently obtained the portfolio of the Minister of Agriculture. During his official career he wrote his 'History of Ireland.' In 1865 he was in Ireland as representative from Canada at the Dublin Exhibition; and during his sojourn, while on a visit to his father, in the county Wexford, delivered a philippic against the then widespread Fenian organisation, and descanted upon the degraded lives led by the Irish in the United States. In 1867 he revisited Europe, this time as the Dominion representative at the Paris *Exposition*, and, on his return, promoted the beneficent scheme of consolidation of the Canadian Colonies. He was publicly entertained in Montreal, on St. Patrick's Day, 1868, in consideration of his services to the State; and a few weeks later, on the 7th April, almost immediately after a brilliant speech in the Parliament, he was assassinated. Thus was he rewarded for having forsaken the paths of revolution, for having recanted so openly and reviled so consistently and furiously his old political creeds; for having, in season and out of season, with tongue and pen, persistently opposed and denounced the Fenian organisation.

As a parliamentary orator his eloquence was of a high order, and as a politician he possessed many statesmanlike attributes. As a literary man he was throughout his life industrious, and his writings are not of an ephemeral character. He wrote a 'History of Ireland,' sundry works in connection with the Irish settlers in America, and the 'Lives of Irish Writers.' His poems fill a volume; and his songs, most of which belong to his earlier life, are national in their tone—impulsive, ardent, enthusiastic—are full of life and dignity, and marked by an undoubted sincerity. 'His poetry,' wrote Sir Charles Gavan Duffy, who knew him well, 'touches me like the breath of spring, and revives the buoyancy and chivalry of youth.'

WILLIAMS.

RICHARD DALTON WILLIAMS was the son of a Tipperary farmer who lived at Grenanstown, at the foot of the Devil's Bit Mountains. Hayes says he was born there; others say he was born in Dublin; but of the place and of the time there is doubt. It is believed he was born about the year 1822. He was educated at Tullabeg School, and went thence to Carlow College, which he left to become a medical student in Dublin. He was a contributor to the *Nation*, was involved in the 1848 movement, and, after John Mitchell's conviction and the suppression of the *United Irishman* paper, Williams assisted O'Doherty in establishing the *Irish Tribune*, a journal of the same character. It was speedily suppressed—before its sixth number—and O'Doherty was tried for sedition, convicted, and transported to Australia. Williams escaped, the jury in his case acquitting him, or disagreeing. He now resumed his medical studies, and received a diploma from the Edinburgh University. Armed with this he emigrated to America, in 1850. He practised at his profession in New Orleans for some time, but with indifferent success. He became Professor of *Belles Lettres* in Spring Hill College—an educational institution at Mobile, in Alabama. He did not long continue at this work, but moved to Louisiana, to again practise medicine at Thibodeaux. Here, on 5th July, 1862, he fell a victim to consumption, a disease which had afflicted him since his youth. He died in utter poverty and loneliness, and his burial-place was marked by a piece of board for a monument, until some Irish-American soldiers, passing through the locality, heard of and saw the grave, and they raised over his ashes a fitting and enduring memorial.

Williams was one of the ablest of the young men who in those troubled times of 1848 gathered together and raised aloft a new standard to eclipse O'Connell. His first poem which appeared in the *Nation* newspaper—the organ of the Young Irelanders—was 'The Munster War-Song,' and was written while he was at Carlow

College, still in his teens. He wrote much while in Dublin, and embellished all he wrote with a playful wit, a grotesque humour, an affectionate sympathy—all lit up by a wide and varied knowledge and a cultivated intelligence. His verses on 'The Dying Girl' were written after a visit to one of the Dublin hospitals. His 'Song of the Irish American Regiments' was written in America, when he was fired to enthusiasm by the outbreak of the Civil War. 'Tears lie in him and a consuming fire,' wrote a kindly, friendly critic. 'There is in him the gentleness and trembling pity of a woman, and the deep earnestness and passionate ardour of the hero.' And he died an exile, struggling vainly for bread, weighed down into his grave by relentless disease, aggravated by poverty bordering on starvation. He is to be numbered amongst the unfortunates in Irish literature who saw no good in their own days—a humorous man withal throughout, who did not end his days in peace.

CASEY.

IN Ireland during the century the literature of rebellion has been prolific in songs, many of which, especially those of 1848, are of more than average merit. The Fenian conspiracy of 1866 was almost exclusively confined to the proletariat, and was conspicuous, in comparison with previous revolutionary movements, for its utter literary deficiency. There are one or two still living who were connected with it, and whose songs will be preserved; but of those who are dead there was but one —John Keegan Casey—who as a song-writer deserves to be remembered. When but twenty years of age he collected and published those effusions which he had contributed to various journals, and the volume was a success. In 1869, when twenty-three years old, he published another book of poems, 'The Rising of the Moon,' the contents of which were of the ultra-national type. The *London Review* in commenting on this volume said, 'Treason is put in a fascinating, tolerant, and intelligent shape, and no Saxon could feel over-vexed at being railed at so eloquently in his own language.' This was written of the work of a peasant's son, who died when twenty-three and a half years of age; who had seen the inside of a prison as a rebel; and whose love-songs are even preferable to his rebel-songs.

He was born in 1846 at Mount Dalton, in the county Westmeath, where his father was a peasant-farmer; he had a taste for learning, and few opportunities for gratifying it. He tried a shopboy's life, but abandoned it for literature and sedition. As a lad, before he was sixteen, he was a contributor to the *Nation* 'Poet's Corner,' and under the *nom de plume* of 'Leo,' wrote frequently and well. The literary ability of all his songs, and the tender simplicity of his love-songs, are very remarkable in one such as he. Had he lived down his hot youth, as other poets have done, there is every indication and promise in his writings that his maturer years would have added much—not discreditable—to the song-literature of Ireland.

DRINKING SONGS

O'ROURKE'S FEAST.*

O'ROURKE's noble fare
  Will ne'er be forgot
By those who were there
  Or those who were not.

His revels to keep,
  We sup and we dine
On seven score sheep,
  Fat bullocks, and swine.

Usquebaugh to our feast
  In pails was brought up,—
A hundred at least—
  And a mether† our cup.

---

* Written from tradition by MacGauran of Leitrim, a contemporary of Carolan, to celebrate a great feast given by The O'Rourke, a chieftain of Leitrim, upon his taking leave of his neighbours to visit Queen Elizabeth. The castle where the feast was given still stands, a ruin. O'Rourke was put to death in England. The translation of MacGauran's Irish song is by Dean Swift.
† A wooden four-handled drinking-vessel.

Oh, there is the sport !—
  We rise with the light
In disorderly sort
  From snoring all night.

Oh, how was I trick'd !
  My pipe it was broke,
My pocket was pick'd,
  I lost my new cloak.

'I'm rifled,' quoth Nell,
  'Of mantle and kercher ;
Why, then, fare them well—
  The de'il take the searcher !'

Come, harper ! strike up !
  'But first, by your favour,
Boy, give us a cup ;—
  Ah, this hath some savour.'

O'Rourke's jolly boys
  Ne'er dreamt of the matter,
Till—roused by the noise
  And the musical clatter—

They bounce from their nest,
  No longer will tarry ;
They rise ready drest,
  Without one Ave-Mary ;

They dance in a round,
  Cutting capers and ramping—
A mercy the ground
  Did not burst with their stamping.

The floor is all wet
   With leaps and with jumps,
While the water and sweat
   Splish-splash in their pumps.

'Bless you, late and early,
   Laughlin O'Enagin !
But, my hand*, you dance rarely,
   Margery Grenagin !

'Bring straw for our bed,
   Shake it down to the feet,
Then over us spread
   The winnowing sheet.

'To show I don't flinch
   Fill the bowl up again,
Then give us a pinch
   Of your sneezing Azean.'

Good Lord ! what a sight
   After all their good cheer,
For people to fight
   In the midst of their beer.

They rise from their feast,
   And hot are their brains ;
A cubic at least
   The length of their skeans.†

What stabs and what cuts !
   What clattering of sticks !

   *   *   *   *   *

   *   *   *   *   *

* An oath.   † Dagger-knives.

With cudgels of oak
Well harden'd in flame,
A hundred heads broke,
A hundred struck lame!

* * * * *

HUGH MACGAURAN.
(*Translated by Dean Swift.*)

SONG IN PRAISE OF DRINKING.

WHEN once I to the Tavern go
   I cannot leave it all the night,
For always there gay, happy lads
   Are drinking to their hearts' delight.

A generous flask is my desire,
   Filled till it overflows the brink;
And loving youngsters to partake.
   To them—and it—and all, I drink.

O bright love! come, sit near my side
   And drink from out my cup, *astore!*
And I will drain it to the dregs,
   And when it's dry, I'll call for more.

Come, tune the fiddle and the flute
   And touch the harp's melodious strings;
I drink my punch most willingly
   When music solace round me flings.

For then my heart is merriest,
   And then my brightest pleasures be
In emptying the methers full,
   With all around me gay and free.

And justly, fairly, worthily,
  Let's drink each others' health *galore;*
It is sufficient wealth to me
  To turn my cup and call for more.

O friends who near me feasting sit,
  Leave not the supper, I implore,
Till we have emptied all our cans
  In loving healths—and called for more.

To every brave man here's a health!
  To every wise and generous soul
Who does not starve to save his coins,
  But spends them in the flowing bowl!

The wretched churls who scraped and saved
  And added to their stingy store,
Are rotting in the churchyard now
  Where they can never call for more.

ANDREW MAGRATH.
(*Rendered by C. M. Collins.*)

MY GRAND RECREATION.

I SELL the best brandy and sherry,
To make my good customers merry;
  But at times their finances
  Run short, as it chances,
And then I feel very sad, very!

Here's brandy! Come, fill up your tumbler
Or ale, if your liking be humbler;
  And, while you've a shilling,
  Keep filling and swilling—
A fig for the growls of the grumbler!

I like, when I'm quite at my leisure,
Mirth, music, and all sorts of pleasure;
    When Margery's bringing
    The glass, I like singing
With bards—if they drink within measure.

Libation I pour on libation,
I sing the past fame of our nation;
    For valorous glory,
    For song and for story,
This, this is my grand recreation.

A. MAGRATH.
(Translated.)

MAGGY LAIDIR.*

Here's first the toast, the pride and boast,
    Our darling Maggy Laidir;
Let old and young, with ready tongue
    And open heart, applaud her.
Again prepare!—here's to the Fair
    Whose smiles with joy have crown'd us;
Then drain the bowl for each gay soul
    That's drinking here around us.

The mether† fill with right goodwill,
    There's sure no joy like drinking!
Our Bishop's name this draught must claim—
    Come, let me have no shrinking!
His name is dear, and with him here
    We'll join old Father Peter,
And as he steers through life's long years,
    May life to him seem sweeter.

* Pronounced *Lauder*.   † Drinking-cup.

Come, mark the call, and drink to all
  Old Ireland's tribes so glorious,
Who still have stood, in fields of blood,
  Unbroken and victorious.
Long as of old may Connaught hold
  Her boast of peerless beauty;
And Leinster show to friend and foe
  Her sons all prompt for duty.

A curse for those who dare oppose
  Our country's claim for freedom;
May none appear the knaves to hear,
  Or none who hear 'em, heed 'em:
May famine fall upon them all,
  May pests and plagues confound them,
And heartfelt care, and black despair,
  Till life's last hour surround them!

May lasting joys attend the boys
  Who love the land that bore us!
Still may they share such friendly fare
  As this that spreads before us.
May social cheer, like what we've here,
  For ever stand to greet them;
And hearts as sound as those around
  Be ready still to meet them!

Come, raise the voice! rejoice, rejoice—
  Fast, fast—the dawn's advancing;
My eyes grow dim, but every limb
  Seems quite agog for dancing.
Sweet girls! begin, 'tis shame and sin
  To see the time we're losing;
Come, lads! be gay—trip, trip away,
  While those who sit keep boozing.

Where's Thady Oge? up, Dan, you rogue!
　　Why stand you shilly-shally;
There's Mora here, and Una's here,
　　And yonder's sporting Sally.
Now frisk it round—aye, there's the sound
　　Our sires were fond of hearing;
The harp rings clear—hear, gossip, hear!
　　Oh, sure such notes are cheering!

Your health, my friend! till life shall end
　　May no bad chance betide us;
Oh may we still, our grief to kill,
　　Have drink like this beside us!
A fig for care!—but who's that there
　　That's of a quarrel thinking?
Put out the clown, or knock him down—
　　We're here for fun and drinking!
　　　　　　　　JOHN O'NEACHTAN.

LIQUOR OF LIFE!

The Bard addresses Whisky:

WHY, liquor of life, do I love you so,
When in all our encounters you lay me low?
More stupid and senseless I every day grow:
　　What a hint—if I'd mend by the warning!
Tatter'd and torn you've left my coat,
I've not a cravat to save my throat,
Yet I'd pardon you all, my sparkling doat,
　　If you'd cheer me again in the morning!

Whisky replies:

When you've heard prayers on Sunday next,
With a sermon beside, or at least—the text,
Come down to the ale-house—however you're vexed,
    And though thousands of cares assault you,
You'll find tippling there;—till morals mend,
A cock shall be placed in the barrel's end,
The jar shall be near you, and I'll be your friend,
    And give you a ' *Cead mille failté.*'

The Bard resumes his address:

You're my soul and my treasure, without and within,
My sister and cousin and all my kin;
'Tis unlucky to wed such a prodigal sin,
    But all other enjoyment is vain, love!
My barley-ricks all turn into you—
My tillage—my plough—and my horses too—
My cows and my sheep—they have bid me adieu:
    I care not—while *you* remain, love!

Come, vein of my heart! then come in haste,
You're like Nectar, at once my liquor and feast,—
My forefathers all had the very same taste
    For the genuine dew of the mountain.
O Usquebaugh! I love its kiss!—
My guardian spirit, I think it is;
Had my christening bowl been filled with this,
    I'd have swallowed it—were it a fountain.

Many's the quarrel and fight we've had,
And many a time you've made me mad,
But while I've a heart—it can never be sad,
    When you smile at me full on the table;

Surely you are my wife and brother—
My only child—my father and mother—
My outside coat—I have no other!
   Oh, I'll stand by you—while I am able.

If family pride can aught avail,
I've the sprightliest kin of all the Gael—
Brandy and Usquebaugh, and Ale!
   But Claret untasted may pass us;
To clash with the clergy were sore amiss,
So, for righteousness' sake, I leave them this—
For Claret the gownsman's comfort is,
   When they've saved us with matins and masses.

                TURLOUGH CAROLAN.
        (*Translated by John D'Alton, M.R.I.A.*)

OCTOBER ALE.

    How void of ease
    He spends his days
Who wastes his time in thinking!
    How like a beast,
    That ne'er can taste
The pleasures of good drinking
  May curses light upon the sot
    That ever kennels sober,
  Or rises e'er without a pot
    Of lovely brown October!

    Let others raise
    Their voice to praise
The Rhenish or the Sherry,
    The sparkling White
    Champagne so bright,
The Claret or Canary.

'Tis true they'd thaw the freezing blood,
And hinder our being sober;
But what for that was e'er so good
As lovely brown October?

What knaves are they
Who cross the sea
To bring such stuff among us?
How blind are we,
Who will not see
How grievously they wrong us!
They spoil the products of the land,
And of her coin disrobe her;
And yet their dregs can never stand
Against our brave October.

My jolly boys,
Let us rejoice,
And cast away all sorrow,
Let's never think,
While thus we drink,
What may fall out to-morrow.
Let's waste our wealth, enjoy content,
And never more live sober:
By Jove, the coin is rightly spent,
That's melted in October!

MATTHEW CONCANEN.
(*From* '*Wexford Wells.*)

NEWCASTLE BEER.

WHEN Fame brought the news of Great Britain's success,
And told at Olympus each Gallic defeat,
Glad Mars sent by Mercury orders express,
To summon the deities all to a treat;

   Blithe Comus was placed
   To guide the gay feast,
And freely declared there was choice of good cheer,
   Yet vow'd, to his thinking,
   For exquisite drinking.
Their nectar was nothing to Newcastle beer.

The great god of war, to encourage the fun,
 And humour the taste of his whimsical guest,
Sent a message that moment to Moore's for a tun
 Of Stingo, the stoutest, the brightest, and best;
   No gods—they all swore—
   Regal'd so before,
With liquor so lively, so potent, and clear;
   And each deified fellow
   Got jovially mellow,
In honour, brave boys, of our Newcastle beer.

Apollo, perceiving his talents refine,
 Repents he drank Helicon water so long;
He bow'd, being asked by the musical Nine,
 And gave the gay board an extempore song.
   But ere he began
   He toss'd off his can—
There's nought like good liquor the fancy to clear—
   Then sang with great merit
   The flavour and spirit
His godship had found in our Newcastle beer.

'Twas Stingo like this made Alcides so bold
 It braced up his nerves and enlivened his powers;
And his mystical club, that did wonders of old,
 Was nothing, my lads, but such liquor as ours.

The horrible crew
That Hercules slew,
Were Poverty, Calumny, Trouble and Fear,—
Such a club would you borrow
To drive away sorrow,
Apply for a jorum of Newcastle beer.

Ye youngsters, so diffident, languid and pale,
　Whom love, like the colic, so rudely infests;
Take a cordial of this, 'twill *probatum* prevail,
　And drive the cur Cupid away from your breasts.
　　Dull whining despise,
　　Grow rosy and wise,
Nor longer the jest of good fellows appear;
　　Bid adieu to your folly,
　　Get drunk and be jolly,
And smoke o'er a tankard of Newcastle beer.

Ye fanciful folk, for whom physic prescribes,
　Whom bolus and potion have harass'd to death;
Ye wretches, whom law and her ill-looking tribes
　Have hunted about 'till you're quite out of breath;
　　Here's shelter and ease,
　　No craving for fees,
No danger, no doctor, no bailiff is near;
　　Your spirits this raises,
　　It cures your diseases,
There's freedom and health in our Newcastle beer!

　　　　　　　　　JOHN CUNNINGHAM.

PUSH ABOUT THE JORUM.

WHEN bickerings hot
To high words got,
   Break out at Gamiorum ;
The flame to cool,
My golden rule
   Is—push about the jorum !
With fist on jug,
Coifs who can lug,
   Or show me that glib speaker,
Who her red rag
In gibe can wag,
   With her mouth full of liquor.
                KANE O'HARA.
          (*From* '*The Golden Pippin.*')

LOVE *VERSUS* THE BOTTLE.

SWEET Chloe advised me, in accents divine,
   The joys of the bowl to surrender ;
Nor lose in the turbid excesses of wine,
   Delights more ecstatic and tender ;
She bade me no longer in vineyards to bask,
Or stagger at orgies, the dupe of a flask,
For the sigh of a sot's but the scent of the cask,
   And a bubble the bliss of the bottle.

To a soul that's exhausted, or sterile, or dry,
   The juice of the grape may be wanted ;
But mine is reviv'd by a love-beaming eye,
   And with Fancy's gay flow'rets enchanted.

Oh, who but an owl would a garland entwine
Of Bacchus's ivy—and myrtle resign?
Yield the odours of love for the vapours of wine,
And Chloe's kind kiss for a bottle!

EDWARD LYSAGHT.

HERE'S TO THE MAIDEN.

HERE's to the maiden of bashful fifteen,
  Here's to the widow of fifty;
Here's to the flaunting extravagant quean,
  And here's to the housewife that's thrifty!

  Chorus: Let the toast pass,
      Drink to the lass,
I'll warrant she'll prove an excuse for the glass.

Here's to the charmer whose dimples we prize,
  And now to the maid who has none, sir;
Here's to the girl with a pair of blue eyes,
  And here's to the nymph with but one, sir!
    Let the toast pass, etc.

Here's to the maid with a bosom of snow,
  And to her that's as brown as a berry;
Here's to the wife with a face full of woe,
  And now to the girl that's merry!
    Let the toast pass, etc.

For let 'em be clumsy, or let 'em be slim,
  Young or ancient, I care not a feather;
So fill a pint bumper quite up to the brim,
  And let us e'en toast them together.
    Let the toast pass, etc.

RICHARD BRINSLEY SHERIDAN.
(*From ' The School for Scandal.'*)

LET'S DRINK LIKE HONEST MEN.

Had I the tun which Bacchus used,
    I'd sit on it all day;
For, while a can it ne'er refused,
    He nothing had to pay.

I'd turn the cock from morn to eve,
    Nor think it toil and trouble;
But I'd contrive, you may believe,
    To make it carry double.

My friend should sit as well as I,
    And take a jovial pot;
For he who drinks—although he's dry—
    Alone, is sure a sot.

But since the tun which Bacchus used
    We have not here—what then,
Since god-like toping is refused,
    Let's drink like honest men.

And let that churl, old Bacchus, sit—
    Who envies him his wine?
While mortal fellowship and wit
    Make whisky more divine?
        Richard Alfred Millikin.

'LET US BE MERRY BEFORE WE GO.'

If sadly thinking, with spirits sinking,
    Could, more than drinking, my cares compose,
A cure for sorrow from sighs I'd borrow,
    And hope to-morrow would end my woes.

But as in wailing there's nought availing,
   And Death unfailing will strike the blow,
Then for that reason, and for a season,
   Let us be merry before we go!

To joy a stranger, a wayworn ranger,
   In ev'ry danger my course I've run;
Now hope all ending, and death befriending,
   His last aid lending, my cares are done;
No more a rover, or hapless lover—
   My griefs are over—my glass runs low;
Then for that reason, and for a season,
   Let us be merry before we go!
JOHN PHILPOT CURRAN.

THE MONKS OF THE SCREW.

WHEN St. Patrick this order established,
   He called us the 'Monks of the Screw;'
Good rules he revealed to our abbot
   To guide us in what we should do.
But first he replenished our fountain
   With liquor the best from on high;
And he said, on the word of a saint,
   That the fountain should never run dry.

'Each year, when your octaves approach,
   In full chapter convened let me find you;
And when to the convent you come,
   Leave your favourite temptation behind you.
And be not a glass in your convent—
   Unless on a festival—found;
And, this rule to enforce, I ordain it
   One festival all the year round.

'My brethren, be chaste—till you're tempted;
   While sober, be grave and discreet;
And humble your bodies with fasting,
   As oft as you've nothing to eat.
Yet, in honour of fasting, one lean face
   Among you I'd always require;
If the abbot should please, he may wear it,
   If not, let it come to the prior.'

Come, let each take his chalice, my brethren,
   And with due devotion prepare,
With hands and with voices uplifted,
   Our hymn to conclude with a prayer.
May this chapter oft joyously meet,
   And this gladsome libation renew,
To the saint, and the founder, and abbot,
   And prior, and Monks of the Screw!

                  JOHN PHILPOT CURRAN.

THE WINE-BIBBER'S GLORY.

        'Quo me Bacche rapis tui plenum?'—HOR.

IF Horatius Flaccus made jolly old Bacchus
   So often his favourite theme;
If in him it was classic to praise his old Massic
   And Falernian to gulp in a stream;
If Falstaff's vagaries 'bout sack and Canaries
   Have pleased us again and again;
Shall we not make merry on Port, Claret, or Sherry,
   Madeira and sparkling Champagne?

First Port, that potation preferred by our nation
    To all the small drink of the French;
'Tis the best standing liquor for layman or vicar,
    The army, the navy, the bench;
'Tis strong and substantial, believe me, no man shall
    Good Port from my dining-room send;
In your soup—after cheese—every way it will please,
    But most *tête-à-tête* with a friend.

Fair Sherry, Port's sister, for years they dismissed her
    To the kitchen to flavour the jellies;
There long she was banish'd, and well-nigh had vanished
    To comfort the kitchen-maids' bellies;
'Till his Majesty fixt, he thought Sherry when sixty
    Years old like himself quite the thing;
So I think it but proper, to fill a tip-topper
    Of Sherry to drink to the King.

Though your delicate Claret by no means goes far, it
    Is famed for its exquisite flavour;
'Tis a nice provocation to *wise* conversation,
    Queer blarney, or harmless palaver;
'Tis the bond of society—no inebriety
    Follows a swig of the blue;
One may drink a whole ocean, but ne'er feel commotion
    Or headache from Chateau Margoux.

But though Claret is pleasant to taste for the present,
    On the stomach it sometimes feels cold;
So to keep it all clever, and comfort your liver,
    Take a glass of Madeira that's old.
When't has sailed for the Indies, a cure for all wind 'tis,
    And colic 'twill put to the rout;
All doctors declare a good glass of Madeira
    The best of all things for the gout.

Then Champagne ! dear Champagne ! ah, how gladly I
    drain a
  Whole bottle of Œil de Perdrix !
To the eye of my charmer, to make my love warmer,
  If cool that love ever could be.
I could toast her for ever—but never, oh never
  Would I her dear name so profane ;
So, if e'er when I'm tipsy, it slips to my lips, I
  Wash it back to my heart with Champagne !
WILLIAM MAGINN, LL.D.

'I FILLED TO THEE.'

I FILLED to thee, to thee I drank,
  I nothing did but drink and fill ;
The bowl by turns was bright and blank,
  'Twas drinking, filling, drinking still !

At length I bid an artist paint
  Thy image in this ample cup,
That I might see the dimpled saint
  To whom I quaffed my nectar up.

Behold how bright that purple lip
  Is blushing through the wave at me !
Every roseate drop I sip
  Is just like kissing wine from thee !

But oh, I drink the more for this !
  For, ever when the draught I drain,
Thy lip invites another kiss,
  And in the nectar flows again !

So here's to thee, my gentle dear!
And may that eye for ever shine
Beneath as soft and sweet a tear
As bathes it in this bowl of mine!

THOMAS MOORE.

SEND ROUND THE BOWL.

OH! think not my spirits are always as light,
    And as free from a pang, as they seem to you now;
Nor expect that the heart-beaming smile of to-night
    Will return with to-morrow to brighten my brow.
No; life is a waste of wearisome hours,
    Which seldom the rose of enjoyment adorns;
And the heart that is soonest awake to the flowers,
    Is always the first to be touched by the thorns.
But send round the bowl and be happy awhile:
    May we never meet worse, in our pilgrimage here,
Than the tear that enjoyment may gild with a smile,
    And the smile that compassion can turn to a tear!

The thread of our life would be dark, Heaven knows!
    If it were not with friendship and love intertwined;
And I care not how soon I may sink to repose,
    When these blessings shall cease to be dear to my mind.
But they who have lovèd the fondest, the purest,
    Too often have wept o'er the dream they believed;
And the heart that has slumbered in friendship securest,
    Is happy indeed if 'twas never deceived.
But send round the bowl; while a relic of truth
    Is in man or in woman, this prayer shall be mine:—
That the sunshine of love may illumine our youth,
    And the moonlight of friendship console our decline.

THOMAS MOORE

COME, SEND ROUND THE WINE.

Come, send round the wine, and leave points of belief,
  To simpleton sages, and reasoning fools;
This moment's a flower too fair and too brief,
  To be wither'd and stained by the dust of the schools.
Your glass may be purple, and mine may be blue,
  But while they are fill'd from the same bright bowl,
The fool that would quarrel for difference of hue,
  Deserves not the comfort they shed o'er the soul.

Shall I ask the brave soldier who fights by my side
  In the cause of mankind, if our creeds agree?
Shall I give up the friend I have valued and tried,
  If he kneel not before the same altar with me?
From the heretic girl of my soul should I fly,
  To seek somewhere else a more orthodox kiss?
No, perish the hearts and the laws that try
  Truth, valour, or love by a standard like this.

Thomas Moore.

ONE BUMPER AT PARTING.

One bumper at parting! though many
  Have circled the board since we met,
The fullest, the saddest of any
  Remains to be crown'd by us yet.
The sweetness that pleasure hath in it
  Is always so slow to come forth,
That seldom, alas! till the minute
  It dies, do we know half its worth.

But come—may our life's happy measure
  Be all of such moments made up;
They're born on the bosom of pleasure,
  They die 'midst the tears of the cup.

As onward we journey, how pleasant
  To pause and inhabit awhile
Those few sunny spots, like the present,
  That 'mid the dull wilderness smile;
But Time, like a pitiless master,
  Cries, 'Onward!' and spurs the gay hours—
Ah, never doth Time travel faster
  Than when his way lies among flowers.
But come—may our life's happy measure
  Be all of such moments made up;
They're born on the bosom of pleasure,
  They die 'midst the tears of the cup.

We saw how the sun looked in sinking,
  The waters beneath him how bright;
And now let our farewell of drinking
  Resemble that farewell of light.
You saw how he finish'd, by darting
  His beam o'er a deep billow's brim—
So, fill up, let's shine at our parting
  In full liquid glory, like him.
And oh, may our life's happy measure
  Of moments like this be made up;
'Twas born on the bosom of pleasure,
  It dies 'mid the tears of the cup.

                THOMAS MOORE.

FILL THE BUMPER FAIR.

FILL the bumper fair!
   Every drop we sprinkle
O'er the brow of care
   Smooths away a wrinkle.
Wit's electric flame
   Ne'er so swiftly passes,
As when through the frame
   It shoots from brimming glasses.
Fill the bumper fair!
   Every drop we sprinkle
O'er the brow of care
   Smooths away a wrinkle.

Sages can, they say,
   Grasp the lightning's pinions,
And bring down its ray
   From the starr'd dominions.
So we, sages, sit,
   And 'mid bumpers brightening,
From the heaven of Wit
   Draw down all its lightning.

Wouldst thou know what first
   Made our souls inherit
This ennobling thirst
   For wine's celestial spirit?
It chanced upon that day,
   When, as bards inform us,
Prometheus stole away
   The living fires that warm us.

The careless youth, when up
    To Glory's fount aspiring,
Took nor urn nor cup
    To hide the pilfer'd fire in.
But oh, his joy! when, round
    The halls of heaven spying,
Among the stars he found
    A bowl of Bacchus lying.

Some drops were in that bowl,
    Remains of last night's pleasure,
With which the sparks of soul
    Mix'd their burning treasure.
Hence the goblet's shower
    Hath such spells to win us,
Hence its mighty power
    O'er that flame within us.
Fill the bumper fair!
    Every drop we sprinkle
O'er the brow of care
    Smooths away a wrinkle.

                THOMAS MOORE.

OH, THE DAYS WHEN I WAS YOUNG.

OH, the days when I was young,
    When I laugh'd in fortune's spite;
Talk'd of love the whole day long,
    And with nectar crown'd the night!
Then it was, old Father Care,
    Little reck'd I of thy frown;
Half thy malice youth could bear,
    And the rest a bumper drown.

Truth, they say, lies in a well—
　Why, I vow I ne'er could see,
Let the water-drinkers tell—
　There it always lay for me.
For when sparkling wine went round
　Never saw I falsehood's mask ;
But still honest truth I found
　In the bottom of each flask.

True, at length my vigour's flown,
　I have years to bring decay ;
Few the locks that now I own,
　And the few I have are grey.
Yet, old Jerome, thou mayst boast,
　While thy spirits do not tire ;
Still beneath thy age's frost,
　Glows a spark of youthful fire.
　　　　RICHARD BRINSLEY SHERIDAN.
　　(*From ' The Duenna.'*)

PATRIOTIC SONGS.

THE SORROWS OF INNISFAIL.

THROUGH the long drear night I lie awake, for the sorrows of Innisfail.
My bleeding heart is ready to break; I cannot but weep and wail.
Oh, shame and grief and wonder! her sons crouch lowly under
      The footstool of the paltriest foe
      That ever yet hath wrought them woe!

How long, O Mother of Light and Song, how long will they fail to see
That men must be *bold*, no less than *strong*, if they truly will to be free?
They sit but in silent sadness, while wrongs that should rouse them to madness,
      Wrongs that might wake the very dead
      Are piled on thy devoted head!

Thy castles, thy towers, thy palaces proud, thy stately mansions all,
Are held by the knaves who crossed the waves to lord it in Brian's hall.
Britannia, alas! is portress in Cobhthach's Golden Fortress,
    And Ulster's and Momonia's lands
    Are in the Robber-stranger's hands.

The tribe of Eogan is worn with woe; the O'Donnell reigns no more;
O'Neill's remains lie mouldering low, on Italy's far-off shore;
And the youths of the Pleasant Valley are scattered and cannot rally,
    While foreign Despotism unfurls
    Its flag 'mid hordes of base-born churls.

The chieftains of Naas were valorous lords, but their valour was crushed by craft—
They fell beneath Envy's butcherly dagger, and Calumny's poisoned shaft.
A few of their mighty legions yet languish in alien regions,
    But most of them, the frank, the free,
    Were slain through Saxon perfidie!

Oh, lived the Princes of Ainy's plains, and the heroes of green Dromgole,
And the chiefs of the Maigue, we still might hope to baffle our doom and dole.
Well then might the dastards shiver who herd by the blue Bride river,
    But ah! those great and glorious men
    Shall draw no glaive on earth agen!

All-powerful God! look down on the tribes who mourn
       throughout the land,
And raise them some deliverer up, of a strong and
       smiting hand!
Oh, suffer them not to perish, the race Thou wert wont
       to cherish,
              But soon avenge their fathers' graves,
              And burst the bonds that keep them slaves!
                     (*From the Irish of* GEOFFREY KEATING.)

KEATING TO HIS LETTER.

FOR the sake of the dear little Isle where I send you,
For those who will welcome, and speed, and befriend
       you;
For the green hills of Erin that still hold my heart there,
Though stain'd with the blood of the patriot and martyr.
              My blessing attend you!
              My blessing attend you!

Adieu to her nobles, may honour ne'er fail them!
To her clergy adieu, may no false ones assail them!
Adieu to her people, adieu to her sages,
Her historians, and all that illumine their pages!
              In distance I hail them,
              More fondly I hail them!

Adieu to her plains all enamelled with flowers!
A thousand adieus to her hills and her bowers!
Adieu to the friendships and hearts long devoted!
Adieu to the lakes on whose bosom I've floated,
              In youth's happy hours,
              In youth's happy hours.

Adieu to her fish-rivers murmuring through rushes!
Adieu to her meadows, her fields, wells, and bushes!
Adieu to her lawns, her moors, and her harbours!
Adieu from my heart, to her forests and arbours,
    All vocal with thrushes!
    All vocal with thrushes!

Adieu to her harvests, for ever increasing!
And her hills of assemblies, all wisdom possessing!
And her people—oh, where is there braver or better?
Then go to the Island of Saints, my dear letter!
    And bring her my blessing!
    And bring her my blessing!
    (*From the Irish of* GEOFFREY KEATING.)

ODE WRITTEN ON LEAVING IRELAND.

  WHAT sorrow wrings my bleeding heart,
   To flee from Innisfail!
  Oh, anguish from her scenes to part,
   Of mountain, wood, and vale!
  Vales that the hum of bees resound,
  And plains where generous steeds abound.

  While wafted by the breeze's wing,
   I see fair Fintan's shore recede,
  More poignant griefs my bosom wring,
   The farther eastward still I speed.
  With Erin's love my bosom warms,
  No soil but hers for me has charms.

  A soil enrich'd with verdant bowers,
   And groves with mellow fruits that teem;
  A soil of fair and fragrant flowers,
   Of verdant turf and crystal stream:

Rich plains of Ir, that bearded corn,
And balmy herbs, and shrubs adorn.

A land that boasts a pious race,
   A land of heroes brave and bold;
Enriched with every female grace
   Are Banba's maids with locks of gold.
Of men, none with her sons compare;
No maidens with her daughters fair.

If Heaven, propitious to my vow,
   Grant the desire with which I burn,
Again the foamy deep to plow,
   And to my native shores return;
'Speed on,' I'll cry, 'my galley fleet,
Nor e'er the crafty Saxon greet.'

No perils of the stormy deep
   I dread—yet sorrow wounds my heart;
To leave thee, Leogaire's fort, I weep;
   From thee, sweet Delvin, must I part?
Oh, hard the task—oh, lot severe,
To flee from all my soul holds dear!

Farewell, ye kind and generous bards,
   Bound to my soul by friendship strong;
And ye Dundargvais' happy lands,
   Ye festive halls—ye sons of song;
Ye generous friends in Meath who dwell,
Beloved, adored, farewell! farewell!

                        GERALD NUGENT.

LAMENT

(FOR THE TYRONIAN AND TYRCONNELLIAN PRINCES
BURIED AT ROME).

O, WOMAN of the Piercing Wail,
   Who mournest o'er yon mound of clay
      With sigh and groan,
Would God thou wert among the Gael!
   Thou would'st not then from day to day
      Weep thus alone.
'Twere long before, around a grave
   In green Tirconnell, one could find
      This loneliness;
Near where Beann-Boirche's banners wave,
   Such grief as thine could ne'er have pined
      Compassionless.

Beside the wave, in Donegal,
   In Antrim's glens, or fair Dromore,
      Or Killilee,
Or where the sunny waters fall,
   At Assaroe, near Erna's shore,
      This could not be.
On Derry's plains—in rich Drumclieff—
   Throughout Armagh the Great, renowned
      In olden years,
No day could pass but woman's grief
   Would rain upon the burial-ground
      Fresh floods of tears!

Oh, no!—from Shannon, Boyne, and Suir,
   From high Dunluce's castle-walls,
      From Lissadill,

Would flock alike both rich and poor,
  One wail would rise from Cruachan's halls
    To Tara's hill;
And some would come from Barrow-side,
  And many a maid would leave her home,
    On Leitrim's plains,
And by melodious Banna's tide,
  And by the Mourne and Erne, to come
    And swell thy strains!

Oh, horses' hoofs would trample down
  The mount whereon the martyr-saint
    Was crucified.
From glen and hill, from plain and town,
  One loud lament, one thrilling plaint,
    Would echo wide.
There would not soon be found, I ween,
  One foot of ground among those bands
    For museful thought,
So many shriekers of the *keen**
  Would cry aloud and clap their hands,
    All woe-distraught!

Two princes of the line of Conn
  Sleep in their cells of clay beside
    O'Donnell Roe:
Three royal youths, alas! are gone,
  Who lived for Erin's weal, but died
    For Erin's woe!
Ah! could the men of Ireland read
  The names those noteless burial-stones
    Display to view,

* The funeral wail.

Their wounded hearts afresh would bleed,
  Their tears gush forth again, their groans
    Resound anew!

The youths whose relics smoulder here
  Were sprung from Hugh, high Prince and Lord
    Of Aileach's lands;
Thy noble brothers, justly dear,
  Thy nephew, long to be deplored
    By Ulster's bands.
Theirs were not souls wherein dull Time
  Could domicile decay or house
    Decrepitude!
They passed from earth ere manhood's prime,
  Ere years had power to dim their brows
    Or chill their blood.

And who can marvel o'er thy grief,
  Or who can blame thy flowing tears,
    That knows their source?
O'Donnell, Dunnasava's chief,
  Cut off amid his vernal years,
    Lies here a corse
Beside his brother Cathbar, whom
  Tirconnell of the Helmets mourns
    In deep despair—
For valour, truth, and comely bloom,
  For all that greatens and adorns
    A peerless pair.

Oh, had these twain, and he, the third,
  The Lord of Mourne, O'Niall's son,
    Their mate in death—

A prince in look, in deed and word—
   Had these three heroes yielded on
      The field their breath,
Oh, had they fallen on Criffan's plain,
   There would not be a town or clan
      From shore to sea,
But would with shrieks bewail the slain,
   Or chant aloud the exulting *rann**
      Of jubilee!

When high the shout of battle rose,
   On fields where Freedom's torch still burned
      Through Erin's gloom,
If one, if barely one of those
   Were slain, all Ulster would have mourned
      The Hero's doom!
If at Athboy, where hosts of brave
   Ulidian horsemen sank beneath
      The shock of spears,
Young Hugh O'Neill had found a grave,
   Long must the north have wept his death
      With heart-wrung tears!

If on the day of Ballach-myre
   The Lord of Mourne had met thus young
      A warrior's fate,
In vain would such as thou desire
   To mourn alone, the champion sprung
      From Niall the great!
No marvel this—for all the dead
   Heaped on the field, pile over pile,
      At Mullach-brack,

* A song.

Were scare an *eric** for his head,
  If death had stayed his footsteps while
    On Victory's track!

If on the Day of Hostages
  The fruit had from the parent bough
    Been rudely torn
In sight of Munster's bands—MacNee's—
  Such blow the blood of Conn, I trow,
    Could ill have borne.
If on the day of Ballach-boy
  Some arm had laid, by foul surprise,
    The chieftain low,
Even our victorious shout of joy
  Would soon give place to rueful cries
    And groans of woe!

If on the day the Saxon host,
  Were forced to fly—a day so great
    For Ashanee—
The chief had been untimely lost,
  Our conquering troops should moderate
    Their mirthful glee.
There would not lack on Lifford's day,
  From Galway, from the glens of Boyle,
    From Limerick's towers,
A marshalled file, a long array
  Of mourners, to bedew the soil
    With tears in showers!

If on the day a sterner fate
  Compelled his flight from Athenree,
    His blood had flowed,

* A compensation or fine.

What numbers all disconsolate,
  Would come unasked, and share with thee
    Affliction's load!
If Derry's crimson field had seen
  His life-blood offered up, though 'twere
    On Victory's shrine,
A thousand cries would swell the *keen*,
  A thousand voices of despair
    Would echo thine!

Oh, had the fierce Dalcassian swarm
  That bloody night on Fergus' banks
    But slain our chief,
When rose his camp in wild alarm—
  How would the triumphs of his ranks
    Be dashed with grief!
How would the troops of Murbach mourn
  If on the Curlew Mountains' day
    Which England rued,
Some Saxon hand had left them lorn,
  By shedding there, amid the fray,
    Their prince's blood!

Red would have been our warriors' eyes
  Had Roderick found on Sligo's field
    A gory grave,
No northern chief would soon arise
  So sage to guide, so strong to shield,
    So swift to save.
Long would Leith-Cuinn have wept if Hugh
  Had met the death he oft had dealt
    Among the foe;

But, had our Roderick fallen too,
  All Erin must, alas, have felt
    The deadly blow!

What do I say? Ah, woe is me!
  Already we bewail in vain
    Their fatal fall!
And Erin, once the great and free,
  Now vainly mourns her breakless chain
    And iron thrall!
Then, daughter of O'Donnell! dry
  Thine overflowing eyes, and turn
    Thy heart aside;
For Adam's race is born to die,
  And sternly the sepulchral urn
    Mocks human pride!

Look not, nor sigh, for earthly throne,
  Nor place thy trust in arm of clay—
    But on thy knees
Uplift thy soul to God alone,
  For all things go their destined way
    As he decrees.
Embrace the faithful crucifix,
  And seek the path of pain and prayer
    Thy Saviour trod!
Nor let thy spirit intermix
  With earthly hope and worldly care
    Its groans to God!

And thou, O mighty Lord! whose ways
  Are far above our feeble minds
    To understand,

Sustain us in these doleful days,
    And render light the chain that binds
        Our fallen land!
Look down upon our dreary state,
    And through the ages that may still
        Roll sadly on,
Watch thou o'er hapless Erin's fate,
    And shield at least from darker ill
        The blood of Conn!

                OWEN WARD.
            (*Translated by Mangan*).

CLARAGH'S LAMENT.

THE tears are ever in my wasted eye,
My heart is crushed, and my thoughts are sad;
For the son of chivalry* was forced to fly,
And no tidings come from the soldier lad.
    Chorus: My heart it danced when he was near,
            My hero! my Cæsar! my Chevalier!
            But while he wanders o'er the sea
            Joy can never be joy to me.

Silent and sad pines the lone cuckoo,
Our chieftains hang o'er the grave of joy;
Their tears fall heavy as the summer's dew
For the lord of their hearts—the banished boy.

Mute are the minstrels that sang of him,
The harp forgets its thrilling tone;
The brightest eyes of the land are dim,
For the pride of their aching sight is gone.

      * The Young Pretender.

The sun refused to lend his light,
And clouds obscured the face of day;
The tiger's whelps preyed day and night,
For the lion of the forest was far away.

The gallant, graceful, young Chevalier,
Whose look is bonny as his heart is gay;
His sword in battle flashes death and fear,
While he hews through falling foes his way.

O'er his blushing cheeks his blue eyes shine
Like dewdrops glitt'ring on the rose's leaf;
Mars and Cupid all in him combine,
The blooming lover and the godlike chief.

His curling locks in wavy grace,
Like beams on youthful Phœbus' brow,
Flit wild and golden o'er his speaking face,
And down his ivory shoulders flow.

Like Ængus is he in his youthful days,
Or MacCein, whose deeds all Erin knows;
MacDary's chiefs, of deathless praise,
Who hung like fate on their routed foes.

Like Connall the besieger, pride of his race;
Or Fergus, son of a glorious sire;
Or blameless Connor, son of courteous Nais,
The chief of the Red Branch—Lord of the Lyre.

The cuckoo's voice is not heard on the gale,
Nor the cry of the hounds in the nutty grove,
Nor the hunter's cheering through the dewy vale,
Since far—far away is the youth of our love.

The name of my darling none must declare,
Though his fame be like sunshine from shore to shore;
But, oh, may Heaven—Heaven hear my prayer!
And waft the hero to my arms once more.

Chorus: My heart—it danced when he was near,
  Ah! now my woe is the young Chevalier,
  'Tis a pang that solace ne'er can know,
  That he should be banish'd by a rightless foe.

JOHN MACDONNELL.
(*From Hardiman's 'Irish Minstrelsy.'*)

OLD ERIN IN THE SEA.

WHO sitteth cold, a beggar old,
  Before the prosperous lands,
With outstretched palms that asketh alms
  From charitable hands!
Feeble and lone she maketh moan—
  A stricken one is she,
That deep and long hath suffered wrong,
  Old Erin in the sea!

How art thou lost, how hardly crost,
  Land of the reverend head!
And, dismal Fate, how harsh thy hate,
  That gives her lack of bread!
Though broad her fields, and rich their yields,
  From Liffey to the Lee,
Her grain but grows to flesh the foes
  Of Erin in the sea!

'Tis but the ban of ruthless man
  That works thy wretchedness;
What nature bears with thee she shares,
  And genial seasons bless.

The very waves that kiss the caves
   Clap their huge hands for glee,
That they should guard so fair a sward
   As Erin by the sea !

Her vales are green, her gales serene,
   Hard granite ribs her coast,
God's fairest smile is on the isle,
   Alas ! and bootless boast ;
No land more curst hath Ocean nurst
   Since first a wave had he ;
No land whose grief had less relief
   Than Erin in the sea !

Can this be she whose history
   Is in the mist of years,
Whose kings of old wore crowns of gold,
   And led ten thousand spears !
Not so I wis ; no land like this
   Could know such bravery,
Or change is wrought, or lore is nought
   For Erin in the sea !

Ah ! truly change most sad and strange—
   Her kings have passed away ;
Her sons, the same in outward frame,
   Full false and tame are they—
Each hating each, alone they teach,
   And but in this agree :
To work thy pains, and bind thy chains,
   Old Erin in the sea !

Where are the men, by tower and glen,
   Who held thee safe of yore?
Full oft that gave their foes a grave
   On thine insulted shore?
Galglach* and Kerne, full sure and stern,
   They did good fight for thee;
Alas! they sleep, and thou must weep,
   Old Erin in the sea!

Soft may they rest within her breast,
   That for their country died;
And where they lie may peace be nigh,
   And lasting love abide!
Ye grace them well; for them that fell
   And her that nourished ye,
For them ye bled, she holds ye dead—
   Old Erin in the sea!

And in your place a wretched race
   Upon the soil have grown,
Unfearing shame, and in the name
   Like to their sires alone.
They shun the claim of patriot fame,
   And cringe the servile knee,
To kiss the yoke their fathers broke
   In Erin in the sea!

Would they unite in valorous fight
   For her that gave them breath,
As they for her—the conqueror,
   Whose direful touch is death,
No more the blight of traitorous might
   On sacred right should be,
But peace, delight, and strength bedight
   Old Erin in the sea!

       * Gallowglass.

Pillage and pest her vales infest,
    Strange tongues her name revile;
Where prayed her saints, false doctrine taints,
    And godless rites defile.
Be they reviled, be they defiled,
    More dear are they to me—
The verdant plains, the holy fanes,
    Of Erin in the sea!

Thine is the page, all rimed with age
    In mighty deeds sublime—
The proud records of willing swords,
    And storied lays of time;
An empire thou, while she that now,
    By Heaven's harsh decree,
Holds thee disgraced, was wild and waste,
    Old Erin in the sea!

Would this were all! Not thine the fall
    By force and battle-rush,
Not men more brave hold thee for slave,
    Nor stouter hearts that crush;
But vengeful ire of son with sire,
    Thy children's perfidy—
Theirs is the strife that slays thy life,
    Old Erin in the sea!

Ye bards of song, ye warriors strong!
    Of high heroic deeds,—
All dust are ye, by mount and lea,
    While she, your mother, bleeds.

And cold the blood, by fort and flood,
   That ran in veins as free
As she was then, when ye were men,
   Old Erin in the sea!

JOHN MACDONNELL.
(Translated by W. B. Guinee.)

CLARAGH'S DREAM.

I LAY in unrest—old thoughts of pain,
   That I struggled in vain to smother,
Like midnight spectres haunted my brain—
   Dark fantasies chased each other,
When lo! a figure—who might it be?
   A tall, fair figure stood near me?
Who might it be? An unreal Banshee?
   Or an angel sent to cheer me?

Though years have rolled since then, yet now
   My memory thrillingly lingers
On her awful charms, her waxen brow,
   Her pale translucent fingers;
Her eyes, that mirrored a wonder world,
   Her mien, of unearthly wildness;
And her waving raven tresses that curled
   To the ground in beautiful wildness.

'Whence comest thou, spirit?' I asked, methought;
   'Thou art not one of the banished?'
Alas for me! she answered nought,
   But rose aloft and vanished;

And a radiance, like to a glory, beamed
  In the light she left behind her;
Long time I wept; and at last me-dreamed
  I left my shieling to find her.

And first I turned to the thund'rous north,
  To Gruagach's mansion kingly;
Untouching the earth, I then sped forth
  To Inver-lough, and the shingly
And shining strand of the fishful Erne,
  And thence to Croghan the golden,
Of whose resplendent palace ye learn
  So many a marvel olden.

I saw the Mourna's billows flow—
  I passed the walls of Shenady,
And stood in the hero-thronged Ardroe,
  Embossed amid greenwoods shady;
And visited that proud pile that stands
  Above the Boyne's broad waters,
Where Ængus dwells with his warrior bands
  And the fairest of Ulster's daughters;

To the halls of Mac-Lir, to Creevroe's height,
  To Tara, the glory of Erin,
To the fairy palace that glances bright
  On the peak of the blue Cnocfeerin,
I vainly hied. I went west and east—
  I travelled seaward and shoreward—
But thus was I greeted in field and at feast—
  'Thy way lies onward and forward!'

At last I reached, I wist not how,
  The royal towers of Ival,
Which under the cliff's gigantic brow
  Still rise without a rival.
And here were Thomond's chieftains all,
  With armour, and swords, and lances,
And here sweet music filled the hall,
  And damsels charmed with dances.

And here, at length, on a silvery throne,
  Half seated, half reclining,
With forehead white as the marble stone,
  And garments so starrily shining,
And features beyond the poet's pen—
  The sweetest, saddest features—
Appeared before me once again,
  That fairest of living creatures!

'Draw near, O mortal!' she said with a sigh,
  'And hear my mournful story;
The guardian spirit of Erin am I,
  But dimmed is mine ancient glory.
My priests are banished, my warriors wear
  No longer victory's garland;
And my child, my son, my beloved heir,*
  Is an exile in a far land!'

I heard no more—I saw no more—
  The bands of slumber were broken,
And palace, and hero, and river, and shore,
  Had vanished and left no token.

* The Young Pretender.

Dissolved was the spell that had bound my will
   And my fancy thus for a season;
But a sorrow, therefore, hangs over me still,
   Despite of the teachings of reason.

JOHN MACDONNELL.
(Translated by J. C. Mangan.)

THE COMING OF PRINCE CHARLIE.

Too long have the churls in dark bondage oppressed me,
   Too long have I cursed them in anguish and gloom;
Yet Hope with no vision of comfort has blessed me—
   The cave is my shelter—the rude rock my home.
Save Doun* and his kindred, my sorrow had shaken
All friends from my side, when at evening, forsaken,
I sought the lone fort, proud to hear him awaken,
   The hymn of deliverance breathing for me.

He told how the heroes were fall'n and degraded,
   And scorn dashed the tear their affliction would claim;
But Phelim and Heber,† whose children betrayed it,
   The land shall relume with the light of their fame.
The fleet is prepared, proud Charles‡ is commanding,
And wide o'er the wave the white sail is expanding,
The dark brood of Luther shall quail at their landing,
   The Gael like a tempest shall burst on the foe.

The bards shall exult, and the harp-strings shall tremble,
   And love and devotion be poured in the strain;
Ere 'Samhain'§ our chiefs shall in Temor ‖ assemble,
   The 'Lion' protect our own pastors again.

* The ruler of the Munster fairies.
† Renegade Irish who joined the foe.
‡ The Pretender.
§ The 1st of November, the festival of Baal-Samen, so called by the Druids.
‖ Tara.

The Gael shall redeem every shrine's desecration,
In song shall exhale our warm heart's adoration,
Confusion shall light on the foe's usurpation,
  And Erin shine out yet triumphant and free.

The secrets of destiny now are before you—
  Away! to each heart the proud tidings to tell :
Your Charles is at hand, let the green flag spread o'er you !
  The treaty they broke your deep vengeance shall swell.
The hour is arrived, and in loyalty blending,
Surround him! sustain! Shall the gorg'd goal descending
Deter you, your own sacred monarch defending?
  Rush on like a tempest and scatter the foe!
                        ANDREW MAGRATH.

OUR ISLAND.

    MAY God, in whose hand
    Is the lot of each land—
Who rules over ocean and dry land—
    Inspire our good King
    From his presence to fling
Ill advisers who'd ruin our island.
Don't we feel 'tis our dear native island !
A fertile and fine little island !
    May Orange and Green
    No longer be seen
Bestain'd with the blood of our island.

    The fair ones we prize,
    Declare they despise,
Those who'd make it a slavish and vile land;

OUR ISLAND.

    Be their smiles our reward,
    And we'll gallantly guard
All the rights and delights of our island—
For, oh, 'tis a lovely green island!
Bright beauties adorn our dear island!
    At St. Patrick's command,
    Vipers quitted our land—
But he's wanted again in our island!

    For her interest and pride,
    We oft fought by the side
Of England, that haughty and high land;
    Nay, we'd do so again,
    If she'd let us remain
A free and a flourishing island.
But she, like a crafty and sly land,
Dissension excites in our island,
    And, our feuds to adjust,
    She would lay in the dust
All the freedom and strength of our island.

    A few years ago—
    Though now she says no—
We agreed with that surly and sly land,
    That each, as a friend,
    Should the other defend,
And the crown be the link of each island:
'Twas the final state-bond of each island;
Independence we swore to each island.
    Are we grown so absurd,
    As to credit her word,
When she's breaking her oath with our island?

　　　　　Let us steadily stand
　　　　　By our King and our land,
　　　And it shan't be a slavish or vile land ;
　　　　　Nor impudent Pitt,
　　　　　Unpunished, commit
　　　An attempt on the rights of our island.
　　　Each voice should resound through our island,
　　　You're my neighbour, but, Bull, this is my land ;
　　　　　Nature's favourite spot—
　　　　　And I'd sooner be shot,
　　　Than surrender the rights of our island !
　　　　　　　　　　　　EDWARD LYSAGHT.

TO HENRY GRATTAN :

'THE MAN WHO LED THE VAN OF IRISH VOLUNTEERS.'

THE gen'rous sons of Erin, in manly virtue bold,
With hearts and hands preparing our country to uphold,
Tho' cruel knaves and bigot slaves disturbed our isle some years,
Now hail the man who led the van of Irish Volunteers.

Just thirty years are ending since first his glorious aid,
Our sacred rights defending, struck shackles from our trade ;
To serve us still, with might and skill, the vet'ran now appears,
That gallant man who led the van of Irish Volunteers.

He sows no vile dissensions ; goodwill to all he bears ;
He knows no vain pretensions, no paltry fears or cares ;
To Erin's and to Britain's sons, his worth his name endears ;
They love the man who led the van of Irish Volunteers.

Opposed by hirelings sordid, he broke oppression's chain !
On statute books recorded, his patriot acts remain ;
The equipoise his mind employs of Commons, Kings, and Peers,
The upright man who led the van of Irish Volunteers.

A British constitution (to Erin ever true),
In spite of state pollution, he gained in '82 ;
He watched it in its cradle, and bedew'd its hearse with tears :
This gallant man who led the van of Irish Volunteers.

While other nations tremble, by proud oppressors gall'd,
On hustings we'll assemble, by Erin's welfare call'd ;
Our Grattan, there we'll meet him, and greet him with three cheers ;
The gallant man who led the van of Irish Volunteers.

EDWARD LYSAGHT.

THE GREEN LITTLE SHAMROCK OF IRELAND.

THERE'S a dear little plant that grows in our isle,
  'Twas Saint Patrick himself, sure, that set it ;
And the sun on his labour with pleasure did smile,
  And with dew from his eye often wet it.
It thrives through the bog, through the brake, through the mireland ;
  And he called it the dear little shamrock of Ireland,
    The sweet little shamrock, the dear little shamrock,
    The sweet little, green little, shamrock of Ireland.

This dear little plant still grows in our land,
    Fresh and fair as the daughters of Erin,
Whose smiles can bewitch, whose eyes can command,
    In each climate that they may appear in ;
And shine through the bog, through the brake, through the mireland ;
    Just like their own dear little shamrock of Ireland.
        The sweet little shamrock, the dear little shamrock,
        The sweet little, green little, shamrock of Ireland.

This dear little plant that springs from our soil,
    When its three little leaves are extended,
Denotes from one stalk we together should toil,
    And ourselves by ourselves be befriended ;
And still through the bog, through the brake, through the mireland,
    From one root should branch, like the shamrock of Ireland,
        The sweet little shamrock, the dear little shamrock,
        The sweet little, green little, shamrock of Ireland.
ANDREW CHERRY.

CUSHLA MA CHREE.*

DEAR Erin, how sweetly thy green bosom rises !
    An emerald set in the ring of the sea !
Each blade of thy meadows my faithful heart prizes,
    Thou queen of the west ! the world's cushla ma chree !

Thy gates open wide to the poor and the stranger—
    There smiles hospitality hearty and free ;
Thy friendship is seen in the moment of danger,
    And the wand'rer is welcomed with cushla ma chree.

        Anglicè, 'Darling of my heart.'

Thy sons they are brave; but, the battle once over,
  In brotherly peace with their foes they agree;
And the roseate cheeks of thy daughters discover
  The soul-speaking blush that says cushla ma chree.

Then flourish for ever, my dear native Erin!
  While sadly I wander an exile from thee;
And, firm as thy mountains, no injury fearing,
  May heaven defend its own cushla ma chree!

JOHN PHILPOT CURRAN.

THE IRISHMAN.

THE savage loves his native shore,
  Though rude the soil and chill the air;
Then well may Erin's sons adore
  Their isle, which nature formed so fair.
What flood reflects a shore so sweet
  As Shannon great, or pastoral Bann?
Or who a friend or foe can meet
  So generous as an Irishman?

His hand is rash, his heart is warm,
  But honesty is still his guide;
None more repents a deed of harm,
  And none forgives with nobler pride;
He may be duped, but won't be dared—
  More fit to practise than to plan;
He dearly earns his poor reward,
  And spends it like an Irishman.

If strange or poor, for you he'll pay,
  And guide to where you safe may be;
If you're his guest, while e'er you stay
  His cottage holds a jubilee.

His inmost soul he will unlock,
   And if he may *your* secrets scan,
Your confidence he scorns to mock,
   For faithful is an Irishman.

By Honour bound in woe or weal,
   Whate'er she bids he dares to do;
Try him with bribes—they won't prevail;
   Prove him in fire—you'll find him true.
He seeks not safety, let his post
   Be where it ought, in danger's van;
And if the field of fame be lost,
   It won't be by an Irishman.

Erin! loved land! from age to age
   Be thou more great, more famed, and free;
May peace be thine, or, should'st thou wage
   Defensive war, cheap victory.
May plenty bloom in every field
   Which gentle breezes softly fan;
And cheerful smiles serenely gild
   The home of every Irishman!

JAMES ORR.

SONG OF AN EXILE.

IN Ireland 'tis evening—from toil my friends hie all,
   And weary walk home o'er the dew-spangled lea;
The shepherd in love tunes his grief-soothing viol,
   Or visits the maid that his partner will be;
The blithe milk-maid trips to the herd that stands lowing;
The west richly smiles, and the landscape is glowing;
The sad-sounding curfew, and torrent fast-flowing,
   Are heard by my fancy, though far, far at sea!

SONG OF AN EXILE.

What has my eye seen since I left the green valleys,
   But ships as remote as the prospect could be;
Unwieldy, huge monsters, as ugly as malice,
   And floats of some wreck, which with sorrow I see!
What's seen but the fowl, that its lonely flight urges,
The lightning, that darts through the sky-meeting surges,
And the sad-scowling sky, that the bitter rain scourges,
   This cheek care sits drooping on, far, far at sea!

How hideous the hold is!—Here, children are screaming—
   There, dames faint through thirst with their babes on their knee!
Here, down every hatch the big breakers are streaming,
   And there, with a crash, half the fixtures break free!
Some court, some contend, some sit dull stories telling;
The mate's mad and drunk, and the tars tasked and yelling;
What sickness and sorrow pervade my rude dwelling!—
   A huge floating lazar-house, far, far at sea!

How changed all may be when I seek the sweet village!
   A hedge-row may bloom where its street used to be;
The floors of my friends may be tortured by tillage,
   And the upstart be served by the fallen grandee;
The axe may have humbled the grove that I haunted,
And shades be my shield that as yet are unplanted,
Nor one comrade live who repined when he wanted
   The sociable sufferer that's far, far at sea!

In Ireland 'tis night—on the flowers of my setting
   A parent may kneel, fondly praying for me;—
The village is smokeless—the red moon is getting
   That hill for a throne which I hope yet to see.

If innocence thrive, many more have to grieve for,
Success, slow but sure, I'll contentedly live for:
Yes, Sylvia, we'll meet, and your sigh cease to heave for
  The swain your fine image haunts, far, far at sea!

JAMES ORR.

JOHN O'DWYER OF THE GLEN.*

BLITHE the bright dawn found me,
Rest with strength had crown'd me,
Sweet the birds sang round me,
  Sport was all their toil.
The horn its clang was keeping,
Forth the fox was creeping,
Round each dame stood weeping
  O'er that prowler's spoil.
Hark! the foe is calling,
Fast the woods are falling,
Scenes and sights appalling
  Mark the wasted soil.

War and confiscation
Curse the fallen nation;
Gloom and desolation
  Shade the lost land o'er.
Chill the winds are blowing,
Death aloft is going;
Peace or hope seems growing
  For our race no more.

* This is supposed to be a very ancient poem, from the allusion to the falling of the woods which destroyed the hiding-places of the flying Irish. Spenser, in his 'View of the State of Ireland,' says: 'I wish that orders were taken for cutting and opening all places through the woods; so that a wide way, of the space of one hundred yards, might be laid open in every of them.'

JOHN O'DWYER OF THE GLEN.

Hark! the foe is calling,
Fast the woods are falling,
Scenes and sights appalling
   Throng our blood-stained shore.

Where's my goat to cheer me?
Now it plays not near me;
Friends no more can hear me;
   Strangers round me stand.
Nobles once high-hearted,
From their homes have parted,
Scatter'd, scared, and started,
   By a base-born band.
Hark! the foe is calling,
Fast the woods are falling,
Scenes and sights appalling
   Thicken round the land.

Oh that death had found me,
And in darkness bound me,
Ere each object round me
   Grew so sweet, so dear!
Spots that once were cheering,
Girls beloved, endearing,
Friends from whom I'm steering,
   Take this parting tear.
Hark! the foe is calling,
Fast the woods are falling,
Scenes and sights appalling
   Plague and haunt me here.

        Translated by THOMAS FURLONG.

ON CLEADA'S HILL THE MOON IS BRIGHT.

On Cleada's* hill the moon is bright,
Dark Avondu† still rolls in light,
All changeless in that mountain's head,
That river still seeks ocean's bed :
The calm blue waters of Loch Lene
Still kiss their own sweet isles of green,
But where's the heart as firm and true
As hill, or lake, or Avondu ?

It may not be, the firmest heart
From all it loves must often part,
A look, a word, will quench the flame
That time or fate could never tame ;
And there are feelings proud and high
That through all changes cannot die,
That strive with love, and conquer too ;
I knew them all by Avondu.

How cross and wayward still is fate
I've learned at last, but learned too late.
I never spoke of love, 'twere vain ;
I knew it, still I dragg'd my chain.

* Cleada and Cahir-bearna (The Hill of the Four Gaps) form part of the chain of mountains which stretches westward from Millstreet to Killarney.
† Avondu means the Blackwater ('Avunduff' of Spenser). There are several rivers of this name in the counties of Cork and Kerry, but the one here mentioned is by far the most considerable. It rises in a boggy mountain called Meenganine, in the latter county, and discharges itself into the sea at Youghal. For the length of its course, and the beauty and variety of scenery through which it flows, it is superior, I believe, to any river in Munster.—CALLANAN.

I had not, never had a hope—
But who 'gainst passion's tide can cope?
Headlong it swept this bosom through,
And left it waste by Avondu.

O Avondu! I wish I were
As once upon that mountain bare,
Where thy young waters laugh and shine
On the wild breast of Meenganine;
I wish I were by Cleada's hill,
Or by Glenluachra's rushy rill.
But no!—I never more shall view
Those scenes I loved by Avondu.

Farewell, ye soft and purple streaks
Of evening on the beauteous Reeks;*
Farewell, ye mists that lov'd to ride
On Cahir-bearna's stormy side;
Farewell, November's moaning breeze,
Wild minstrel of the dying trees;
Clara! a fond farewell to you,
No more we meet by Avondu.

No more—but thou, O glorious hill!
Lift to the moon thy forehead still;
Flow on, flow on, thou dark swift river,
Upon thy free wild course for ever.
Exult, young heart, in lifetime's spring,
And taste the joys pure love can bring;
But, wanderer, go—they're not for you!
Farewell, farewell, sweet Avondu!

JAMES JOSEPH CALLANAN.

* Macgillacuddy's Reeks in the neighbourhood of Killarney; they are the highest mountains in Munster.

DARK ROSALEEN.*

Oh, my Dark Rosaleen,
    Do not sigh, do not weep!
The priests are on the ocean green,
    They march along the deep.
There's wine from the royal Pope,
    Upon the ocean green;
And Spanish ale shall give you hope,
    My Dark Rosaleen!
    My own Rosaleen!
Shall glad your heart, shall give you hope,
Shall give you health, and help, and hope,
    My Dark Rosaleen!

Over hills and through dales,
    Have I roamed for your sake;
All yesterday I sailed with sails
    On river and on lake.
The Erne, at its highest flood,
    I dashed across unseen,
For there was lightning in my blood,
    My Dark Rosaleen!
    My own Rosaleen!
Oh, there was lightning in my blood,
Red lightning lightened through my blood
    My Dark Rosaleen!

All day long, in unrest,
    To and fro do I move.
The very soul within my breast
    Is wasted for you, love!

* This is allegorical throughout. Rosaleen is Ireland.

The heart in my bosom faints
　　To think of you, my queen,
My life of life, my saint of saints,
　　My Dark Rosaleen!
　　My own Rosaleen!
To hear your sweet and sad complaints,
My life, my love, my saint of saints,
　　My Dark Rosaleen!

Woe and pain, pain and woe,
　　Are my lot, night and noon,
To see your bright face clouded so,
　　Like to the mournful moon.
But yet will I rear your throne
　　Again in golden sheen;
'Tis you shall reign, shall reign alone,
　　My Dark Rosaleen!
　　My own Rosaleen!
'Tis you shall have the golden throne,
'Tis you shall reign, and reign alone,
　　My Dark Rosaleen!

Over dews, over sands,
　　Will I fly, for your weal;
Your holy, delicate white hands
　　Shall girdle me with steel.
At home, in your emerald bowers,
　　From morning's dawn till e'en,
You'll pray for me, my flower of flowers,
　　My Dark Rosaleen!
　　My fond Rosaleen!
You'll think of me through daylight's hours,
My virgin flower, my flower of flowers,
　　My Dark Rosaleen!

I could scale the blue air,
　I could plough the high hills,
Oh, I could kneel all night in prayer,
　To heal your many ills!
And one beamy smile from you
　Would float like light between
My toils and me, my own, my true,
　My Dark Rosaleen!
　My fond Rosaleen!
Would give me life and soul anew,
A second life, a soul anew,
　My Dark Rosaleen!

Oh, the Erne shall run red
　With redundance of blood,
The earth shall rock beneath our tread,
　And flames wrap hill and wood;
And gun-peal and slogan-cry,
　Wake many a glen serene,
Ere you shall fade, ere you shall die,
　My Dark Rosaleen!
　My own Rosaleen!
The Judgment Hour must first be nigh,
Ere you can fade, ere you can die,
　My Dark Rosaleen!
　　　　　　Translated by J. C. MANGAN.

DUHALLOW.

FAR away from my friends,
   On the chill hills of Galway,
My heart droops and bends,
   And my spirit pines alway—
'Tis as not when I roved
   With the wild rakes of Mallow—
All is here unbeloved,
   And I sigh for Duhallow.

My sweetheart was cold,
   Or in sooth I'd have wept her—
Ah! that love should grow old
   And decline from his sceptre!
While the hearts' feelings yet
   Seem so tender and callow!
But I deeplier regret
   My lost home in Duhallow!

My steed is no more,
   And my hounds roam unyelling;
Grass waves at the door
   Of my dark-windowed dwelling;
Through sunshine and storm
   Corrach's acres lie fallow;
Would Heaven I were warm
   Once again in Duhallow!

In the blackness of night,
   In the depth of disaster,
My heart were more light
   Could I call myself master

Of Corrach once more,
   Than if here I might wallow
In gold thick as gore
   Far away from Duhallow!

I lov'd Italy's show
   In the years of my greenness,
Till I saw the deep woe,
   The debasement, the meanness,
That rot that bright land!
   I have since grown less shallow,
And would now rather stand
   In a bog in Duhallow!

This place I'm in here,
   On the grey hills of Galway,
I like for its cheer
   Well enough in a small way;
But the men are all short,
   And the women all sallow;
Give M'Quillan his quart
   Of brown ale of Duhallow!

My sporting day's o'er,
   And my love-day's gone after,
Not earth could restore
   Me my old life and laughter.
Burns now my breast's flame
   Like a dim wick of tallow,
Yet I love thee the same
   As at twenty, Duhallow!

But my hopes, like my rhymes,
   Are consumed and expended;
What's the use of old times
   When *our* time is now ended?

Drop the talk! Death will come
For the debt that we all owe,
And the grave is a home,
Quite as old as Duhallow.
Translated by J. C. MANGAN.

CÁHAL MÓR OF THE WINE-RED HAND.

(A VISION OF CONNAUGHT IN THE THIRTEENTH CENTURY.)

I WALKED entranced
  Through a land of morn;
The sun, with wondrous excess of light
  Shone down and glanced
    Over seas of corn,
And lustrous gardens aleft and right.
  Even in the clime
    Of resplendent Spain
Beams no such sun upon such a land;
  But it was the time,
    'Twas in the reign,
Of Cáhal Mór of the Wine-red Hand.

  Anon stood nigh
    By my side a man
Of princely aspect and port sublime.
  Him queried I,
    'Oh, my lord and khan,
What clime is this, and what golden time?'
  When he—'The clime
    Is a clime to praise,

The clime is Erin's, the green and bland;
   And it is the time,
     These be the days
Of Cáhal Mór of the Wine-red Hand!'
   Then I saw thrones
     And circling fires,
And a dome rose near me, as by a spell,
   Whence flowed the tones
     Of silver lyres
And many voices in wreathed swell;
   And their thrilling chime
     Fell on mine ears
As the heavenly hymn of an angel-band—
   'It is now the time,
     These be the years,
Of Cáhal Mór of the Wine-red Hand!
   I sought the hall,
     And, behold!—a change
From light to darkness, from joy to woe!
   Kings, nobles, all,
     Looked aghast and strange;
The minstrel-group sate in dumbest show!
   Had some great crime
     Wrought this dread amaze,
This terror? None seemed to understand.
   'Twas then the time,
     We were in the days,
Of Cáhal Mór of the Wine-red Hand.
   I again walked forth;
     But lo! the sky
Showed fleckt with blood, and an alien sun
   Glared from the north,
     And there stood on high,

Amid his shorn beams, A SKELETON !
It was by the stream
Of the castled Maine,
One autumn-eve, in the Teuton's land
That I dreamed this dream
Of the time and reign
Of Cáhal Mór of the Wine-red hand !
J. C. MANGAN.

LAMENT FOR BAṄBA.*

OH, my land ! oh, my love !
What a woe, and how deep
Is thy death to my long-mourning soul !
God alone, God above,
Can awake thee from sleep—
Can release thee from bondage and dole !
Alas, alas, and alas,
For the once proud people of Banba !

As a tree in its prime,
Which the axe layeth low,
Didst thou fall, O, unfortunate land !
Not by Time, nor thy crime,
Came the shock and the blow.
They were given by a false felon hand !
Alas, alas, and alas,
For the once proud people of Banba !

Oh, my grief of all griefs
Is to see how thy throne
Is usurped, whilst thyself art in thrall !
Other lands have their chiefs,

* Ireland.

Have their kings ; thou alone
Art a wife—yet a widow withal.
  Alas, alas, and alas,
   For the once proud people of Banba!

  The high house of O'Neill
   Is gone down to the dust,
The O'Brien is clanless and banned ;
 And the steel, the red steel,
  May no more be the trust
Of the faithful and brave in the land !
  Alas, alas, and alas,
   For the once proud people of Banba!

 True, alas ! Wrong and wrath
  Were of old all too rife,
Deeds were done which no good man admires ;
 And, perchance, Heaven hath
  Chastened us for the strife
And the blood-shedding ways of our sires !
  Alas, alas, and alas,
   For the once proud people of Banba!

 But, no more ! This our doom,
  While our hearts yet are warm,
Let us not over-weakly deplore !
For the hour soon may loom
 When the Lord's mighty hand
Shall be raised for our rescue once more !
  And our grief shall be turned into joy
   For the still proud people of Banba!
    Translated by J. C. MANGAN.

THE BRIGHTEST OF THE BRIGHT.
(ALLEGORICAL.)

The brightest of the bright met me on my path so lonely;
  The crystal of all crystals was her flashing dark-blue eye;
Melodious more than music was her spoken language only;
  And glories were her cheeks, of a brilliant crimson dye.

With ringlets above ringlets her hair in many a cluster
  Descended to the earth, and swept the dewy flowers;
Her bosom shone as bright as a mirror in its lustre;
  She seemed like some fair daughter of the celestial powers.

She chanted me a chant, a beautiful and grand hymn,
  Of him who should be shortly Eire's* reigning king—
She prophesied the fall of the wretches who had banned him;
  And somewhat else she told me which I dare not sing.

Trembling with many fears, I called on Holy Mary,
  As I drew nigh this fair, to shield me from all harm;
When, wonderful to tell, she fled far to the fairy
  Green mansion of Sliabh Luachra in terror and alarm!

O'er mountain, moor, and marsh, by greenwood, lough, and hollow,
  I tracked her distant footsteps with a throbbing heart;
Through many an hour and day did I follow on and ow,
  Till I reached the magic palace reared of old by Druid art.

* Erin's.

There a wild and wizard band, with mocking fiendish laughter,
  Pointed out me her I sought, who sat low beside a clown;
And I felt as though I never could dream of pleasure after
  When I saw the maid so fallen whose charms deserved a crown.

Then, with burning speech and soul, I looked at her, and told her
  That to wed a churl like that was for her the shame of shames,
When a bridegroom such as I was longing to enfold her
  To a bosom that her beauty had kindled into flames.

But answer made she none; she wept with bitter weeping,
  Her tears ran down in rivers, but nothing could she say;
She gave me then a guide for my safe and better keeping,—
  The Brightest of the Bright, whom I met upon the way.

SUMMING UP.

Oh, my misery, my woe, my sorrow and my anguish,
  My bitter source of dolor is evermore that she
The Loveliest of the Lovely should thus be left to languish
  Amid a ruffian horde till the Heroes cross the sea.

EGAN O'REILLY.

THE FAIR HILLS OF EIRE,* O!

TAKE a blessing from my heart to the land of my birth,
  And the fair Hills of Eire, O!
And to all that yet survive of Eibhear's tribe on earth,
  On the fair Hills of Eire, O!

* A dissyllable: Erin.

In that land so delightful the wild thrush's lay
Seems to pour a lament forth for Eire's decay—
Alas! alas! why pine I a thousand miles away
    From the fair Hills of Eire, O!

The soil is rich and soft—the air is mild and bland,
    Of the fair Hills of Eire, O!
Her barest rock is greener to me than this rude land—
    Oh, the fair Hills of Eire, O!
Her woods are tall and straight, grove rising over grove;
Trees flourish in her glens below, and on her heights above,
Oh, in heart and in soul, I shall ever, ever love
    The fair Hills of Eire, O!

A noble tribe, moreover, are the now hapless Gael,
    On the fair Hills of Eire, O!
A tribe in battle's hour unused to shrink or fail
    On the fair Hills of Eire, O!
For this is my lament in bitterness outpoured,
To see them slain or scattered by the Saxon sword—
Oh, woe of woes, to see a foreign spoiler horde
    On the fair Hills of Eire, O!

Broad and tall rise the *Cruachs* in the golden morning's glow
    On the fair Hills of Eire, O!
O'er her smooth grass for ever sweet cream and honey flow
    On the fair Hills of Eire, O!
Oh, I long, I am pining, again to behold
The land that belongs to the brave Gael of old;
Far dearer to my heart than a gift of gems or gold
    Are the fair Hills of Eire, O!

The dewdrops lie bright 'mid the grass and yellow corn
    On the fair Hills of Eire, O!
The sweet-scented apples blush redly in the morn
    On the fair Hills of Eire, O!
The watercress and sorrel fill the vales below;
The streamlets are hushed till the evening breezes blow;
While the waves of the Suir, noble river! ever flow
    Near the fair Hills of Eire, O!

A fruitful clime is Eire's, through valley, meadow, plain,
    And the fair land of Eire, O!
The very 'Bread of Life' is in the yellow grain
    On the fair Hills of Eire, O!
Far dearer unto me than the tones music yields
Is the lowing of the kine and the calves in her fields,
And the sunlight that shone long long ago on the shields
    Of the Gaels, on the fair Hills of Eire, O!
              DONOGH MACCON-MARA.

O EIRE, MY SOUL, WHAT A WOE IS THINE!

O SPIRIT OF SONG, awake! arise!
  For thee I pine by night and by day;
With none to cheer me, or hear my sighs
  For the fate of him who is far away*
    O Eire, my soul, what a woe is thine!

That glorious youth of a kingly race,
  Whose arm is strong to hew tyrants down,
How long shall it be ere I see his face,
  How long shall it be ere he wins the crown?
    O Eire, my soul! etc.

        * Prince Charlie.

Why, bards, arise ye not, each and all—
   Why sing ye not strains in warlike style?
He comes with his heroes, to disenthral
     By the might of the sword, our long-chained isle!
        O Eire, my soul! etc.

Kings Philip and James, and their marshalled hosts,
   A brilliant phalanx, a dazzling band,
Will sail full soon for our noble coasts,
     And reach in power *Inis Eilge's* strand,
        O Eire, my soul! etc.

They will drive afar to the surging sea
   The sullen tribe of the dreary tongue;
The Gaels again shall be rich and free;
     The praise of the Bards shall be loudly sung!
        O Eire, my soul! etc.

Oh, dear to my heart is the thought of that day!
   When it dawns we will quaff the beaded ale;
We'll pass it in pleasure, merry and gay,
     And drink to all sneakers out of our pale,
        O Eire, my soul! etc.

O Mother of Saints, to thee be the praise
   Of the downfall that waits the Saxon throng!
The priests shall assemble and chant sweet lays,
     And each bard and lyrist shall echo the song!
        O Eire, my soul! etc.

JOHN O'TUOMY.

A WELCOME FOR 'KING' CHARLES.

O Patrick, my friend, have you heard the commotion,
  The clangour, the shouting, so lately gone forth?
The troops have come over the blue-billowed ocean,
  And Thurot commands in the camp of the North.
Up, up, to your post!—one of glory and danger—
  Our legions must now neither falter nor fail:
We'll chase from the island the hosts of the stranger,
  Led on by the conquering Prince of the Gael!

And you, my poor countrymen, trampled for ages,
  Grasp each of you now his sharp sword in his hand!
The war that Prince Charlie so valiantly wages
  Is one that will shatter the chains of our land.
Hurrah for our leader! hurrah for Prince Charlie!
  Give praise to his efforts with music and song;
Our nobles will now, in the juice of the barley,
  Carouse to his victories all the day long!

Rothe marshals his brave-hearted forces to waken
  The soul of the nation to combat and dare,
While Georgy is feeble and Cumberland shaken,
  And Parliament gnashes its teeth in despair.
The lads with the dirks from the hills of the Highlands
  Are marching with pibroch and shout to the field,
And Charlie, Prince Charlie, the King of the Islands
  Will force the usurping old German to yield!

Oh, this is the joy, this the revel in earnest,
  The story to tell to the ends of the earth,
That our youths have uprisen, resolving, with sternest
  Intention, to fight for the land of their birth.

We will drive out the stranger from green-valleyed Erin—
    King George and his crew shall be scarce in the land,
And the Crown of Three Kingdoms shall he alone wear in
    The Islands—our Prince—the man born to command!
                    WILLIAM HEFFERNAN.

MAYO.

ON the deck of Patrick Lynch's boat I sat in a woeful
    plight,
Through my sighing all the weary day, and weeping all
    the night,
Were it not that full of sorrow from my people forth I go,
By the blessed sun, 'tis royally I'd sing thy praise, Mayo.

When I dwelt at home in plenty, and my gold did much
    abound,
In the company of fair young maids the Spanish ale went
    round—
'Tis a bitter change from those gay days that now I'm
    forced to go,
And must leave my bones in Santa Cruz, far from my
    own Mayo.

They are altered girls in Irrul now; 'tis proud they're
    grown and high,
With their hair-bags and their top-knots, for I pass their
    buckles by;
But it's little now I heed their airs, for God will have it so,
That I must depart for foreign lands, and leave my sweet
    Mayo.

'Tis my grief that Patrick Loughlin is not Earl of Irrul still,
And that Brian Duff no longer rules as Lord upon the hill;
And that Colonel Hugh MacGrady should be lying dead and low,
And I sailing, sailing swiftly from the county of Mayo.
     Translated by GEORGE FOX.

SOUL AND COUNTRY.

ARISE! my slumbering soul, arise!
 And learn what yet remains for thee
  To dree or do!
The signs are flaming in the skies;
 A struggling world would yet be free,
  And live anew.
The earthquake hath not yet been born,
 That soon shall rock the lands around,
  Beneath their base.
Immortal freedom's thunder horn,
 As yet, yields but a doleful sound
  To Europe's race.

Look round, my soul, and see and say
 If those about thee understand
  Their mission here;
The will to smite—the power to slay—
 Abound in every heart and hand,
  Afar, anear.

But, God! must yet the conqueror's sword
   Pierce *mind*, as heart, in this proud year?
      Oh, dream it not!
It sounds a false, blaspheming word,
   Begot and born of moral fear—
      And ill-begot!

To leave the world a name is nought;
   To leave a name for glorious deeds
      And works of love—
A name to waken lightning thought,
   And fire the soul of him who reads,
      This tells above.
Napoleon sinks to-day before
   The ungilded shrine, the *single* soul
      Of Washington;
Truth's name, alone, shall man adore,
   Long as the waves of time shall roll
      Henceforward on!

My countrymen! my words are weak,
   My health is gone, my soul is dark,
      My heart is chill—
Yet would I fain and fondly seek
   To see you borne in freedom's bark
      O'er ocean still.
Beseech your God, and bide your hour—
   He cannot, will not, long be dumb;
      Even now His tread
Is heard o'er earth with coming power;
   And coming, trust me, it will come,
      Else were He dead!

                J. C. MANGAN.

THE POET'S PROPHECY.

In the time of my boyhood I had a strange feeling,
  That I was to die in the noon of my day;
Not quietly into the silent grave stealing,
  But torn, like a blasted oak, sudden away.

That, even in the hour when enjoyment was keenest,
  My lamp should quench suddenly, hissing in gloom,
That even when mine honours were freshest and greenest,
  A blight should rush over and scatter their bloom.

It might be a fancy—it might be the glooming
  Of dark visions taking the semblance of truth,
And it might be the shade of the storm that is coming,
  Cast thus in its morn through the sunshine of youth.

But be it a dream or a mystic revealing,
  The bodement has haunted me year after year,
And whenever my bosom with rapture was filling,
  I paused for the footfall of fate at mine ear.

With this feeling upon me all feverish and glowing,
  I rushed up the rugged way panting to Fame;
I snatched at my laurels while yet they were growing,
  And won for my guerdon the half of a name.

My triumphs I viewed from the least to the brightest,
  As gay flowers plucked from the fingers of Death;
And whenever joy's garments flowed richest and lightest,
  I looked for the skeleton lurking beneath.

O friend of my heart! if that doom should fall on me,
  And thou shouldst live on to remember my love—
Come oft to the tomb when the turf lies upon me,
  And list to the even wind mourning above.

Lie down by that bank where the river is creeping
    All fearfully under the still autumn tree,
When each leaf in the sunset is silently weeping,
    And sigh for departed days—thinking of me.

But when o'er the minstrel thou'rt lonelily sighing,
    Forgive, if his failings should flash on thy brain;
Remember the heart that beneath thee is lying
    Can never awake to offend thee again.

Remember how freely that heart that to others
    Was dark as the tempest-dawn frowning above,
Burst open to thine with the zeal of a brother's,
    And showed all its hues in the light of thy love.

GERALD GRIFFIN.

THE POET'S GRIEF.

My spirit o'er an early tomb,
    With ruffled wing sits drooping;
And real forms of blighted bloom
Have in my heart left little room
    For forms of fancy's grouping.
The heart—the eye I loved to light
    With song, are dark and hollow;
And if, when that young eye was bright,
I took a haughty minstrel flight,
It was to tempt the inborn might
    Of that young heart to follow!

No more—oh, never more to gaze
    Shall be to me as glory!
No more—oh, never more my lays
Shall sway him with a hope to raise
    His country, and her story!

And when the loved ones in the numb,
   Deaf trance of death are wreathèd
(Though sweet may be her song to some),
The singer feels the hour is come
For lyre and lyrist to be dumb—
   Her best of song is breathèd.

'Tis true, it was a joy to see
   The slave for freedom wrestle,
Stirred by my random minstrelsy;
But 'tis not in the lofty tree
   The sweetest song-birds nestle—
They are a shy and chary race:
   And though they soar, and squander
Rich music over nature's face,
To one deep, lonely dwelling-place
No foot may find—no eye may trace,
   They still return the fonder.

O God!—but prayers avail'd me not!
   The darkening angel enter'd,
And made one universal blot—
A world-wide desert—of the spot
   Where all my hope was centred!
The heart—the eye I loved to light
   With song, are dark and hollow:
What marvel if my spirit slight
The guerdon of the minstrel's flight?
I cannot tempt the inborn might
   Of that young heart to follow!

J. FRASER.

GOUGANE BARRA.

There is a green island in lone Gougane Barra,
Whence Allu of songs rushes forth like an arrow;
In deep-valleyed Desmond a thousand wild fountains
Come down to that lake, from their home in the mountains.
There grows the wild ash; and a time-stricken willow
Looks chidingly down on the mirth of the billow,
As, like some gay child that sad monitor scorning,
It lightly laughs back to the laugh of the morning.

And its zone of dark hills—oh! to see them all bright'ning,
When the tempest flings out its red banner of lightning,
And the waters come down, 'mid the thunder's deep rattle,
Like clans from their hill at the voice of the battle;
And brightly the fire-crested billows are gleaming,
And wildly from Mallow the eagles are screaming;
Oh, where is the dwelling, in valley or high land,
So meet for a bard as this lone little island?

How oft, when the summer sun rested on Clara
And lit the blue headland of sullen Ivara,
Have I sought thee, sweet spot, from my home by the ocean,
And trod all thy wilds with a minstrel's devotion,
And thought on the bards who, oft gathering together
In the cleft of thy rocks and the depth of thy heather,
Dwelt far from the Saxon's dark bondage and slaughter,
As they raised their last song by the rush of thy water!

High sons of the lyre! oh, how proud was the feeling
To dream while alone through that solitude stealing;
Though loftier minstrels green Erin can number,
I alone waked the strain of her harp from its slumber,
And glean'd the grey legend that long had been sleeping,
Where oblivion's dull mist o'er its beauty was creeping,
From the love which I felt for my country's sad story,
When to love her was shame, to revile her was glory!

Last bard of the free! were it mine to inherit
The fire of thy harp and the wing of thy spirit,
With the wrongs which, like thee, to my own land have bound me,
Did your mantle of song throw its radiance around me;
Yet, yet on those bold cliffs might Liberty rally,
And abroad send her cry o'er the sleep of each valley.
But rouse thee, vain dreamer! no fond fancy cherish;
Thy vision of Freedom in bloodshed must perish.

I soon shall be gone—though my name may be spoken
When Erin awakes, and her fetters are broken—
Some minstrel will come in the summer eve's gleaming,
When Freedom's young light on his spirit is beaming,
To bend o'er my grave with a tear of emotion,
Where calm Avonbuee seeks the kisses of ocean,
And a wild wreath to plant from the banks of that river
O'er the heart and the harp that are silent for ever.

JAMES JOSEPH CALLANAN.

THE VIRGIN MARY'S BANK.

THE evening-star rose beauteous above the fading day,
As to the lone and silent beach the Virgin came to pray;

And hill and wave shone brightly in the moonlight's
   mellow fall,
But the bank of green where Mary knelt was brightest of
   them all.

Slow moving o'er the waters, a gallant bark appear'd,
And her joyous crew look'd from the deck as to the land
   she near'd;
To the calm and shelter'd haven she floated like a swan,
And her wings of snow o'er the waves below in pride and
   beauty shone.

The master saw our Lady as he stood upon the prow,
And mark'd the whiteness of her robe and the radiance
   of her brow;
Her arms were folded gracefully upon her stainless breast,
And her eyes look'd up among the stars to Him her soul
   lov'd best.

He show'd her to his sailors, and he hail'd her with a
   cheer;
And on the kneeling Virgin they gazed with laugh and
   jeer,
And madly swore a form so fair they never saw before;
And they curs'd the faint and lagging breeze that kept
   them from the shore.

The ocean from its bosom shook off the moonlight sheen,
And up its wrathful billows rose to vindicate their queen;
And a cloud came o'er the heavens, and a darkness o'er
   the land,
And the scoffing crew beheld no more that Lady on the
   strand.

Out burst the pealing thunder, and the lightning leap'd about,
And rushing with his watery war, the tempest gave a shout;
And that vessel from a mountain wave came down with thund'ring shock,
And her timbers flew like scatter'd spray on Inchidony's rock.

Then loud from all that guilty crew one shriek rose wild and high:
But the angry surge swept over them and hush'd their gurgling cry;
And with a hoarse exulting tone the tempest pass'd away,
And down, still chafing from their strife, the indignant waters lay.

When the calm and purple morning shone out on high Dunmore,
Full many a mangled corpse was seen on Inchidony's shore;
And to this day the fisherman shows where the scoffers sank;
And still he calls that hillock green the 'Virgin Mary's Bank.'

JAMES JOSEPH CALLANAN.

O SAY, MY BROWN DRIMIN.*

O SAY, my brown Drimin, thou silk of the kine,
Where, where are thy strong ones, last hope of thy line?
Too deep and too long is the slumber they take,
At the loud call of Freedom why don't they awake?

* A pet cow: allegorical for Ireland.

My strong ones have fallen—from the bright eye of day
All darkly they sleep in their dwelling of clay;
The cold turf is o'er them;—they hear not my cries,
And since Louis no aid gives I cannot arise.

Oh! where art thou, Louis,—our eyes are on thee?
Are thy lofty ships walking in strength o'er the sea?
In Freedom's last strife if you linger or quail,
No morn e'er shall break on the night of the Gael.

But should the king's son,* now bereft of his right,
Come, proud in his strength, for his country to fight,
Like leaves on the trees will new people arise,
And deep from their mountains shout back to my cries.

When the prince, now an exile, shall come for his own,
The isles of his father, his rights and his throne,
My people in battle the Saxon will meet,
And kick them before, like old shoes from their feet.

O'er mountains and valleys they'll press on their rout,
The five ends of Erin shall ring to their shout;
My sons all united shall bless the glad day
When the flint-hearted Saxons they've chased far away.
    Translated by JAMES JOSEPH CALLANAN.

LAMENT FOR IRELAND.

How dimm'd is the glory that circled the Gael,
And fall'n the high people of green Innisfail!
The sword of the Saxon is red with their gore,
And the mighty of nations is mighty no more!

  * The Pretender.

Like a bark on the ocean, long shattered and tost,
On the land of your fathers at length you are lost;
The hand of the spoiler is stretched on your plains,
And you're doom'd from your cradles to bondage and chains.

Oh where is the beauty that beam'd on thy brow?
Strong hand in the battle, how weak art thou now!
That heart is now broken that never would quail,
And thy high songs are turned into weeping and wail.

Bright shades of our sires! from your home in the skies,
Oh blast not your sons with the scorn of your eyes!
Proud spirit of Gollam, how red is thy cheek,
For thy freemen are slaves, and thy mighty are weak!

O'Nial of the Hostages, Con, whose high name
On a hundred red battles has floated to fame,
Let the long grasses sigh undisturbed o'er thy sleep;
Arise not to shame us, awake not to weep.

In thy broad wing of darkness enfold us, O Night!
Withhold, O bright sun, the reproach of thy light!
For freedom or valour no more can'st thou see
In the home of the brave, in the isles of the free.

Affliction's dark waters your spirits have bow'd,
And oppression hath wrapped all your land in its shroud,
Since first from the Brehon's pure justice you stray'd,
And bent to those laws the proud Saxon has made.

We know not our country, so strange is her face;
Her sons, once her glory, are now her disgrace;
Gone, gone is the beauty of fair Innisfail,
For the stranger now rules in the land of the Gael.

Where, where are the woods that oft rung to your cheer,
Where you waked the wild chase of the wolf and the deer?
Can those dark heights, with ramparts all frowning and riven,
Be the hills where your forests wav'd brightly in heaven?

O bondsmen of Egypt, no Moses appears,
To light your dark steps through this desert of tears!
Degraded and lost ones, no Hector is nigh
To lead you to freedom, or teach you to die!
 O'GNIVE (*translated by* JAMES JOSEPH CALLANAN).

ADARE.

O SWEET ADARE! O lovely vale!
 O soft retreat of sylvan splendour!
Nor summer sun, nor morning gale,
 E'er hailed a scene more softly tender.
How shall I tell the thousand charms
 Within thy verdant bosom dwelling,
Where, lulled in Nature's fost'ring arms,
 Soft peace abides and joy excelling!

Ye morning airs, how sweet at dawn
 The slumbering boughs your song awaken,
Or linger o'er the silent lawn,
 With odour of the harebell taken!
Thou rising sun, how richly gleams
 Thy smile from far Knockfierna's mountain,
O'er waving woods and bounding streams,
 And many a grove and glancing fountain!

Ye clouds of noon, how freshly there,
  When summer heats the open meadows,
O'er parchèd hill and valley fair,
  All coolly lie your veiling shadows!
Ye rolling shades and vapours grey,
  Slow creeping o'er the golden heaven,
How soft ye seal the eye of day,
  And wreath the dusky brow of even!

In sweet Adare the jocund Spring
  His notes of odorous joy is breathing;
The wild birds in the woodland sing,
  The wild flowers in the vale are wreathing.
There winds the Mague, as silver-clear,
  Among the elms so sweetly flowing;
There, fragrant in the early year,
  Wild roses on the banks are blowing.

The wild-duck seeks the sedgy bank,
  Or dives beneath the glistening billow,
Where graceful droop, and clustering dank,
  The osier bright and rustling willow.
The hawthorn scents the leafy dale,
  In thicket lone the stag is belling,
And sweet along the echoing vale
  The sound of vernal joy is swelling.

GERALD GRIFFIN.

ORANGE AND GREEN.

Come, pledge again thy heart and hand—
  One grasp that ne'er shall sever:
Our watchword be, 'Our native land!'
  Our motto, 'Love for ever.'

And let the Orange lily be
   Thy badge, my patriot brother—
The everlasting Green for *me;*
   And we for one another.

Behold how green the gallant stem
   On which the flower is blowing;
How in one heavenly breeze and beam
   Both flower and stem are glowing!
The same good soil, sustaining both,
   Makes both united flourish;
But cannot give the Orange growth,
   And cease the Green to nourish.

Yea, more—the hand that plucks the flow'r
   Will vainly strive to cherish;
The stem blooms on—but in that hour
   The flower begins to perish.
Regard them, then, of equal worth,
   While lasts their genial weather;
The time's at hand when into earth
   The two shall sink together.

E'en thus be, in our country's cause,
   Our party feelings blended;
Till lasting peace, from equal laws,
   On both shall have descended.
Till then the Orange lily be
   Thy badge, my patriot brother—
The everlasting Green for *me;*
   And—we for one another.

JOHN D. FRASER.

O BAY OF DUBLIN!

O Bay of Dublin! my heart you're troublin',
   Your beauty haunts me like a fevered dream;
Like frozen fountains that the sun sets bubblin',
   My heart's blood warms when I but hear your name.
And never till this life-pulse ceases,
   My earliest thought you'll cease to be;
Oh! there's no one here knows how fair that place is,
   And no one cares how dear it is to me.

Sweet Wicklow Mountains! the sunlight sleeping
   On your green banks is a picture rare:
You crowd around me, like young girls peeping,
   And puzzling me to say which is most fair;
As though you'd see your own sweet faces,
   Reflected in that smooth and silver sea.
Oh! my blessin' on those lovely places,
   Though no one cares how dear they are to me.

How often when at work I'm sitting,
   And musing sadly on the days of yore,
I think I see my Katey knitting,
   And the children playing round the cabin door;
I think I see the neighbours' faces
   All gather'd round, their long-lost friend to see.
Oh! though no one knows how fair that place is,
   Heaven knows how dear my poor home was to me.
                        LADY DUFFERIN.

THE BELLS OF SHANDON.

With deep affection
And recollection
I often think of
   Those Shandon bells,
Whose sounds so wild would,
In the days of childhood,
Fling round my cradle
   Their magic spells.
On this I ponder
Where'er I wander,
And thus grow fonder,
   Sweet Cork, of thee;
With thy bells of Shandon,
That sound so grand on
The pleasant waters
   Of the river Lee.

I've heard bells chiming
Full many a clime in,
Tolling sublime in
   Cathedral shrine,
While at a glib rate
Brass tongues would vibrate
But all their music
   Spoke nought like thine:
For memory dwelling
On each proud swelling
Of the belfry knelling
   Its bold notes free.

Made the bells of Shandon
Sound far more grand on
The pleasant waters
  Of the river Lee.

I've heard bells tolling
Old 'Adrian's Mole' in,
Their thunder rolling
  From the Vatican,
And cymbals glorious
Swinging uproarious
In the gorgeous turrets
  Of Nôtre Dame;
But thy sounds were sweeter
Than the dome of Peter
Flings o'er the Tiber,
  Pealing solemnly;—
Oh, the bells of Shandon
Sound far more grand on
The pleasant waters
  Of the river Lee.

There's a bell in Moscow,
While on tower and kiosk O!
In Saint Sophia
  The Turkman gets,
And loud in air
Calls men to prayer
From the tapering summit
  Of tall minarets.
Such empty phantom
I freely grant them;
But there's an anthem
  More dear to me—

'Tis the bells of Shandon,
That sound so grand on
The pleasant waters
Of the river Lee.
    FRANCIS SYLVESTER MAHONY.
      (*Father Prout.*)

DIRGE OF RORY O'MORE.
A.D. 1642.

UP the sea-sadden'd valley, at evening's decline,
A heifer walks lowing, 'the silk of the kine;'*
From the deep to the mountain she roams, and again
From the mountain's green urn to the purple-rimm'd main.

Whom seek'st thou, sad mother? Thine own is not thine!
He dropp'd from the headland; he sank in the brine!
'Twas a dream! but in dream at thy foot did he follow,
Through the meadow-sweet on by the marish and mallow!

Was he thine? Have they slain him? Thou seek'st him, not knowing
Thyself too art theirs, thy sweet breath and sad lowing!
Thy gold horn is theirs; thy dark eye and thy silk!
And that which torments thee, thy milk, is their milk!

'Twas no dream, motherland! 'Twas no dream, Innisfail!
Hope dreams, but grief dreams not—the grief of the Gael!
From Leix and Ikerrin, to Donegal's shore,
Rolls the dirge of thy last and thy bravest—O'More!
    Translated by AUBREY T. DE VERE.

* Allegorical for Ireland.

AM I REMEMBERED IN ERIN?

AM I remember'd in Erin?
  I charge you speak me true—
Has my name a sound, a meaning,
  In the scenes my boyhood knew?
Does the heart of the mother ever
  Recall her exile's name?
For to be forgot in Erin,
  And on earth, is all the same.

O mother! Mother Erin!
  Many sons your age hath seen—
Many gifted, constant lovers
  Since your mantle first was green.
Then how may I hope to cherish
  The dream that I could be
In your crowded memory number'd
  With that palm-crown'd companie?

Yet faint and far, my mother,
  As the hope shines on my sight,
I cannot choose but watch it
  Till my eyes have lost their light;
For never among your brightest,
  And never among your best,
Was heart more true to Erin
  Than beats within my breast.

THOMAS D'ARCY M'GEE.

THE DEATH OF O'CAROLAN.

THERE is an empty seat by many a board,
    A guest is missed in hostelry and hall—
There is a harp hung up in Alderford
    That was in Ireland sweetest harp of all.
The hand that made it speak, woe's me, is cold ;
    The darkened eyeballs roll inspired no more ;
The lips—the potent lips—gape like a mould,
    Where late the golden torrents floated o'er.

In vain the watchman looks from Mayo's towers
    For him whose presence filled all hearts with mirth ;
In vain the gathered guests outsit the hours,
    The honoured chair is vacant by the hearth.
From Castle-Archdall, Moneyglass, and Trim,
    The courteous messages go forth in vain ;
Kind words no longer have a joy for him
    Whose lowly lodge is in death's dark domain.

Kilronan Abbey is his castle now,
    And there till doomsday peacefully he'll stay ;
In vain they weave new garlands for his brow,
    In vain they go to meet him by the way.
In kindred company he does not tire,
    The native dead and noble lie around,
His lifelong song has ceased, his wood and wire
    Rest, a sweet harp unstrung, in holy ground.

Last of our ancient Minstrels ! thou who lent
    A buoyant motive to a foundering race—
Whose saving song, into their being blent,
    Sustained them by its passion and its grace.

God rest you!   May your judgment-dues be light,
  Dear Turlogh! and the purgatorial days
Be few and short, till clothed in holy white,
  Your soul may come before the Throne of rays.
                    THOMAS D'ARCY M'GEE.

ADIEU TO INNISFAIL.*

ADIEU!—The snowy sail
Swells her bosom to the gale
And our bark from Innisfail
        Bounds away.
While we gaze upon thy shore
That we never shall see more,
And the blinding tears flow o'er,
        We pray:—

Ma vuirneen! be thou long
In peace the queen of song—
In battle proud and strong
        As the sea.
Be saints thine offspring still,
True heroes guard each hill,
And harps by every rill
        Sound free!

Though round her Indian bowers
The hand of Nature showers
The brightest blooming flowers
        Of our sphere;
Yet not the richest rose
In an *alien* clime that blows,
Like the briar at home that grows
        Is dear.

* Ireland.

Though glowing breasts may be
In soft vales beyond the sea,
Yet ever, *gra ma cree*,
    Shall I wail
For the heart of love I leave
In the dreary hours of eve,
On thy stormy shores to grieve,
    Innisfail!

But mem'ry o'er the deep
On her dewy wing shall sweep,
When in midnight hours I weep
    O'er thy wrongs;
And bring me, steeped in tears,
The dead flowers of other years,
And waft unto my ears
    Home's songs.

When I slumber in the gloom
Of a nameless foreign tomb,
By a distant ocean's boom,
    Innisfail!
Around thy em'rald shore
May the clasping sea adore,
And each wave in thunder roar,
    'All hail!'

And when the final sigh
Shall bear my soul on high,
And on chainless wing I fly
    Through the blue,
Earth's latest thought shall be,
As I soar above the sea,
'Green Erin, dear, to thee
    Adieu!'

    RICHARD DALTON WILLIAMS.

ERIN! THE TEAR AND THE SMILE IN THINE EYES.

Erin! the tear and the smile in thine eyes
Blend like the rainbow that hangs in thy skies!
   Shining through sorrow's stream
   Sadd'ning through pleasure's beam,
   Thy suns with doubtful gleam
      Weep while they rise.

Erin! thy silent tear shall never cease,
Erin! thy languid smile ne'er shall increase,
   Till, like the rainbow's light,
   Thy various tints unite,
   And form in Heaven's sight
      One arch of peace!

                Thomas Moore.

THE HARP THAT ONCE THROUGH TARA'S HALLS.

The harp that once through Tara's halls
   The soul of music shed,
Now hangs as mute on Tara's walls
   As if that soul were fled.
So sleeps the pride of former days,
   So glory's thrill is o'er,
And hearts, that once beat high for praise,
   Now feel that pulse no more.

No more to chiefs and ladies bright
   The harp of Tara swells:
The chord alone, that breaks at night,
   Its tale of ruin tells.

Thus Freedom now so seldom wakes,
　The only throb she gives
Is when some heart indignant breaks,
　To show that still she lives.
Thomas Moore.

RICH AND RARE WERE THE GEMS SHE WORE.

Rich and rare were the gems she wore,
And a bright gold ring on her wand she bore,
But, oh! her beauty was far beyond
Her sparkling gems or snow-white wand.

'Lady, dost thou not fear to stray,
So lone and lovely, through this bleak way?
Are Erin's sons so good or so cold,
As not to be tempted by woman or gold?'

'Sir Knight! I feel not the least alarm,
No son of Erin will offer me harm:
For, though they love women and golden store,
Sir Knight! they love honour and virtue more!'

On she went, and her maiden smile
In safety lighted her round the green isle;
And blest for ever is she who relied
Upon Erin's honour and Erin's pride.
Thomas Moore.

THE MEETING OF THE WATERS.

There is not in the wide world a valley so sweet,
As that vale in whose bosom the bright waters meet;
Oh, the last rays of feeling and life must depart,
Ere the bloom of that valley shall fade from my heart!

Yet it was not that Nature had shed o'er the scene
Her purest of crystal and brightest of green;
'Twas *not* her soft magic of streamlet or hill,
Oh no—it was something more exquisite still.

'Twas that friends, the beloved of my bosom, were near,
Who made ev'ry dear scene of enchantment more dear,
And who felt how the best charms of Nature improve,
When we see them reflected from looks that we love.

Sweet vale of Avoca! how calm could I rest
In thy bosom of shade, with the friends I love best,
Where the storms that we feel in this cold world should cease,
And our hearts, like thy waters, be mingled in peace!

THOMAS MOORE.

LET ERIN REMEMBER THE DAYS OF OLD.

LET Erin remember the days of old,
   Ere her faithless sons betray'd her;
When Malachi wore the collar of gold,
   Which he won from her proud invader;
When her kings, with standard of green unfurl'd,
   Led the Red-Branch Knights to danger;
Ere the emerald gem of the western world
   Was set in the crown of a stranger.

On Lough Neagh's bank as the fisherman strays,
   When the clear cold eve's declining,
He sees the round towers of other days
   In the wave beneath him shining:
Thus shall memory often, in dreams sublime,
   Catch a glimpse of the days that are over;
Thus, sighing, look through the waves of time
   For the long-faded glories they cover.

THOMAS MOORE.

OH, THE SHAMROCK!

Through Erin's Isle,
To sport awhile,
As Love and Valour wander'd,
With Wit, the sprite,
Whose quiver bright
A thousand arrows squander'd;
Where'er they pass,
A triple grass
Shoots up, with dew-drops streaming,
As softly green
As emerald seen
Through purest crystal gleaming.
Oh, the Shamrock, the green, immortal Shamrock!
Chosen leaf
Of Bard and Chief,
Old Erin's native Shamrock!

Says Valour, 'See,
They spring for me,
Those leafy gems of morning!'
Says Love, 'No, no,
For me they grow,
My fragrant path adorning.'
But Wit perceives
The triple leaves,
And cries, 'Oh, do not sever
A type that blends
Three godlike friends,
Love, Valour, Wit, for ever!'

Oh, the Shamrock, the green, immortal Shamrock!
    Chosen leaf
    Of Bard and Chief,
Old Erin's native Shamrock!

    So firmly fond
    May last the bond
They wove that morn together,
    And ne'er may fall
    One drop of gall
On Wit's celestial feather!
    May Love, as twine
    His flowers divine,
Of thorny falsehood weed 'em!
    May Valour ne'er
    His standard rear
Against the cause of Freedom!
Oh, the Shamrock, the green, immortal Shamrock!
    Chosen leaf
    Of Bard and Chief,
Old Erin's native Shamrock!
                            THOMAS MOORE.

THE MINSTREL-BOY.

THE Minstrel-boy to the war is gone,
    In the ranks of death you'll find him;
His father's sword he has girded on,
    And his wild harp slung behind him.
'Land of Song!' said the warrior-bard,
    'Though all the world betrays thee,
One sword, at least, thy rights shall guard,
    One faithful harp shall praise thee!'

The Minstrel fell!—but the foeman's chain
    Could not bring his proud soul under;
The harp he loved ne'er spoke again,
    For he tore its chords asunder;
And said, 'No chains shall sully thee,
    Thou soul of love and bravery!
Thy songs were made for the brave and free,
    They shall never sound in slavery!'

THOMAS MOORE.

OH FOR THE SWORDS OF FORMER TIME!

OH for the swords of former time!
    Oh for the men who bore them,
When, armed for Right, they stood sublime,
    And tyrants crouched before them!
When pure yet, ere courts began
    With honours to enslave him,
The best honours worn by man
    Were those which Virtue gave him.
Oh for the swords of former time!
    Oh for the men who bore them,
When, armed for Right, they stood sublime,
    And tyrants crouched before them!

Oh for the kings who flourished then!
    Oh for the pomp that crowned them,
When hearts and hands of freeborn men
    Were all the ramparts round them!
When, safe built on bosoms true,
    The throne was but the centre
Round which Love a circle drew,
    That Treason durst not enter.

Oh for the kings who flourished then !
Oh for the pomp that crowned them,
When hearts and hands of freeborn men
Were all the ramparts round them !

THOMAS MOORE.

THE BOYNE'S ILL-FATED RIVER.

As vanquished Erin wept beside
    The Boyne's ill-fated river,
She saw where Discord, in the tide,
    Had dropped his loaded quiver.
'Lie hid,' she cried, 'ye venomed darts,
    Where mortal eye may shun you ;
Lie hid—for oh, the stain of hearts
    That bled for me is on you !'

But vain her wish, her weeping vain—
    As Time too well hath taught her :
Each year the fiend returns again,
    And dives into that water ;
And brings triumphant, from beneath,
    His shafts of desolation,
And sends them, winged with worse than death,
    Throughout her maddening nation.

Alas for her who sits and mourns
    Even now beside that river—
Unwearied still the fiend returns,
    And stored is still his quiver.
'When will this end, ye Powers of Good ?'
    She weeping asks for ever ;
But only hears, from out that flood,
    The demon answer, 'Never !'

THOMAS MOORE.

THE PRAYER OF EMAN OGE.

God of this Irish Isle,
   Blessed and old,
Wrapt in the morning's smile,
   In the sea's fold—
Here where thy saints have trod,
   Here where they prayed,
Hear me, O saving God,
   May I be saved!
God of the circling sea,
   Far-rolling and deep,
Its caves are unshut to Thee—
   Its bounds Thou dost keep—
Here, from this strand
   Whence saints have gone forth,
Father! I own Thy hand
   Humbled to earth.
God of this blessed light
   Over me shining,
On the wide way of right
   I go, unrepining.
No more despising
   My lot or my race,
But toiling, uprising,
   To Thee through thy grace.
              T. D. M'GEE.

THE HEART'S RESTING-PLACE.

Twice have I sailed the Atlantic o'er,
   Twice dwelt an exile in the west;
Twice did kind nature's skill restore
   The quiet of my troubled breast;

As moss upon a rifted tree,
   So Time its gentle cloaking did;
But though the wound no eye could see,
   Deep in my heart the barb was hid.

I felt a weight where'er I went—
   I felt a void within my brain;
My day-hopes and my dreams were blent,
   With sable threads of mental pain;
My eye delighted not to look
   On forest old or rapids grand;
The stranger's joy I scarce could brook,
   My heart was in my own dear land.

Where'er I turned, some emblem still
   Roused consciousness upon my track;
Some hill was like an Irish hill,
   Some wild bird's whistle called me back.
A sea-bound ship bore off my peace,
   Between its white, cold wings of woe;
Oh, if I had but wings like these,
   Where my peace went I too would go.
                       T. D. M'GEE.

ORANGE AND GREEN.

The night was falling dreary
   In merry Bandon town,
When in his cottage, weary,
   An Orangeman lay down.
The summer sun in splendour
   Had set upon the vale,
And shouts of 'No surrender!'
   Arose upon the gale.

Beside the waters, laving
    The feet of aged trees,
The Orange banners waving,
    Flew boldly in the breeze;
In mighty chorus meeting,
    A hundred voices join;
And fife and drum were beating
    The *Battle of the Boyne.*

Ha! tow'rd his cottage hieing,
    What form is speeding now,
From yonder thicket flying,
    With blood upon his brow?
'Hide, hide me, worthy stranger,
    Though Green my colour be,
And in the day of danger
    May Heaven remember thee!

'In yonder vale contending
    Alone against that crew,
My life and limbs defending,
    An Orangeman I slew.
Hark! hear that fearful warning,
    There's death in every tone.
Oh, save my life till morning,
    And Heaven prolong your own!'

The Orange heart was melted
    In pity to the Green;
He heard the tale and felt it
    His very soul within.
'Dread not that angry warning
    Though death be in its tone;
I'll save your life till morning,
    Or I will lose my own.'

Now, round his lowly dwelling
    The angry torrent press'd,
A hundred voices swelling,
    The Orangeman addressed:
'Arise, arise and follow
    The chase along the plain!
In yonder stony hollow
    Your only son is slain!'

With rising shouts they gather
    Upon the track amain,
And leave the childless father
    Aghast with sudden pain.
He seeks the righted stranger,
    In covert where he lay;
'Arise!' he said; 'all danger
    Is gone and past away!

'I had a son, one only,
    One lovèd as my life;
Thy hand has left me lonely,
    In that accursed strife.
I pledged my word to save thee
    Until the storm should cease;
I keep the pledge I gave thee—
    Arise, and go in peace!'

The stranger soon departed
    From that unhappy vale;
The father, broken-hearted,
    Lay brooding o'er that tale.
Full twenty summers after
    To silver turned his beard;
And yet the sound of laughter
    From him was never heard.

    *   *   *

ORANGE AND GREEN.

The night was falling dreary
   In merry Wexford town,
When in his cabin, weary,
   A peasant laid him down.
And many a voice was singing
   Along the summer vale,
And Wexford town was ringing
   With shouts of 'Granua Uile.'[*]

Beside the waters laving
   The feet of aged trees,
The Green flag, gaily waving,
   Was spread against the breeze.
In mighty chorus meeting,
   Loud voices filled the town,
A fife and drum were beating,
   'Down, Orangemen! lie down!'

Hark! 'mid the stirring clangour
   That woke the echoes there,
Loud voices, high in anger,
   Rise on the evening air.
Like billows on the ocean,
   He sees them hurry on;
And, 'mid the wild commotion,
   An Orangeman alone.

'My hair,' he said, 'is hoary,
   And feeble is my hand,
And I could tell a story
   Would shame your cruel band.
Full twenty years and over
   Have changed my heart and brow,
And I am grown a lover
   Of peace and concord now.

     * Pronounced Gran-u-wale.

'It was not thus I greeted
　　Your brother of the Green;
When fainting and defeated
　　I freely took him in.
I pledged my word to save him
　　From vengeance rushing on;
I kept the pledge I gave him,
　　Though he had killed my son.'

That aged peasant heard him,
　　And knew him as he stood,
Remembrance kindly stirr'd him,
　　And tender gratitude.
With gushing tears of pleasure,
　　He pierced the listening train,
'I'm here to pay the measure
　　Of kindness back again!'

Upon his bosom falling,
　　That old man's tears came down;
Deep memory recalling
　　That cot and fatal town.
'The hand that would offend thee,
　　My being first shall end;
I'm living to defend thee,
　　My saviour and my friend!'

He said, and, slowly turning,
　　Address'd the wondering crowd—
With fervent spirit burning
　　He told the tale aloud.
Now pressed the warm beholders,
　　Their aged foe to greet;
They raised him on their shoulders
　　And chaired him through the street.

As he had saved the stranger
   From peril scowling dim,
So in his day of danger
   Did Heav'n remember him.
By joyous crowds attended,
   The worthy pair were seen,
And their flags that day were blended
   Of Orange and of Green.

GERALD GRIFFIN.

THE HOMEWARD BOUND.

PALER and thinner the morning moon grew,
Colder and sterner the rising wind blew;
The pole-star had set in a forest of cloud,
And the icicles crackled on spar and on shroud,
When a voice from below we heard feebly cry:
'Let me see, let me see my own land ere I die.'

'Ah, dear sailor, say, have we sighted Cape Clear?
Can you see any sign?   Is the morning light near?
You are young, my brave boy; thanks, thanks for your hand—
Help me up, till I get a last glimpse of the land.
Thank God, 'tis the sun that now reddens the sky;
I shall see, I shall see my own land ere I die.

'Let me lean on your strength, I am feeble and old,
And one half of my heart is already stone-cold.
Forty years work a change! when I first crossed the sea
There were few on the deck that could grapple with me;
But my youth and my prime in Ohio went by,
And I'm come back to see the old spot ere I die.'

'Twas a feeble old man, and he stood on the deck,
His arm round a kindly young mariner's neck,
His ghastly gaze fixed on the tints of the east,
As a starveling might stare at the noise of a feast.
The morn quickly rose and revealed to his eye
The land he had prayed to behold, and then die!

Green, green was the shore, though the year was near done;
High and haughty the capes the white surf dash'd upon;
A grey ruined convent was down by the strand,
And the sheep fed afar, on the hills of the land!
'God be with you, dear Ireland!' he gasped with a sigh;
'I have lived to behold you—I'm ready to die.'

He sunk by the hour, and his pulse 'gan to fail,
As we swept by the headland of storied Kinsale;
Off Ardigna Bay it came slower and slower,
And his corpse was clay-cold as we sighted Tramore.
At Passage we waked him, and now he doth lie
In the lap of the land he beheld but to die.

T. D. M'GEE.

FEAGH M'HUGH.

    FEAGH M'HUGH of the mountain—
        Feagh M'Hugh of the glen—
    Who has not heard of the Glenmalur chief,
        And the feats of his hard-riding men?
    Came you the seaside from Carmen—
        Crossed you the plains from the west—
    No rhymer you met but could tell you,
        Of Leinster men, who is the best.

Or seek you the Liffey or Dodder—
    Ask in the bawns of the Pale—
Ask them whose cattle they fodder,
    Who drinks without fee of their ale.
From Ardamine north to Kilmainham,
    He rules, like a king, of few words,
And the Marchmen of seven score castles
    Keep watch for the sheen of his swords.

The vales of Kilmantan are spacious—
    The hills of Kilmantan are high—
But the horn of the Chieftain finds echoes,
    From the water-side up to the sky.
The lakes of Kilmantan are gloomy,
    Yet bright rivers stream from them all—
So dark is our Chieftain in battle,
    So gay in the camp or the hall.

The plains of Clan Saxon are fertile,
    Their Chiefs and their Tanists are brave,
But the first step they take o'er the border,
    Just measures the length of a grave;
Thirty score of them forayed to Arklow,
    Southampton and Essex their van—
Our Chief crossed their way, and he left of
    Each score of them, living a man.

Oh, many the tales that they cherish,
    In the glens of Kilmantan to-day!
And though church, rath, and native speech perish,
    His glory's untouched by decay.
Feagh M'Hugh of the mountain—
    Feagh M'Hugh of the glen—
Who has not heard of the Glenmalur Chief,
    And the feats of his hard-riding men?

                      T. D. M'GEE.

THE EXILE'S DEVOTION.

I'D rather be the bird that sings
    Above the martyr's grave,
Than fold in fortune's cage my wings
    And feel my soul a slave;
I'd rather turn one simple verse
    True to the Gaelic ear,
Than sapphic odes I might rehearse
    With senates list'ning near.

O Native Land! dost ever mark,
    When the world's din is drown'd,
Betwixt the daylight and the dark
    A wandering solemn sound,
That on the western wind is borne
    Across thy dewy breast?
It is the voice of those who mourn
    For thee, far in the West!

For them and theirs, I oft essay
    Your ancient art of song,
And often sadly turn away,
    Deeming my rashness wrong;
For well I ween, a loving will
    Is all the art I own;
Ah me, could love suffice for skill,
    What triumphs I had known!

My native land, my native land,
    Live in my memory still!
Break on my brain, ye surges grand!
    Stand up, mist-covered hill!

Still in the mirror of the mind
  The land I love I see;
Would I could fly on the western wind,
  My native land, to thee!
                    THOMAS D'ARCY M'GEE.

BEN-HEDER (THE HILL OF HOWTH).

I RAMBLED away, on a festival day,
  From vanity, glare, and noise,
To calm my soul, where the wavelets roll,
  In solitude's holy joys.
By the lonely cliffs whence the white gull starts,
  Where the clustering sea-pinks blow,
And the Irish rose, on the purple quartz,
  Bends over the waves below.
Where the ramaline clings, and the samphire swings,
  And the long laminaria trails,
And the sea-bird springs on his snowy wings
  To blend with the distant sails.

I leaned on a rock, and the cool waves there
  Plash'd on the shingles round:
And the breath of Nature lifted my hair—
Dear God! how the face of Thy child is fair!—
And a gush of memory, tears, and pray'r,
  My spirit a moment drown'd.
I bowed me down to the rippling wave—
  For a swift sail glided near—
And the spray, as it fell upon pebble and shell,
  Received, it may be, a tear.

For well I remember the festal days
On this shore, that Hy-Brassil seemed—
The friends I trusted, the dreams I dream'd,
    Hopes high as the cloud above—
Perchance of Fame, or a land redeem'd,
    Perchance 'twas a dream of love.
When first I trod on this breezy sod,
    To me it was holy ground,
For genius and beauty—rays of God—
    Like a swarm of stars shone round.
Well! well! I have learned rude lessons since then
    In life's disenchanted hall;
I have scanned the motives and ways of men,
    And the skeleton grins through all.

Of the great heart-treasure of hope and trust
    I exulted to feel mine own,
Remains, in that down-trod temple's dust,
    But faith in God alone.
I have seen too oft the domino torn
    And the mask from the face of men,
To have aught save a smile of tranquil scorn
    For all I believed in then.
The day is dark as the night with woes,
    And my dreams are of battles lost,
Of eclipse, phantoms, wrecks, and foes,
    And of exiles tempest-tost.

No more, no more! on the dreary shore
    I hear a caonia-song;
With the early dead is my lonely bed—
    You shall not call me long;
I fade away to the home of clay,
    With not one dream fulfilled:

My wreathless brow in the dust I bow,
  My heart and harp are stilled.
Oh, would I might rest, when my soul departs,
  Where the clustering sea-pinks blow,
And the Irish rose, on the purple quartz,
  Droops over the waves below;
Where the crystals gleam in the caves about,
  Like virtue in humble souls,
And the Victor Sea, with a thunder-shout,
  Through the breach in the rock-wall rolls!
              RICHARD DALTON WILLIAMS.

ST. KEVIN AND KATHLEEN.

COME, Kathleen, pure and soft as dew,
  The lake is heaving at our feet,
The stars ascend the eternal blue,
  Primeval granite makes our seat.
Beneath eternal skies above,
  'Mid everlasting hills around,
I speak of love—immortal love!—
  Such as in Eden first was found.
Let each look through the other's soul,
  Until each thought within that lies,
Like spar o'er which these clear waves roll,
  Unveil its lustre to our eyes.

I bless thee, Kathleen, o'er and o'er,
  For all the joy thy smiles have brought me,
And mysteries of loving lore
  Thy very presence oft hath taught me.

For beauty innocent as thine—
   Such lovely soul in lovely form—
Still makes diviner aught divine,
   And calms the spirit's wildest storm.
Whene'er I muse—how oft!—on thee,
   Half seen, each high and holy feeling
Of love and immortality
   Take shape, like angels round me wheeling.

To thee I owe the purest flow'rs
   Of song that o'er my pathway burst,
And holy thought, at midnight hours,
   From thine unconscious beauty nurst.
There is no stain on flowers like these,
   That from my heart to thine are springing;
And thoughts of thee are like the breeze,
   When bells for midnight mass are ringing.
Without thy knowledge from thee beams
   Some gentle and refining light,
That fills my heart with childhood's dreams,
   And I grow purer in thy sight.

Thou art no Queen—no hero I—
   But thou'rt the fairest Christian maid
To whom the worship of a sigh,
   By Christian bard was ever paid.
And this I am—Sire—God above,
   Who made my soul of that rich flame,
All adoration, song, and love,
   That from thine own great Spirit came!
Than mine no purer, warmer zeal
   For justice and sublime desire
Of freedom, truth, and human weal
   Glows in the seraph ranks of fire.

ST. KEVIN AND KATHLEEN.

I've bower'd thee in a lonely shrine—
   My bosom's convent-garden, sweet—
Where song and pray'r their signs combine,
   Where love and adoration meet.
I've rob'd thee like Ban-Tierna olden
   Of Eirè, in a vesture green;
And clasp'd thee with a girdle golden
   O'er all my dream-world Saint and Queen.
I've starr'd thy hands with Irish gems,
   And sought to wreathe thy rich brown hair,
The oakwood's dewy diadems,
   And won the sacred shamrocks there.

Oh, would that thou couldst read my heart,
   Or that my lips might be unseal'd,
And by love's lamp, in every part,
   My spirit's inmost crypt reveal'd!
Within, like maid in minstrel tale,
   One lovely vision sleeping lies;
Beside her Hope, with forehead pale,
   And timid Joy with downcast eyes.
'Tis Love, in long enchantment bound,
   I know not how, in torpor there:
The spells obey but one sweet sound—
   When Kathleen sings, they melt in air.

See! over yonder mountains, crack'd
   And sunder'd by volcanic fire,
Sings Glendalough's white cataract—
   Fit chord of such a granite lyre.
And then the cloud-born waterfall
   Summons aloud, from rock and wood,
The child-like springs, and leads them all,
   With laughter to this gloomy flood.

And thus thy love my heart shall lave—
When sorrow's rocks, faith-cloven, sever,
Giving a glimpse of God—and save
Life's current pure and fresh for ever!

R. D. WILLIAMS.

LOVE-SONGS, AND SONGS OF THE AFFECTIONS.

THE COOLIN.

HAD you seen my sweet Coolin at the day's early dawn,
When she moves through the wild wood or the wide dewy lawn;
There is joy, there is bliss in her soul-cheering smile,
She's the fairest of the flowers of our green-bosom'd isle.

In Belanagar dwells the bright blooming maid,
Retired like the primrose that blows in the shade;
Still dear to the eyes that fair primrose may be,
But dearer and sweeter is my Coolin to me.

Then, boy, rouse you up! go and bring me my steed,
Till I cross the green vale and the mountains with speed;
Let me hasten far forward, my lov'd one to find,
And hear that she's constant, and feel that she's kind.

O dearest! thy love from thy childhood was mine,
O sweetest! this heart from life's opening was thine;
And though coldness by kindred or friends may be shown,
Still! still, my sweet Coolin, that heart is thine own.

Thou light of all beauty, be true still to me;
Forsake not thy swain, love, though poor he may be:
For rich in affection, in constancy tried,
We may look down on wealth in its pomp and its pride.

Remember the night, love! when safe in the shade
We marked the wild havoc the wild wind had made;
Think! think how I sheltered thee—watched thee with care;
Oh, think of the words, love, that fell from us there!

MAURICE DUGAN.

SINCE CŒLIA'S MY FOE.

SINCE Cœlia's my foe,
To a desert I'll go
    Where some river
    For ever
Shall echo my woe.

The trees shall appear
More relenting than her,
    In the morning
    Adorning
Each leaf with a tear.

When I make my sad moan
To the rocks all alone,
    From each hollow
    Will follow
Some pitiful groan.

But with silent disdain
She requites all my pain,
    To my mourning
    Returning
No answer again.

Ah, Cœlia, adieu!
When I cease to pursue,
    You'll discover
    No lover
Was ever so true.

Your sad shepherd flies
From those dear cruel eyes,
    Which not seeing,
    His being
Decays, and he dies.

Yet 'tis better to run
To the fate we can't shun,
    Than for ever
    To strive for
What cannot be won.

What, ye gods, have I done
That Amyntor alone
    Is so treated,
    And hated,
For loving but one?

                  THOMAS DUFFET.

COME ALL YOU PALE LOVERS.

COME all you pale lovers that sigh and complain,
While your beautiful tyrants but laugh at your pain,
    Come practise with me
    To be happy and free,
In spite of inconstancy, pride, or disdain.
    I see and I love, and the bliss I enjoy
    No rival can lessen nor envy destroy.

My mistress so fair is, no language or art
Can describe her perfection in every part;
  Her mien's so genteel,
  With such ease she can kill—
By each look, with new passion, she captures my heart.

Her smile's the kind message of love from her eyes;
When she frowns 'tis from others her flame to disguise.
  Thus her scorn or her spite
  I convert to delight,
As the bee gathers honey wherever he flies.

My vows she receives from her lover unknown,
And I fancy kind answers although I have none.
  How blest should I be
  If our hearts did agree,
Since already I find so much pleasure alone.
  I see and I love, and the bliss I enjoy
  No rival can lessen, nor envy destroy.
       THOMAS DUFFET.

PEGGY BROWNE.

OH, dark—sweetest girl—are my days doomed to be,
While my heart bleeds in silence and sorrow for thee:
In the green spring of life to the grave I go down,
Oh, shield me, and save me, my lov'd Peggy Browne!

I dreamt that at evening my footsteps were bound
To yon deep-spreading wood where the shades fall
  around;
I sought, 'midst new scenes, all my sorrows to drown,
But the cure of my grief rests with thee, Peggy Browne.

'Tis soothing, sweet maiden, thy accents to hear,
For like wild fairy music they melt on the ear;
Thy breast is as fair as the swans clothed in down,
Oh, peerless and perfect's my own Peggy Browne.

Dear, dear is the bark to its own cherished tree,
But dearer, far dearer, is my lov'd one to me :
In my dreams I draw near her uncheck'd by a frown,
But my arms spread in vain to embrace Peggy Browne.
CAROLAN.
(Translated by Thomas Furlong.)

GENTLE BRIDEEN.

O GENTLE, fair maiden, thou hast left me in sadness;
   My bosom is pierced with Love's arrow so keen;
For thy mien it is graceful, thy glances are gladness,
   And thousands thy lovers, O gentle Brideen!

The grey mist of morning in autumn was fleeting,
   When I met the bright darling down in the boreen ;*
Her words were unkind, but I soon won a greeting;
   Sweet kisses I stole from the lips of Brideen!

Oh, fair is the sun in the dawning all tender,
   And beauteous the roses beneath it are seen!
Thy cheek is the red rose! thy brow the sun-splendour!
   And, cluster of ringlets! my dawn is Brideen!

Then shine, O bright sun, on thy constant true lover;
   Then shine, once again, in the leafy boreen,
And the clouds shall depart that around my heart hover,
   And we'll walk amid gladness, my gentle Brideen.
CAROLAN.
(Translated by George Sigerson, M.D.)

* *Anglice*, a narrow lane.

BRIDGET CRUISE.

Oh, turn thee to me, my only love!
   Let not despair confound me;
Turn, and may blessings from above
   In life and death surround thee.

This fond heart throbs for thee alone—
   Oh, leave me not to languish!
Look on these eyes, whence sleep hath flown,
   Bethink thee of my anguish:
My hopes, my thoughts, my destiny—
All dwell, all rest, sweet girl, on thee.

Young bud of beauty, for ever bright,
   The proudest must bow before thee:
Source of my sorrow and my delight—
   Oh, must I in vain adore thee?
Where, where, through earth's extended round,
Where may such loveliness be found?
   Talk not of fair ones known of yore;
Speak not of Deirdre the renowned—
     She whose gay glance each minstrel hail'd;
   Nor she whom the daring Dardan bore
From her fond husband's longing arms;
Name not the dame whose fatal charms,
     When weighed against a world, prevail'd;
To each might blooming beauty fall,
   Lovely, thrice lovely, might they be;
But the gifts and graces of each and all
   Are minglèd, sweet maid, in thee!

How the entranc'd ear fondly lingers
  On the turns of thy thrilling song!
How brightens each eye as thy fair white fingers
  O'er the chords fly gently along!
The noble, the learn'd, the ag'd, the vain,
Gaze on the songstress, and bless the strain.
How winning, dear girl, is thine air,
How glossy thy golden hair!
Oh, lov'd one, come back again,
  With thy train of adorers about thee!
Oh come, for in grief and in gloom we remain—
  Life is not life without thee!

My memory wanders—my thoughts have stray'd—
  My gathering sorrows oppress me—.
Oh, look on thy victim, bright peerless maid!
  Say one kind word to bless me.
Why, why on thy beauty must I dwell,
When each tortur'd heart knows its power too well?
Or why need I say that favour'd and bless'd
  Must be the proud land that bore thee?
Oh, dull is the eye and cold the breast
  That remains unmov'd before thee!

CAROLAN.

(Translated by Thomas Furlong.)

CAROLAN ON HIS WIFE'S DEATH.

WERE mine the choice of intellectual fame,
  Of spellful song, and eloquence divine,
Painting's sweet power, Philosophy's pure flame,
  And Homer's lyre, and Ossian's harp were mine,

The splendid arts of Erin, Greece, and Rome,
  In Mary lost, would lose their wonted grace;
All would I give to snatch her from the tomb,
  Again to fold her in my fond embrace.

Desponding, sick, exhausted with my grief,
  Awhile the founts of sorrow cease to flow;
In vain!—I rest not—sleep brings no relief;
  Cheerless, companionless, I wake to woe.
Nor birth, nor beauty, shall again allure,
  Nor fortune win me to another bride;
Alone I'll wander, and alone endure,
  'Till death restore me to my dear one's side.

Once ev'ry thought and ev'ry scene was gay,
  Friends, mirth, and music, all my hours employ'd,—
Now doom'd to mourn my last sad years away,
  My life a solitude!—my heart a void!
Alas, the change!—to change again no more!
  For ev'ry comfort is with Mary fled;
And ceaseless anguish shall her loss deplore,
  Till age and sorrow join me with the dead.

Adieu, each gift of nature and of art,
  That erst adorn'd me in life's early prime!—
The cloudless temper, and the social heart,
  The soul ethereal, and the flights sublime!
Thy loss, my Mary, chas'd them from my breast!
  Thy sweetness cheers, thy judgment aids no more;
The muse deserts a heart with grief opprest—
  And flown is ev'ry joy that charm'd before.

CAROLAN.
(*From Walker's 'Irish Bards.'*)

A SONG FOR MABEL KELLY.

*   *   *   *   *

As when the softly blushing rose
Close by some neighbouring lily grows,
Such is the glow thy cheeks diffuse,
And such their bright and blended hues!

The timid lustre of thine eye
With nature's purest tints can vie;
With the sweet bluebell's azure gem,
That droops upon its modest stem!

The poets of Ierne's plains
To thee devote their choicest strains,
And oft their harps for thee are strung,
And oft thy matchless charms are sung.

Nor doubt I of thy voice's art,
Nor hear with unimpassion'd heart;
Thy health, thy beauties, ever dear,
Oft crown my glass with sweetest cheer!

Since the fam'd fair of ancient days,
Whom bards and worlds conspir'd to praise,
Not one like thee has since appear'd,
Like thee, to every heart endear'd.

How blest the bard, O lovely maid,
To find thee in thy charms array'd!—
Thy pearly teeth—thy flowing hair—
Thy neck, beyond the cygnet, fair!

As when the simple birds at night
Fly round the torch's fatal light—
Wild, and with ecstasy elate,
Unconscious of approaching fate—

So the soft splendours of thy face,
And thy fair form's enchanting grace,
Allure to death unwary Love,
And thousands the bright ruin prove!

Ev'n he[*] whose hapless eyes no ray
Admit from beauty's cheering day;
Yet, though he cannot see the light,
He feels it warm, and knows it bright.

In beauty, talents, taste refin'd,
And all the graces of the mind,
In *all*, unmatch'd thy charms remain,
Nor meet a rival on the plain.

Thy slender foot—thine azure eye—
Thy smiling lip, of scarlet dye—
Thy tapering hand, so soft and fair,
The bright redundance of thy hair—

Oh, blest be the auspicious day
That gave them to thy poet's lay!
O'er rival bards to lift his name,
Inspire his verse and swell his fame!

CAROLAN.
(*Translated by Miss Brooke.*)

[*] Carolan was blind; see memoir.

HOW TO MANAGE A MAN.

The lass that would know how to manage a man,
    Let her listen and learn it from me :
His courage to quail, or his heart to trepan,
    As the time and occasions agree, agree ;
    As the time and occasions agree.

The girl that has beauty, though small be her wit,
    May wheedle the clown or the beau ;
The rake may repel, or may draw in the cit,
    By the use of that pretty word—'No !'
    By the use of that pretty word—'No !'

When a dose is contriv'd to lay virtue asleep,
    A present, a treat, or a ball ;
She still must refuse, if her empire she'd keep,
    And 'No' be her answer to all ; .
    And 'No' be her answer to all.

But when Master Dapperwit offers his hand,
    Her partner in wedlock to go ;
A house, and a coach, and a jointure in land—
    She's an idiot if then she says 'No !'
    She's an idiot if then she says 'No !'

Whene'er she's attack'd by a youth full of charms,
    Whose courtship proclaims him a man ;
When pressed to his bosom and clasped in his arms,
    Then let her say 'No,' if she can !
    Then let her say 'No,' if she can !

                        Matthew Concanen.

I HATE A LONG COURTSHIP.

I LOVE thee, by Heaven!—I cannot say more ;
    Then set not my passion a-cooling.
If thou yield'st not at once, I must e'en give thee o'er,
    For I'm but a novice at fooling.

I know how to love, and to make that love known,
    But I hate all protesting and arguing ;
Had a goddess my heart, she should e'en be alone,
    If she made any words to a bargain.

I'm a Quaker in love, and but barely affirm
    Whate'er my fond eyes have been saying ;
Prithee be thou so too, seek for no better term,
    But e'en throw thy *yea* or thy *nay* in.

I cannot bear love, like a Chancery-suit,
    The age of a patriarch depending ;
Then pluck up a spirit, no longer be mute,
    Give it, one way or other, an ending.

Long courtship's the vice of a phlegmatic fool ;
    Like the grace of fanatical sinners,
Where the stomachs are lost, and the victuals grow cool,
    Before men sit down to their dinners.

MATTHEW CONCANEN.

CUPID'S REVENGE.

As through the woods Panthea stray'd,
    And sought in vain her wand'ring sheep,
Beneath a myrtle's verdant shade
    She found the God of Love asleep.

His quiver underneath his head,
  His bow unbent beside him lay,
His golden arrows round him spread,
  Toss'd by the winds in wanton play.

With terror struck the nymph recedes,
  And softly on her tiptoes trod;
Malice at length to fear succeeds,
  And she returns and robs the god.

As to purloin his bow she tries—
  Of all his scattered shafts possess'd—
The beaming lustre of her eyes
  Play'd on his face, and broke his rest.

Cupid awaking, scarce descry'd,
  'Twixt slumber and surprise, the maid,
And rubbed his drowsy lids, and cry'd,
  'Who thought the sun could pierce this shade?'

At length, recovered from his fright,
  Thus his mistaken thoughts express'd,
' Art thou return'd, my soft delight?
  Approach, my Psyche, to my breast!'

The frighted virgin scarcely view'd,
  Sprung from his sight with eager haste;
No trembling hare by hounds pursued,
  Or fear'd so much, or fled so fast.

Seeking a shaft to stop her flight,
  He found himself of all bereft;
His loss soon set his knowledge right,
  And show'd the plunderer by the theft.

Panthea, stop !' aloud he cries ;
  'Why wouldst thou, fair one, fly from me?
Restore my arrows—thy own eyes
  Have darts, as sharp, enough for thee.'

Unmov'd by this, her pace she mends,
  Regardless of his pain and care—
Th' entreating god no more attends
  Than it had been some lover's prayer.

Cupid, provok'd, for vengeance tries—
  'My leaden shafts, these are not lost ;
Within my pow'r the method lies,
  And thou shalt find it to thy cost !

'Enjoy thy plunder—use my darts —
  Thy crime shall be thy punishment ;
At random wound despairing hearts,
  Nor, for the pangs you give, relent.

'Beauty was made to be enjoy'd—
  I'll mar the end for which 'twas giv n;
Fill up with pride thy reasons void,
  And useless make that gift of heav'n.

'Still cruelty shall taint thy breast,
  And all thy smiling hopes destroy;
In all my mother's beauty drest,
  Be thou a stranger to her joy !

'Since all the shafts thy glances throw
  Shall still be poison'd with disdain,
Nor shalt thou e'er the pleasure know
  Of loving and being loved again.

'Secure in scorn thy charms shall lie,
  Bloom unenjoyed—untasted, fade,
Till thou at last repenting die,
  An old, ill-natur'd, envious maid.'

He said—and from his quiver drew
  A leaden, hate-procuring dart,
And brac'd his bow, from whence it flew
  Unerring to the fair one's heart.
MATTHEW CONCANEN.

'I'D WED IF I WERE NOT TOO YOUNG.'

IN holiday gown, and my new-fangled hat,
  Last Monday I tript to the fair;
I held up my head, and I'll tell you for what,
  Brisk Roger I guess'd would be there.
He woos me to marry whenever we meet,
  There's honey, sure, dwells on his tongue;
He hugs me so close, and he kisses so sweet,
  I'd wed—if I were not too young.

Fond Sue, I'll assure you, laid hold on the boy
  (The vixen would fain be his bride);
Some token she claim'd, either ribbon or toy,
  And swore that she'd not be deny'd.
A top-knot he bought her, and garters of green—
  Pert Susan was cruelly stung:
I hate her so much, that, to kill her with spleen,
  I'd wed—if I were not too young.

He whispered such soft, pretty things in mine ear!
  He flattered, he promised, and swore!
Such trinkets he gave me, such laces and gear,
  That, trust me—my pockets ran o'er.

Some ballads he bought me—the best he could find—
  And sweetly their burthen he sung;
Good faith, he's so handsome, so witty, and kind,
  I'd wed—if I were not so young.

The sun was just setting, 'twas time to retire
  (Our cottage was distant a mile);
I rose to begone—Roger bow'd like a squire,
  And handed me over the stile.
His arm he threw round me—Love laughed in his eye—
  He led me the meadows among;
There prest me so close, I agreed, with a sigh,
  To wed—for I was not too young.
                JOHN CUNNINGHAM.

A LOVE PASTORAL.

HER sheep had in clusters crept close by the grove,
  To hide from the rigours of day;
And Phillis herself, in a woodbine alcove,
  Among the fresh violets lay:
A youngling it seems had been stole from its dam
  ('Twixt Cupid and Hymen a plot),
That Corydon might, as he searched for his lamb,
  Arrive at this critical spot.

As through the gay hedge for his lambkin he peeps,
  He saw the sweet maid with surprise;
'Ye gods, if so killing,' he cried, 'when she sleeps,
  I'm lost when she opens her eyes!
To tarry much longer would hazard my heart,
  I'll onwards my lambkin to trace:'
In vain honest Corydon strove to depart,
  For love had him nail'd to the place.

'Hush, hush'd be these birds! what a bawling they keep!'
   He cried; 'you're too loud on the spray.
Don't you see, foolish lark, that the charmer's asleep?
   You'll wake her as sure as 'tis day!
How dare that fond butterfly touch the sweet maid!
   Her cheek he mistakes for the rose;
I'd put him to death, if I was not afraid
   My boldness would break her repose.'

Young Phillis look'd up with a languishing smïle,
   'Kind shepherd,' she said, 'you mistake;
I laid myself down just to rest me awhile,
   But, trust me, have still been awake.'
The shepherd took courage, advanc'd with a bow,
   He placed himself close by her side,
And managed the matter, I cannot tell how,
   But yesterday made her his bride.

JOHN CUNNINGHAM.

FRIENDSHIP.

FOND Love with all his winning wiles
Of tender looks and flattering smiles,
Of accents that might Juno charm,
Or Dian's colder ear alarm;
No more shall play the tyrant's part,
No more shall lord it o'er my heart.

To Friendship, sweet benignant power!
I consecrate my humble bower,
My lute, my muse, my willing mind,
And fix her in my heart enshrined;
She, heaven-descended queen, shall be
My tutelar divinity.

Soft Peace descends to guard her reign
From anxious fear and jealous pain;
She no delusive hope displays,
But calmly guides our tranquil days;
Refines our pleasures, soothes our care,
And gives the joys of Eden here.

     ELIZABETH RYVES.

LOVE AND GOLD.

Though love and each harmonious maid
To gentle Sappho lent their aid,
Yet, deaf to her enchanting tongue,
Proud Phaon scorned her melting song.

Mistaken nymph! hadst thou adored
Fair Fortune, and her smiles implored;
Had she indulgent owned thy claim,
And given thee wealth instead of fame;

Though harsh thy voice, deformed and old,
Yet such th' omnipotence of gold,
The youth had soon confess'd thy charms,
And flown impatient to thy arms.

     ELIZABETH RYVES.

THE SYLPH LOVER.

Here in this fragrant bower I dwell,
 And nightly here repose;
My couch a lily's snowy bell,
 My canopy a rose.

The honey-dew each morn I sip
That hangs upon the violet's lip;
And like the bee, from flower to flower
I careless rove at noontide hour.

Regardless as I lately strayed
   Along the myrtle grove,
Enchanting music round me played,
   Soft as the voice of love.
Thus its sweet murmurs seem'd to say:
'Fond, thoughtless wanton, come away;
For while you rove, a rival's charms
Wins thy Myrtilla to his arms.'

ELIZABETH RYVES.

ON SONGS.

O TENDER songs!
Heart-heavings of the breast, that longs
   Its best-beloved to meet;
You tell of love's delightful hours,
Of meetings amid jasmine bowers,
And vows, like perfume of young flowers,
   As fleeting—but more sweet.

O glorious songs!
That rouse the brave 'gainst tyrant wrongs,
   Resounding near and far;
Mingled with trumpet and with drum,
Your spirit-stirring summons come,
And urge the hero from his home,
   And arm him for the war.

O mournful songs!
When sorrow's host, in gloomy throngs,
   Assail the widowed heart;
You sing, in softly-soothing strain,
The praise of those whom death hath ta'en,
And tell that we shall meet again,
   And meet no more to part.

O lovely songs—
Breathings of heaven! to you belongs
   The empire of the heart.
Enthroned in memory, still reign
O'er minds of prince, and peer, and swain,
With gentle power, that knows not wane,
   Till thought and life depart.
                THOMAS DERMODY.

WHEN I SAT BY MY FAIR.

WHEN I sat by my fair, and she tremblingly told
   The soft wishes and doubts of her heart,
How quickly old Time then delightfully rolled,
   For love lent the plume from his dart!
From the blush of her cheek, how my bosom caught flame,
And her eyes spoke a fondness her lips would not name.

But her cheek, that once rivalled the summer's full rose,
   Now as April's sad primrose is pale;
In her eye, now, no bright sensibility glows,
   Though I breathe forth truth's rapturous tale;
And thy moments, old Time, that on downy feet fled,
Ah me! are now fettered and weighty as lead.

Yet surely, though much of her passion is past,
  Some sparks of affection remain;
And the clouds, that her meek-beaming brow have o'ercast,
  May be melted in pity's soft rain.
If not, my wrung breast to distraction I bare;
For distraction itself is less hard than despair.
THOMAS DERMODY.

THE LINNET.

My fond social linnet, to thee
  What dear winning charms did belong!
On my hand thou wouldst carol with glee,
  On my bosom attend to my song.
Sweet bird, in return for my strain,
Thou warbled'st thine own o'er again.

Love, jealous a bird should thus share
  My affections, shot speedy his dart:
To my swain now I sang every air;
  The linnet soon took it to heart.
Sweet bird, in how plaintive a strain
Thou warbled'st thine own jealous pain!

But faithless my lover I found,
  And in vain to forget him I tried:
The linnet perceived my heart's wound,
  He sickened, he drooped, and he died.
Sweet bird, why to death yield the strain?
Thy song would have lightened my pain.
THOMAS DERMODY.

(*Said to have been written when he was ten years old.*)

MY BURIAL-PLACE.

Ah me ! and must I like the tenant lie
   Of this dark cell—all hushed the witching song?
And will not Feeling bend his streaming eye
   On my green sod, as slow he wends along,
And, smiting his rapt bosom, softly sigh,
   'His genius soared above the vulgar throng'?

Will he not fence my weedless turf around,
   Sacred from dull-eyed Folly's vagrant feet;
And there, soft swelling in aërial sound,
   Will he not list, at eve, to voices sweet;
Strew with the spring's first flowers the little mound,
   And often muse within the lone retreat?

Yes, though I not affect the immortal lay,
   Nor bold effusions of the learned quill,
Nor often have I wound my tedious way
   Up the steep summit of the muse's hill;
Yet, sometimes have I poured the incondite lay,
   And sometimes have I felt the rapturous thrill.

Him, therefore, whom, even once, the sacred muse
   Has blest, shall be to feeling ever dear;
And, soft as sweet, sad April's gleamy dews,
   On my cold clay shall fall the genial tear;
While, pensive as the springing herb he views,
   He cries, 'Though mute, there is a poet here!'

                      THOMAS DERMODY.

KATE OF GARNAVILLA.

Have you been at Garnavilla?
   Have you seen at Garnavilla
Beauty's train trip o'er the plain
   With lovely Kate of Garnavilla?
Oh, she's pure as virgin snows
   Ere they light on woodland hill, O;
Sweet as dewdrop on wild rose
   Is lovely Kate of Garnavilla!

Philomel, I've listened oft
   To thy lay, nigh weeping willow:
Oh, the strains more sweet, more soft,
   That flows from Kate of Garnavilla.
      Have you been, etc.

As a noble ship I've seen,
   Sailing o'er the swelling billow,
So I've marked the graceful mien
   Of lovely Kate of Garnavilla.
      Have you been, etc.

If poet's prayers can banish cares
   No cares shall come to Garnavilla;
Joy's bright rays shall gild her days,
   And dove-like peace perch on her pillow.
      Charming maid of Garnavilla!
      Lovely maid of Garnavilla!
      Beauty, grace, and virtue wait
      On lovely Kate of Garnavilla.

            EDWARD LYSAGHT.

THE SPRIG OF SHILLELAH.

OH! Love is the soul of a neat Irishman,
He loves all that is lovely, loves all that he can,
   With his sprig of shillelah and shamrock so green!
His heart is good-humoured, 'tis honest and sound,
No envy or malice is there to be found;
He courts and he marries, he drinks and he fights,
For love, all for love, for in that he delights,
   With his sprig of shillelah and shamrock so green!

Who has e'er had the luck to see Donnybrook Fair?
An Irishman, all in his glory, is there,
   With his sprig of shillelah and shamrock so green!
His clothes spick and span new, without e'er a speck,
A neat Barcelona tied round his white neck;
He goes to a tent, and he spends half-a crown,
He meets with a friend, and for love knocks him down,
   With his sprig of shillelah and shamrock so green!

At evening returning, as homeward he goes,
His heart soft with whisky, his head soft with blows,
   From a sprig of shillelah and shamrock so green!
He meets with his Sheelah, who, frowning a smile,
Cries, 'Get you gone, Pat,' yet consents all the while.
To the priest they soon go, and nine months after that,
A baby cries out, 'How d'ye do, Father Pat,
   With your sprig of shillelah and shamrock so green?'

Bless the country, say I, that gave Patrick his birth,
Bless the land of the oak, and its neighbouring earth,
   Where grow the shillelah, and shamrock so green!

May the sons of the Thames, the Tweed, and the Shannon,
Drub the foes who dare plant on our confines a cannon;
United and happy, at Loyalty's shrine,
May the rose and the thistle long flourish and twine
   Round the sprig of shillelah and shamrock so green!
EDWARD LYSAGHT.

KITTY OF COLERAINE.

As beautiful Kitty one morning was tripping,
   With a pitcher of milk from the fair of Coleraine,
When she saw me she stumbled, the pitcher down tumbled,
   And all the sweet butter-milk watered the plain.
'Oh! what shall I do now? 'twas looking at you, now;
   Sure, sure, such a pitcher I'll ne'er meet again;
'Twas the pride of my dairy! O Barney M'Cleary,
   You're sent as a plague to the girls of Coleraine!'

I sat down beside her, and gently did chide her,[1]
   That such a misfortune should give her such pain;
A kiss then I gave her, and, ere I did leave her,
   She vowed for such pleasure she'd break it again.
'Twas hay-making season—I can't tell the reason—
   Misfortunes will never come single, 'tis plain;
For very soon after poor Kitty's disaster,
   The devil a pitcher was whole in Coleraine.
EDWARD LYSAGHT.

BY CŒLIA'S ARBOUR.

By Cœlia's arbour, all the night,
   Hang, humid wreath—the lover's vow;
And haply at the morning's light
   My love will twine thee round her brow.

And if upon her bosom bright
  Some drops of dew should fall from thee;
Tell her they are not drops of night,
  But tears of sorrow shed by me.
                RICHARD BRINSLEY SHERIDAN.

HAD I A HEART FOR FALSEHOOD FRAMED.

HAD I a heart for falsehood framed,
  I ne'er could injure you;
For though your tongue no promise claim'd,
  Your charms would make me true.
To you no soul shall bear deceit,
  No stranger offer wrong;
But friends in all the aged you'll meet,
  And lovers in the young.

But when they learn that you have blest
  Another with your heart,
They'll bid aspiring passion rest,
  And act a brother's part.
Then, lady, dread not here deceit,
  Nor fear to suffer wrong;
For friends in all the aged you'll meet,
  And brothers in the young.
                RICHARD BRINSLEY SHERIDAN.

IF I HAD THOUGHT THOU COULDST HAVE DIED.

IF I had thought thou couldst have died,
  I might not weep for thee;
But I forgot, when by thy side,
  That thou couldst mortal be.

It never through my mind had pass'd
    The time would e'er be o'er,
And I on thee should look my last,
    And thou shouldst smile no more!

And still upon that face I look,
    And think 'twill smile again;
And still the thought I will not brook,
    That I must look in vain!
But when I speak—thou dost not say,
    What thou ne'er left'st unsaid;
And now I feel, as well I may,
    Sweet Mary! thou art dead!

If thou would'st stay, e'en as thou art,
    All cold and all serene,
I still might press thy silent heart,
    And where thy smiles have been!
While e'en thy chill bleak corse I have,
    Thou seemest still mine own;
But there—I lay thee in thy grave,
    And I am now alone!

I do not think, where'er tnou art,
    Thou hast forgotten me;
And I, perhaps, may soothe this heart,
    In thinking too of thee.
Yet there was round thee such a dawn
    Of light unseen before,
As fancy never could have drawn,
    And never can restore!

CHARLES WOLFE.

MARY MAGUIRE.

OH that my love and I
From life's crowded haunts could fly
To some deep shady vale, by the mountain,
Where no sound could make its way
Save the thrush's lively lay,
And the murmur of the clear-flowing fountain:
Where no stranger should intrude
On our hallowed solitude,
Where no kinsman's cold glance could annoy us;
Where peace and joy might shed
Blended blessings o'er our bed,
And love—love alone still employ us.

Still, sweet maiden, may I see
That I vainly talk of thee;
In vain in lost love I lie pining:
I may worship from afar
The beauty-beaming star
That o'er my dull pathway keeps shining:
But in sorrow and in pain
Fond hope will remain,
For rarely from hope can we sever;
Unchanged in good or ill,
One dear dream is cherished still—
Oh, my Mary, I must love thee for ever.

How fair appears the maid,
In loveliness arrayed,
As she moves forth at dawn's dewy hour;
Her ringlets richly flowing,
And her cheek all gaily glowing,
Like the rose in her blooming bower.

Oh, lonely be his life,
  May his dwelling want a wife,
And his nights be long, cheerless, and dreary,
  Who cold or calm could be,
  With a winning one like thee—
Or for wealth forsake thee, my Mary!
Translated by THOMAS FURLONG.

OH, MARY DEAR!

OH, Mary dear! bright peerless flower—
  Pride of the plains of Nair—
Behold me droop through each dull hour,
  In soul-consuming care.
In friends—in wine—where joy was found—
  No joy I now can see;
But still, while pleasure reigns around,
  I sigh, and think of thee.

The cuckoo's notes I love to hear,
  When summer warms the skies;
When fresh the banks and braes appear,
  And flowers around us rise:
That blithe bird sings her song so clear,
  And she sings where the sunbeams shine—
Her voice is sweet, but, Mary dear,
  Not half so sweet as thine.

From town to town I've idly strayed,
  I've wandered many a mile;
I've met with many a blooming maid,
  And owned her charms the while;

I've gazed on some that then seemed fair,
   But when thy looks I see,
I find there's none that can compare,
   My Mary dear, with thee!

           Translated by THOMAS FURLONG.

SLEEP, MY CHILD! (CUSHEEN LOO!)

SLEEP, my child! for the rustling trees,
Stirr'd by the breath of summer breeze,
And fairy songs of sweetest note,
Around us gently float.

Sleep! for the weeping flowers have shed
Their fragrant tears upon thy head,
The voice of love hath sooth'd thy rest,
And thy pillow is a mother's breast.
                Sleep, my child!

Weary hath pass'd the time forlorn
Since to your mansion I was borne,
Though bright the feast of its airy halls
And the voice of mirth resounds from its walls.
                Sleep, my child!

Full many a maid and blooming bride
Within that splendid dome abide—
And many a hoar and shrivell'd sage,
And many a matron bow'd with age.
                Sleep, my child!

Oh thou who hearest this song of fear,
To the mourner's home these tidings bear;
Bid him bring the knife of the magic blade,
At whose lightning-flash the charm will fade.
                Sleep, my child!

Haste! for to-morrow's sun will see
The hateful spell renewed for me;
Nor can I from that home depart,
Till life shall leave my withering heart
                    Sleep, my child!

Sleep, my child! for the rustling trees,
Stirr'd by the breath of summer breeze,
And fairy songs of sweetest note,
Around us gently float.
              JAMES JOSEPH CALLANAN.

THINK NO MORE ON ME.

AND must we part? Then fare thee well;
But he that wails it—he can tell
How dear thou wert, how dear thou art,
And ever must be to this heart;
But now 'tis vain—it cannot be;
Farewell! and think no more on me.

Oh yes! this heart would sooner break,
Than one unholy thought awake;
I'd sooner slumber into clay
Than cloud thy spirit's beauteous ray;
Go, free as air—as angel free—
And, lady, think no more on me.

Oh! did we meet when brighter star
Sent its fair promise from afar,
I then might hope to call thee mine;
The minstrel's heart and harp were thine;
But now 'tis past—it cannot be;
Farewell! and think no more on me.

Or do!—but let it be the hour
When Mercy's all-atoning power
From His high throne of glory hears
Of souls like thine, the prayers, the tears.
Then, whilst you bend the suppliant knee,
Then—then, O lady! think on me.

JAMES JOSEPH CALLANAN.

WHY ARE YOU WANDERING HERE?

'Why are you wandering here, I pray?'
An old man asked a maid one day.
'Looking for poppies, so bright and red,
Father,' said she, 'I'm hither led.'
'Fie! fie!' she heard him cry,
'Poppies, 'tis known to all who rove,
Grow in the field, and not in the grove—
Grow in the field, and not in the grove.

'Tell me again,' the old man said,
'Why are you loitering here, fair maid?'
'The nightingale's song, so sweet and clear,
Father,' said she, 'I come to hear.'
'Fie! fie!' she heard him cry,
'Nightingales all, so people say,
Warble by night, and not by day—
Warble by night, and not by day.'

The sage looked grave, the maiden shy,
When Lubin jumped o'er the stile hard by;
The sage looked graver, the maid more glum,
Lubin he twiddled his finger and thumb.

'Fie! fie!' the old man's cry;
'Poppies like these, I own, are rare,
And of such nightingales' songs beware—
And of such nightingales' songs beware.'
JAMES KENNEY.

THE GREEN LEAVES ALL TURN YELLOW.

A SAGE once to a maiden sung,
    While summer leaves were growing;
Experience dwelt upon his tongue,
    With love her heart was glowing:
'The summer bloom will fade away,
    And will no more be seen;
These flowers, that look so fresh and gay,
    Will not be ever green—
        For the green leaves all turn yellow.

''Tis thus with the delights of love,
    The youthful heart beguiling;
Believe me, you will find them prove
    As transient—though as smiling:
Not long they flourish, ere they fade;
    As sadly I have seen;
Yes, like the summer flowers, fair maid,
    Oh! none are ever green—
        For the green leaves all turn yellow.'
JAMES KENNEY.

I WAS THE BOY FOR BEWITCHING THEM.

I WAS the boy for bewitching them,
    Whether good-humour'd or coy;
All cried when I was beseeching them,
    'Do what you will with me, joy.'

'Daughters, be cautious and steady,'
   Mothers would cry out for fear;
'Won't you take care now of Teddy—
   Och! he's the divil, my dear.'
For I was the boy for bewitching them,
   Whether good-humour'd or coy;
All cried when I was beseeching them,
   'Do what you will with me, joy.'

From every quarter I gather'd them,
   Very few rivals had I;
If I found any I leathered* them,
   And that made them look mighty shy.
Pat Mooney, my Shelah once meeting,
   I twigg'd him beginning his clack;
Says he, 'At my heart I've a beating:'
   Says I, 'Then have one at your back.'
        For I was the boy, etc.

Many a lass that would fly away
   When other wooers but spoke,
Once if I looked her a die-away,
   There was an end of the joke.
Beauties, no matter how cruel,
   Hundreds of lads though they'd crost,
When I came nigh to them, jewel,
   They melted like mud in the frost.
        For I was the boy, etc.
            JAMES KENNEY.

* *Anglicè*, belaboured.

MY LIFE IS LIKE THE SUMMER ROSE.

My life is like the summer rose,
   That opens to the morning sky;
But ere the shades of evening close,
   Is scattered on the ground—to die.
Yet on the rose's humble bed
The sweetest dews of night are shed,
As if she wept the waste to see—
But none shall weep a tear for me!

My life is like the autumn leaf,
   That trembles in the moon's pale ray;
Its hold is frail—its date is brief,
   Restless—and soon to pass away!
Yet, ere that leaf shall fall and fade,
The parent tree will mourn its shade,
The winds bewail the leafless tree,
But none shall breathe a sigh for me!

My life is like the prints which feet
   Have left on Tampa's desert strand;
Soon as the rising tide shall beat,
   All trace will vanish from the sand;
Yet, as if grieving to efface
All vestige of the human race,
On that lone shore loud moans the sea,
But none, alas! shall mourn for me.

                  RICHARD HENRY WILDE.

GILLE MA CHREE.

Gille ma chree,*
Sit down by me;
We now are joined and ne'er shall sever:
This hearth's our own,
Our hearts are one,
And peace is ours for ever!

When I was poor,
Your father's door
Was closed against your constant lover;
With care and pain,
I tried in vain
My fortunes to recover.
I said, 'To other lands I'll roam,
Where Fate may smile on me, love;
I said, 'Farewell, my own old home!'
And I said, 'Farewell to thee, love!'
    Sing, *Gille ma chree,* etc.

I might have said,
My mountain maid,
Come live with me, your own true lover:
I know a spot,
A silent cot,
Your friends can ne'er discover,
Where gently flows the waveless tide
By one small garden only;
Where the heron waves his wings so wide,
And the linnet sings so lonely!
    Sing, *Gille ma chree,* etc.

 * Brightener of my heart.

I might have said,
My mountain maid,
A father's right was never given
True hearts to curse
With tyrant force
That have been blest in heaven.
But then I said, 'In after years,
When thoughts of home shall find her,
My love may mourn with secret tears
Her friends thus left behind her.'
         Sing, *Gille ma chree*, etc.

'Oh no,' I said;
'My own dear maid,
For me, though all forlorn for ever,
That heart of thine
Shall ne'er repine
O'er slighted duty—never.
From home and thee, though wandering far,
A dreary fate be mine, love—
I'd rather live in endless war,
Than buy my peace with thine, love.'
         Sing, *Gille ma chree*, etc.

Far, far away,
By night and day,
I toiled to win a golden treasure;
And golden gains
Repaid my pains
In fair and shining measure.
I sought again my native land,
Thy father welcomed me, love;
I poured my gold into his hand
And my guerdon found in thee, love.

  Sing, *Gille ma chree*,
  Sit down by me;
We now are joined, and ne'er shall sever:
  This hearth's our own,
  Our hearts are one,
And peace is ours for ever!
GERALD GRIFFIN.

I LOVE MY LOVE IN THE MORNING.

I LOVE my love in the morning,
 For she, like morn, is fair—
Her blushing cheek, its crimson streak;
 Its clouds, her golden hair;
Her glance, its beam, so soft and kind;
 Her tears, its dewy showers;
And her voice, the tender whispering wind
 That stirs the early bowers.

I love my love in the morning,
 I love my love at noon,
For she is bright as the lord of light,
 Yet mild as autumn's moon:
Her beauty is my bosom's sun,
 Her faith my fostering shade,
And I will love my darling one
 Till even the sun shall fade.

I love my love in the morning,
 I love my love at even;
Her smile's soft play is like the ray
 That lights the western heaven:

I loved her when the sun was high,
   I loved her when he rose,
But best of all when evening's sigh
   Was murmuring at its close.
                    GERALD GRIFFIN.

THE TIE IS BROKE, MY IRISH GIRL.

THE tie is broke, my Irish girl,
   That bound thee here to me;
My heart has lost its single pearl,
   And thine at last is free—
Dead as the earth that wraps thy clay,
   Dead as the stone above thee—
Cold as this heart that breaks to say
   It never more can love thee.

I press thee to my aching breast—
   No blush comes o'er thy brow;
Those gentle arms that once caress'd
   Fall round me deadly now.
The smiles of Love no longer part
   Those dead, blue lips of thine;
I lay my hand upon thy heart,
   'Tis cold at last to mine.

Were we beneath our native heaven,
   Within our native land,
A fairer grave to thee were given
   Than this wild bed of sand;
But thou wert single in thy faith,
   And single in thy worth,
And thou should'st die a lonely death,
   And lie in lonely earth.

Then lay thee down and take thy rest,
  My last, last ook is given—
The earth is smooth above *thy* breast,
  And mine is yet unriven!
No Mass—no parting rosary—
  My perished love can have;
But her husband's sighs embalm her corse,
  A husband's tears her grave.
                            GERALD GRIFFIN.

MY MARY OF THE CURLING HAIR.

My Mary of the curling hair,
The laughing teeth and bashful air,
Our bridal morn is dawning fair,
  With blushes in the skies.
    Come! come! come, my darling—
    Come softly, and come, my love!
      My love! my pearl!
      My own dear girl!
    My mountain maid, arise!

Wake, linnet of the osier grove!
Wake, trembling, stainless, virgin dove!
Wake, nestling of a parent's love!
  Let Moran see thine eyes.
            Come, come, etc.

I am no stranger, proud and gay,
To win thee from thy home away,
And find thee, for a distant day,
  A theme for wasting sighs.
            Come, come, etc.

But we were known from infancy,
Thy father's hearth was home to me,
No selfish love was mine for thee,
   Unholy and unwise.
          Come, come, etc.

And yet, (to see what love can do!)
Though calm my hope has burned, and true,
My cheek is pale and worn for you,
   And sunken are mine eyes!
          Come, come, etc.

But soon my love shall be my bride,
And happy by our own fireside;
My veins shall feel the rosy tide
   That lingering hope denies.
          Come, come, etc.

My Mary of the curling hair,
The laughing teeth and bashful air,
Our bridal morn is dawning fair,
   With blushes in the sky.
     Come! come! come, my love—
     Come softly! and come, my love!
       My love! my pearl!
       My own dear girl!
     My mountain maid, arise!
          GERALD GRIFFIN.

THE BLIND PIPER.

ONE winter's day, long, long ago,
    When I was a little fellow,
A piper wandered to our door,
    Grey-headed, blind, and yellow:
And, oh! how glad was my young heart,
    Though earth and sky looked dreary,
To see the stranger and his dog—
    Poor 'Pinch,' and Caoch* O'Leary.

And when he stowed away his 'bag,'
    Cross-barred with green and yellow,
I thought and said, 'In Ireland's ground
    There's not so fine a fellow.'
And Fineen Burke, and Shaun Magee,
    And Eily, Kate, and Mary,
Rushed in, with panting haste, to see
    And welcome Caoch O'Leary.

Oh, God be with those happy times!
    Oh, God be with my childhood!
When I, bare-headed, roamed all day,
    Bird-nesting in the wild wood.
I'll not forget those sunny hours,
    However years may vary;
I'll not forget my early friends,
    Nor honest Caoch O'Leary.

* Blind.

Poor Caoch and 'Pinch' slept well that night,
    And in the morning early
He called me up to hear him play
    '*The wind that shakes the barley;*'
And then he stroked my flaxen hair,
    And cried, 'God mark my deary!'
And how I wept when he said, 'Farewell,
    And think of Caoch O'Leary!'

And seasons came and went, and still
    Old Caoch was not forgotten,
Although we thought him dead and gone,
    And in the cold grave rotten;
And often, when I walked and talked
    With Eily, Kate, and Mary,
We thought of childhood's rosy hours,
    And spoke of Caoch O'Leary.

Well, twenty summers had gone past,
    And June's red sun was sinking,
When I, a man, sat by my door,
    Of twenty sad things thinking.
A little dog came up the way,
    His gait was slow and weary,
And at his tail a lame man limped—
    'Twas 'Pinch' and Caoch O'Leary!

Old Caoch, but oh, how wobegone!
    His form is bowed and bending,
His fleshless hands are stiff and wan,
    Ay, time is even blending
The colours on his threadbare 'bag;'
    And 'Pinch' is twice as hairy
And thin-spare, as when first I saw
    Himself and Caoch O'Leary.

'God's blessing here!' the wanderer cried,
　'Far, far be hell's black viper;
Does anybody hereabouts
　Remember Caoch the Piper?'
With swelling heart I grasped his hand;
　The old man murmured, 'Deary,
Are you the silky-headed child
　That loved poor Caoch O'Leary?'

'Yes, yes,' I said;—the wanderer wept
　As if his heart was breaking.
'And where, *a vic ma chree*,'* he sobbed,
　'Is all the merry-making
I found here twenty years ago?'
　'My tale,' I sighed, 'might weary;
Enough to say, there's none but me
　To welcome Caoch O'Leary.'

Vo, vo! vo, vo!' the old man cried,
　And wrung his hands in sorrow;
'Pray let me in, *astore ma chree*,
　And I'll *go home* to-morrow.
My "peace is made;" I'll calmly leave
　This world so cold and dreary;
And you shall keep my pipes and dog,
　And pray for Caoch O'Leary.'

With 'Pinch' I watched his bed that night;
　Next day his wish was granted—
He died; and Father James was brought,
　And the Requiem Mass was chanted.

* Son of my heart.

The neighbours came; we dug his grave
  Near Eily, Kate, and Mary,
And there he sleeps his last sweet sleep.
  God rest you, Caoch O'Leary!

JOHN KEEGAN.

THE DYING MOTHER'S LAMENT.

'O GOD! it is a dreadful night—how fierce the dark winds blow!
It howls like mourning *banshee*, its breathings speak of woe;
'Twill rouse my slumbering orphans—blow gently, O wild blast!
My wearied, hungry darlings are hushed in peace at last.

'And how the cold rain tumbles down in torrents from the skies,
Down, down, upon our stiffened limbs, into my children's eyes:
O God of heaven, stop your hand until the dawn of day,
And out upon the weary world again we'll take our way!

'But ah! my prayers are worthless—oh, louder roars the blast,
And darker frown the pitchy clouds, the rain falls still more fast!
O God, *if* you be merciful, have mercy *now*, I pray!
O God, forgive my wicked words—I know not what I say.

'To see my ghastly babies—my babes so meek and fair—
To see them huddled in that ditch, like wild beasts in their lair;

Like wild beasts! No! the vixen cubs that sport on
    yonder hill
Lie warm this hour, and, I'll engage, of food they've had
    their fill.

'O blessed Queen of Mercy, look down from that black
    sky;
You've felt a mother's misery, then hear a mother's cry.
I mourn not my own wretchedness, but let my children
    rest;
Oh, watch and guard them this wild night, and then I
    shall be blest.'

Thus prayed the wanderer, but in vain—in vain her
    mournful cry;
God did not hush that piercing wind, nor brighten that
    dark sky;
But when the ghastly winter's dawn its sickly radiance
    shed,
The mother and her wretched babes lay stiffened, grim,
    and dead!

JOHN KEEGAN.

THE HOLLY AND IVY GIRL.

'COME buy my nice fresh Ivy, and my Holly-sprigs so
    green;
I have the finest branches that ever yet were seen.
Come buy from me, good Christians, and let me home, I
    pray,
And I'll wish 'Merry Christmas Time' and a 'Happy
    New Year's Day.'

THE HOLLY AND IVY GIRL

'Ah! won't you buy my Ivy? the loveliest ever seen!
Ah! won't you buy my Holly-boughs?—all you who love the green!
Do take a little branch of each, and on my knees I'll pray,
That God may bless your Christmas, and be with your New Year's Day.

'The wind is black and bitter, and the hailstones do not spare
My shivering form, my bleeding feet, and stiff entangled hair;
Then, when the skies are pitiless, be merciful, I say—
So Heaven will light your Christmas and the coming New Year's Day.'

'Twas a dying maiden sung, while the cold hail rattled down,
And fierce winds whistled mournfully o'er Dublin's dreary town;
One stiff hand clutched her Ivy-sprigs and Holly-boughs so fair,
With the other she kept brushing the hail-drops from her hair.

So grim and statue-like she seemed, 'twas evident that Death
Was lurking in her footsteps, whilst her hot impeded breath
Too plainly told her early doom, though the burden of her lay
Was still of life, and Christmas joys, and a Happy New Year's Day.

The ghost-like singer still sang on, but no one came to
   buy;
The hurrying crowd passed to and fro, but did not heed
   her cry:
She uttered one low piercing moan—then cast her boughs
   away,
And smiling cried, 'I'll rest with God before the New
   Year's Day.'

JOHN KEEGAN.

BRIDEEN* BAN MO STORE.

I AM a wand'ring minstrel man,
   And Love my only theme;
I've stray'd beside the pleasant Bann,
   And eke the Shannon's stream;
I've piped and played to wife and maid
   By Barrow, Suir, and Nore,
But never met a maiden yet
   Like *Brideen ban mo store.*

My girl hath ringlets rich and rare,
   By Nature's fingers wove—
Loch Carra's swan is not so fair
   As is her breast of love;
And when she moves, in Sunday sheen,
   Beyond our cottage door,
I'd scorn the high-born Saxon queen
   For *Brideen ban mo store.*

It is not that thy smile is sweet,
   And soft thy voice of song—
It is not that thou fleest to meet
   My comings lone and long!

* Little Bridget.

But that beneath thy breast doth rest
  A heart of purest core,
Whose pulse is known to me alone,
  My *Brideen ban mo store.*
                                EDWARD WALSH.

OVER THE HILLS AND FAR AWAY.

ONCE I bloom'd a maiden young;
A widow's woe now moves my tongue;
My true love's bark ploughs ocean's spray,
Over the hills and far away.
  Chorus: Oh had I worlds I'd yield them now,
        To place me on his tall bark's prow,
        Who was my choice through childhood's day,
        Over the hills and far away!

Oh, may we yet our lov'd one meet,
With joy-bells' chime and wild drums' beat;
While summoning war-trump sounds dismay,
Over the hills and far away!
        Oh, had I worlds, etc.

Oh, that my hero had his throne,
That Erin's cloud of care were flown,
That proudest prince would own his sway,
Over the hills and far away!
        Oh, had I worlds, etc.

My bosom's love, that prince afar,
Our king, our joy, our orient star;
More sweet his voice than wild bird's lay,
Over the hills and far away!
        Oh had I worlds etc.

A high green hill I'll quickly climb,
And tune my heart in song sublime,
And chant his praise the livelong day,
Over the hills and far away!
    Oh, had I worlds, etc.
   Translated by EDWARD WALSH.

MY CLUSTER OF NUTS (MO CRAOIBHIN CNO).

My heart is far from Liffey's tide
 And Dublin town;
It strays beyond the southern side
 Of Knockmeeldown,
Where Cappaquin hath woodlands green,
 Where Avonmore's waters flow,
Where dwells unsung, unsought, unseen,
 Mo craoibhin cno,
Low clustering in her leafy screen,
 Mo craoibhin cno.

The high-bred dames of Dublin town
 Are rich and fair,
With wavy plume and silken gown,
 And stately air;
Can plumes compare with thy dark brown hair?
 Can silks with thy neck of snow?
Or measur'd pace with thine artless grace,
 Mo craoibhin cno,
When harebells scarcely show thy trace,
 Mo craoibhin cno?

I've heard the songs by Liffey's wave
    That maidens sung—
They sung their land, the Saxon's slave,
    In Saxon tongue—
Oh, bring me here that Gaelic dear
    Which cursed the Saxon foe,
When thou didst charm the raptured ear,
    Mo craoibhin cno!
And none but God's good angels near,
    Mo craoibhin cno!

I've wandered by the rolling Lee,
    And Lene's green bowers;
I've seen the Shannon's wide-spread sea,
    And Limerick's towers;
And Liffey's tide, where halls of pride
    Frown o'er the flood below:
My wild heart strays to Avonmore's side,
    Mo craoibhin cno!
With love and thee for aye to bide,
    Mo craoibhin cno!

                EDWARD WALSH.

THE IRISH EMIGRANT.

I'M sitting on the stile, Mary,
    Where we sat side by side,
On a bright May morning long ago,
    When first you were my bride.
The corn was springing fresh and green,
    And the lark sang loud and high,
And the red was on your lip, Mary,
    And the lovelight in your eye.

The place is little changed, Mary,
　　The day as bright as then ;
The lark's loud song is in my ear,
　　And the corn is green again.
But I miss the soft clasp of your hand,
　　And your breath warm on my cheek,
And I still keep list'ning for the words
　　You nevermore may speak.

'Tis but a step down yonder lane,
　　And the little church stands near ;
The church where we were wed, Mary,—
　　I see the spire from here.
But the graveyard lies between, Mary,
　　And my steps would break your rest ;
For I've laid you, darling, down to sleep,
　　With your baby on your breast.

I'm very lonely, now, Mary,
　　For the poor make no new friends ;
But oh, they love the better far
　　The few our Father sends !
And you were all I had, Mary,
　　My blessing and my pride !
There's nothing left to care for now
　　Since my poor Mary died !

I'm bidding you a long farewell,
　　My Mary, kind and true !
But I'll not forget you, darling,
　　In the land I'm going to !

They say there's bread and work for all,
   And the sun shines always there;
But I'll not forget old Ireland,
   Were it fifty times as fair!
LADY DUFFERIN.

TERENCE'S FAREWELL.

So, my Kathleen, you're going to leave me
   All alone by myself in this place;
But I'm sure you will never deceive me,—
   Oh no, if there's truth in that face!
Though England's a beautiful city,
   Full of illigant boys, oh what then?
You wouldn't forget your poor Terence
   You'll come back to ould Ireland again.

Och, those English, deceivers by nature,
   Though maybe you'd think them sincere,
They'll say you're a sweet charming creature,
   But don't you believe them, my dear.
O Kathleen, agra! don't be minding
   The flattering speeches they'd make;
But tell them a poor lad in Ireland
   Is breaking his heart for your sake.

It's folly to keep you from going,
   Though, faith, it's a mighty hard case;
For, Kathleen, you know there's no knowing
   When next I shall see your sweet face.
And when you come back to me, Kathleen,
   None the better will I be off then;
You'll be speaking such beautiful English,
   Sure I won't know my Kathleen again.

Ah now, where's the need of this hurry?
  Don't fluster me so in this way :
I forgot, 'twixt the grief and the flurry,
  Every word I was maning to say.
Now just wait a minute, I bid ye;
  Can I talk if you bother me so?—
O Kathleen, my blessing go wid ye,
  Every inch of the way that you go.
                              LADY DUFFERIN.

MY OWN DARLING KATEY.

I WAS working in the fields near fair Boston city,
  Thinking sadly of Kilkenny—and a girl that's there;
When a friend came and tould me—late enough, and more's the pity!—
  'There's a letter waitin' for ye, in the postman's care!'
Oh, my heart was in my mouth all the while that he was spaking,
  For I knew it was from Katey!—she's the girl that can spell!
And I couldn't speak for crying, for my heart had nigh been breaking,
  With longing for a word from the girl I love well.
Oh! I knew it was from Katey. Who could it be but Katey?
  The poor girl that loves me well, in sweet Kilkenny Town.

Oh, 'twas soon I reached the place, and I thanked them for the trouble
  They wor taking with my letter, a-sorting with such care;

And they asked me, 'Was it single?' and I tould them
    'twas a double!
For wasn't it worth twice as much as any letter there?
Then they sorted and they searched, but something
    seemed the matter,
And my heart it stopped beating when I thought what
    it might be:
Och! boys, would you believe it? they had gone and
    lost my letter,
My poor Katey's letter that had come so far to me.
    For I knew, etc.

I trimbled like an aspen, but I said, "'Tis fun you're
    making,
Of the poor foolish Paddy that's so aisy to craze;
Och! gintlemen, then look again, maybe you wor mis-
    taken,
For letters, as you know, boys, are as like as pase!"
Then they bade me search myself, when they saw my
    deep dejection,
But, och! who could sarch when the tears blind the
    sight?
Moreover (as I tould them), I'd another strong objection,
In regard of niver larning to read nor to write.
For I wasn't cute like Katey, my own darling Katey, etc.

Then they laughed in my face, and they asked me (though
    in kindness),
What good would letters do me that I couldn't under-
    stand.
And I answered, 'Were they cursed with deafness and
    with blindness,
Would they care less for the clasp of a dear loved
    hand?'

Oh, the folks that read and write (though they're so
    mighty clever),
  See nothin' but the words, and they're soon read
    through ;
But Katey's unread letter would be speaking to me ever
  Of the dear love that she bears me, for it shows she is
    true !
Oh, well I know my Katey, my own darling Katey,
  The poor girl that loves me well in sweet Kilkenny
    Town.

LADY DUFFERIN.

THE BLIND MAN TO HIS BRIDE.

WHEN first, beloved, in vanished hours,
  The blind man sought thy hand to gain,
They said thy cheek was bright as flowers
  New freshened by the summer's rain.
The beauty which made them rejoice
  My darkened eyes might never see ;
But well I knew thy gentle voice,
  And that was all in all to me.

At length, as years rolled swiftly on,
  They talked to me of time's decay,
Of roses from thy soft cheek gone,
  Of ebon tresses turned to grey.
I heard them, but I heeded not ;
  The withering change I could not see ;
Thy voice still cheered my darkened lot,
  And that was all in all to me.

And still, beloved, till life grows cold,
  We'll wander 'neath the genial sky,
And only know that we are old
  By counting happy hours gone by.

Thy cheek may lose its blushing hue,
Thy brow less beautiful may be,
But oh, the voice which first I knew,
Still keeps the same sweet tone to me.
Hon. Caroline Norton.

MY IRISH WIFE.

I would not give my Irish wife
   For all the dames of Saxon land—
I would not give my Irish wife
   For the Queen of France's hand.
For she to me is dearer
   Than castles strong, or lands, or life—
An outlaw—so I'm near her
   To love till death my Irish wife.

Oh, what would be this home of mine—
   A ruined, hermit-haunted place,
But for the light that nightly shines,
   Upon its walls from Kathleen's face?
What comfort in a mine of gold—
   What pleasure in a royal life,
If the heart within lay dead and cold,—
   If I could not wed my Irish wife?

I knew the law forbade the banns—
   I knew my kin abhorred her race—
Who never bent before their clans,
   Must bow before their ladies' grace.
Take all my forfeited domain,
   I cannot wage with kinsmen strife—
Take knightly gear and noble name,
   And I will keep my Irish wife.

My Irish wife has clear blue eyes,
    My heaven by day, my stars by night—
And, twin-like, Truth and Fondness lie
    Within her swelling bosom white.
My Irish wife has golden hair—
    Apollo's harp had once such strings—
Apollo's self might pause to hear
    Her bird-like carol when she sings.

I would not give my Irish wife
    For all the dames of Saxon land—
I would not give my Irish wife
    For the Queen of France's hand.
For she to me is dearer
    Than castles strong, or lands, or life—
In death I would be near her,
    And rise beside my Irish wife!

                THOMAS D'ARCY M'GEE.

IF WILL HAD WINGS, HOW FAST I'D FLEE.

If will had wings, how fast I'd flee
To the home of my heart o'er the seething sea!
If wishes were power—if words were spells,
I'd be this hour where my own love dwells.

My own love dwells in the storied land,
Where the Holy Wells sleep in yellow sand;
And the emerald lustre of Paradise beams
Over homes that cluster round singing streams.

I, sighing, alas! exist alone—
My youth is as grass on an unsunn'd stone,
Bright to the eye, but unfelt below—
As sunbeams that lie over Arctic snow.

My heart is a lamp that love must relight,
Or the world's fire-damp will quench it quite.
In the breast of my dear my life-tide springs—
Oh, I'd tarry none here, if will had wings.

For she never was weary of blessing me,
When morn rose dreary on thatch and tree;
She evermore chanted her song of faith,
When darkness daunted on hill and heath.

If will had wings, how fast I'd flee
To the home of my heart o'er the seething sea!
If wishes were power—if words were spells,
I'd be this hour where my own love dwells.
THOMAS D'ARCY M'GEE.

THE MAN OF THE NORTH COUNTRIE.

HE came from the North, and his words were few,
But his voice was kind and his heart was true;
And I knew by his eyes no guile had he,
So I married the man of the North Countrie.

Oh, Garryowen may be more gay
Than this quiet street of Ballibay;
And I know the sun shines softly down
On the river that passes my native town.

But there's not—I say it with joy and pride—
Better man than mine in Munster wide;
And Limerick Town has no happier hearth
Than mine has been with my Man of the North.

I wish that in Munster they only knew
The kind, kind neighbours I came unto:
Small hate or scorn would ever be
Between the South and the North Countrie.

     THOMAS D'ARCY M'GEE.

NONE REMEMBER THEE, SAVE ME!

NONE remember thee! thou whose heart
 Poured love on all around;
Thy name no anguish can impart—
 'Tis a forgotten sound.
Thy old companions pass me by,
With a cold bright smile, and a vacant eye,
 And none remember thee,
   Save me!

None remember thee! thou wert not
 Beauteous as some things are;
My glory beamed upon thy lot,
 My pale and quiet star!
Like a winter bud that too soon hath burst,
Thy cheek was fading from the first—
 And none remember thee,
   Save me!

None remember thee! they could spy
  Nought when they gazed on thee,
But thy soul's deep love in thy quiet eye—
  It hath passed from their memory.
The gifts of genius were not thine,
Proudly before the world to shine—
  And none remember thee,
      Save me!

None remember thee now thou'rt gone!
  Or they could not choose but weep,
When they thought of thee, my gentle one,
  In thy long and lonely sleep.
Fain would I murmur thy name, and tell
How fondly together we used to dwell—
  But none remember thee,
      Save me!
            Hon. Caroline Norton.

SONG OF THE PEASANT WIFE.

Come, Patrick, clear up the storms on your brow;
You were kind to me once—will you frown on me now?
Shall the storm settle here, when from heaven it departs,
And the cold from without find its way to our hearts?
No, Patrick, no! sure the wintriest weather,
Is easily borne when we bear it together.

Though the rain's dropping through from the roof to the floor,
And the wind whistles free where there once was a door,
Can the rain, or the snow, or the storm wash away
All the warm vows we made in our love's early day?
No, Patrick, no! sure the dark stormy weather
Is easily borne, if we bear it together.

When you stole out to woo me when labour was done,
And the day that was closing to us seemed begun,
Did we care if the sunset was bright on the flowers,
Or if we crept out amid darkness and showers?
No, Patrick! we talked, while we braved the wild weather,
Of all we could bear, if we bore it together.

Soon, soon, will these dark dreary days be gone by,
And our hearts be lit up with a beam from the sky!
Oh, let not our spirits, embittered with pain,
Be dead to the sunshine that came to us then!
Heart in heart, hand in hand, let us welcome the weather,
And, sunshine or storm, we will bear it together.

      Hon. Caroline Norton.

THE DYING GIRL.

From a Munster vale they brought her,
 From the pure and balmy air,
An Ormond peasant's daughter,
 With blue eyes and golden hair.
They brought her to the city,
 And she faded slowly there,
Consumption has no pity
 For blue eyes and golden hair.

When I saw her first reclining
 Her lips were mov'd in pray'r,
And the setting sun was shining
 On her loosen'd golden hair.
When our kindly glances met her,
 Deadly brilliant was her eye,
And she said that she was better,
 While we knew that she must die.

She speaks of Munster valleys,
  The pattern, dance, and fair,
And her thin hand feebly dallies
  With her scattered golden hair.
When silently we listened
  To her breath with quiet care,
Her eyes with wonder glisten'd—
  And she asked us, what was there?

The poor thing smiled to ask it,
  And her pretty mouth laid bare,
Like gems within a casket,
  A string of pearlets rare.
We said that we were trying
  By the gushing of her blood
And the time she took in sighing,
  To know if she were good.

Well, she smil'd and chatted gaily,
  Though we saw in mute despair
The hectic brighten daily,
  And the death-dew on her hair.
And oft her wasted fingers
  Beating time upon the bed,
O'er some old tune she lingers,
  And she bows her golden head.

At length the harp is broken,
  And the spirit in its strings
As the last decree is spoken
  To its source exulting springs.
Descending swiftly from the skies,
  Her guardian angel came;
He struck God's lightning from her eyes,
  And bore Him back the flame.

Before the sun had risen
  Through the lark-loved morning air,
Her young soul left its prison,
  Undefiled by sin or care.
I stood beside the couch in tears
  Where pale and calm she slept,
And though I've gaz'd on death for years,
  I blush not that I wept.
I check'd with effort pity's sighs
  And left the matron there,
To close the curtains of her eyes,
  And bind her golden hair.
          RICHARD DALTON WILLIAMS.

KATHLEEN.

My Kathleen dearest! in truth or seeming
  No brighter vision ere blessed mine eyes
Than she for whom, in Elysian dreaming,
  Thy trancèd lover too fondly sighs.
Oh, Kathleen fairest! if elfin splendour
  Hath ever broken my heart's repose,
'Twas in the darkness, ere purely tender,
  Thy smile, like moonlight o'er ocean, rose.

Since first I met thee thou knowest thine are
  This passion-music, and each pulse's thrill—
The flowers seem brighter, the stars diviner,
  And God and Nature more glorious still.
I see around me new fountains gushing—
  More jewels spangle the robes of night;
Strange harps resounding—fresh roses blushing—
  Young worlds emerging in purer light.

KATHLEEN.

No more thy song-bird in clouds shall hover—
  Oh, give him shelter upon thy breast,
And bid him swiftly, his long flight over,
  From heav'n drop into that love-built nest!
Like fairy flow'rets is Love thou fearest,
  At once that springeth like mine from earth—
'Tis Friendship's ivy grows slowly, dearest,
  But Love and Lightning have instant birth.
The mirthful fancy and artful gesture—
  Hair black as tempest, and swan-like breast,
More graceful folded in simple vesture
  Than proudest bosoms in diamonds drest—
Nor these, the varied and rare possession
  Love gave to conquer, are thine alone;
But, oh! there crowns thee divine expression,
  As saints a halo, that's all thine own.
Thou art as poets, in olden story,
  Have pictur'd woman before the fall—
Her angel beauty's divinest glory—
  The pure soul shining, like God, through all.
But vainly, humblest of leaflets springing,
  I sing the queenliest flower of love:
Thus soars the skylark, presumptuous singing
  The orient morning enthroned above.
Yet hear, propitious, belovèd maiden,
  The minstrel's passion is pure as strong,
Though nature fated, his heart, love-laden,
  Must break, or utter its woes in song.
Farewell! if never my soul may cherish
  The dreams that bade me to love aspire,
By Mem'ry's altar! thou shalt not perish,
  First Irish pearl of my Irish lyre!

                RICHARD DALTON WILLIAMS.

THE SISTER OF CHARITY.

Sister of charity, gentle and dutiful,
    Loving as seraphim, tender, and mild,
In humbleness strong, and in purity beautiful,
    In spirit heroic, in manners a child,
Ever thy love like an angel reposes,
    With hovering wings o'er the sufferer here,
Till the arrows of death are half-hidden in roses,
    And hope-speaking prophecy smiles on the bier.

When life, like a vapour, is slowly retiring,
    As clouds in the dawning to heaven uprolled,
Thy prayer, like a herald, precedes him expiring,
    And the cross on thy bosom his last looks behold;
And oh! as the spouse to thy words of love listens,
    What hundredfold blessings descend on thee then—
Thus the flower-absorbed dew in the bright iris glistens,
    And returns to the lilies more richly again.

Sister of charity, child of the holiest,
    Oh, for thy living soul, ardent as pure—
Mother of orphans, and friend of the lowliest—
    Stay of the wretched, the guilty, the poor;
The embrace of the Godhead so plainly enfolds thee,
    Sanctity's halo so shines thee around,
Daring the eye that unshrinking beholds thee,
    Nor droops in thy presence abashed to the ground.

Dim is the fire of the sunniest blushes,
    Burning the breast of the maidenly rose,
To the exquisite bloom that thy pale beauty flushes
    When the incense ascends and the sanctuary glows;

And the music, that seems heaven's language, is pealing,
    Adoration has bowed him in silence and sighs,
And man, intermingled with angels, is feeling
    The passionless rapture that comes from the skies.

Oh! that this heart, whose unspeakable treasure
    Of love hath been wasted so vainly on clay,
Like thine, unallured by the phantom of pleasure,
    Could rend every earthly affection away;
And yet in thy presence, the billows subsiding
    Obey the strong effort of reason and will,
And my soul, in her pristine tranquillity gliding,
    Is calm as when God bid the ocean be still.

Thy soothing, how gentle! thy pity, how tender!
    Choir music thy voice is—thy step angel grace,
And thy union with Deity shines in a splendour,
    Subdued, but unearthly, thy spiritual face.
When the frail chains are broken, a captive that bound thee
    Afar from thy home is the prison of clay,
Bride of the Lamb, and earth's shadows around thee
    Disperse in the blaze of eternity's day.

Still mindful, as now, of the sufferer's story,
    Arresting the thunders of wrath ere they roll,
Intervene, as a cloud between us and His glory,
    And shield from His lightnings the shuddering soul.
As mild as the moonbeam in autumn descending,
    That lightning, extinguished by mercy, shall fall,
While He hears with the wail of a penitent blending
    Thy prayer, Holy Daughter of Vincent de Paul.

                    RICHARD DALTON WILLIAMS.

MY COLLEEN RUE.

My fairy girl, my darling girl,
   If I were near thee now,
The sunlight of your eyes would chase
   The sorrow from my brow;
Your lips would whisper o'er and o'er
   The words so fond and true,
They whispered long and long ago,
   My gentle Colleen Rue.

No more by Inny's bank I sit,
   Or rove the meadows brown,
But count the weary hours away
   Pent in this dismal town;
I cannot breathe the pasture air,
   My father's homestead view,
Or see another face like thine,
   My gentle Colleen Rue.

Thy laugh was like the echo sent
   From Oonagh's crystal hall;
Thy eyes the moonlight's flashing glance
   Upon a waterfall;
Thy hair the amber clouds at eve,
   When lovers haste to woo;
Thy teeth Killarney's snowy pearls,
   My gentle Colleen Rue.

Oh, sweetheart! I can see thee stand
   Beside the orchard stile,
The dawn upon thy regal brow,
   Upon thy mouth a smile;

The apple-bloom above thy head,
  Thy cheeks its glowing hue,
The sunflash in thy radiant eyes,
  My gentle Colleen Rue.

But drearily and wearily
  The snow is drifting by,
And drearily and wearily
  It bears my lonely sigh,
Far from this lonely Connaught town,
  To Inny's wave of blue,
To the homestead in the fairy glen,
  And gentle Colleen Rue.

JOHN KEEGAN CASEY.

DONAL KENNY.

'COME, piper, play the "*Shaskan Reel*,"
  Or else the "*Lasses on the Heather*,"
And, Mary, lay aside your wheel
  Until we dance once more together.
At fair and pattern oft before
  Of reels and jigs we've tripped full many;
But ne'er again this loved old floor
  Will feel the foot of Donal Kenny.'

Softly she rose and took his hand,
  And softly glided through the measure,
While, clustering round, the village band
  Looked half in sorrow, half in pleasure.
Warm blessings flowed from every lip,
  As ceased the dancers' airy motion:
O blessed Virgin! guide the ship
  Which bears bold Donal o'er the ocean!

'Now God be with you all!' he sighed,
   Adown his face the bright tears flowing;
'God guard you well, *avic*,' they cried,
   'Upon the strange path you are going.'
So full his breast, he scarce could speak,
   With burning grasp the stretched hands taking,
He pressed a kiss on every cheek,
   And sobbed as if his heart was breaking.

'Boys, don't forget me when I'm gone,
   For sake of all the days passed over—
The days you spent on heath and bawn,
   With *Donal Rue*, the rattlin' rover.
Mary, *agra*, your soft brown eye
   Has willed my fate,' he whispered lowly;
'Another holds thy heart: good-bye!
   Heaven grant you both its blessings holy!'

A kiss upon her brow of snow,
   A rush across the moonlit meadow,
Whose broom-clad hazels, trembling slow,
   The mossy boreen* wrapped in shadow;
Away o'er Tully's bounding rill,
   And far beyond the Inny river;
One cheer on Carrick's rocky hill,
   And Donal Kenny's gone for ever.

     *   *   *   *   *

The breezes whistled through the sails,
   O'er Galway Bay the ship was heaving,
And smothered groans and bursting wails
   Told of the grief and pain of leaving.

* *Anglicè*, narrow lane.

One form among that exiled band
    Of parting sorrow gave no token,
Still was his breath, and cold his hand:
    For Donal Kenny's heart was broken.
JOHN KEEGAN CASEY.

MARY DONN ASTHORE.*

IN valleys lone I pluck'd the flowers,
    And wove them in her hair,
And never in the greenwood bowers
    Was forest queen as fair.
She gave a silent glance at me,
    With love-light flowing o'er;
Oh! well that love's returned to thee,
    My Mary Donn Asthore.

The sloethorn woos the poplar brown,
    Where shines the sunlit hill,
Its blossoms waft an odour down
    O'er heather, slope, and rill.
Her hand is as that blossom white,
    As pure her bosom's core—
My well of joy, my life's delight,
    My Mary Donn Asthore.

I've strung my harp to many a lay,
    With soothing magic sound,
I've sung to lords and ladies gay
    Throughout old Ireland's ground;

* Brown-haired treasure.

But now I find its tones are vain,
   The ancient songs to pour;
Thy name alone, that fills the strain,
   My Mary Donn Asthore.
JOHN KEEGAN CASEY.

THE WREATH YOU WOVE.

THE wreath you wove, the wreath you wove
   Is fair—but oh! how fair,
If Pity's hand had stolen from Love
   One leaf to mingle there!

If every rose with gold were tied,
   Did gems for dew-drops fall,
One faded leaf where Love had sighed
   Were sweetly worth them all!

The wreath you wove, the wreath you wove
   Our emblem well may be;
Its bloom is yours, but hopeless love
   Must keep its tears for me!
THOMAS MOORE.

WOMAN.

AWAY, away—you're all the same,
   A fluttering, smiling, jilting throng!
Oh, by my soul, I burn with shame,
   To think I've been your slave so long!

Slow to be warmed and quick to rove
   From folly kind, and cunning loth;
Too cold for bliss, too weak for love,
   Yet feigning all that's best in both.

Still panting o'er a crowd to reign,
   More joy it gives to woman's breast
To make ten frigid coxcombs vain,
   Than one true, manly lover blest!

Away, away—your smile's a curse!
   Oh, blot me from the race of men,
Kind pitying Heaven! by death or worse,
   Before I love such things again.
                    THOMAS MOORE.

OH! STILL REMEMBER ME.

Go where glory waits thee,
But while fame elates thee,
   Oh, still remember me!
When the praise thou meetest
To thine ear is sweetest,
   Oh, then remember me!
Other arms may press thee,
Dearer friends caress thee,
All the joys that bless thee,
   Sweeter far may be;
But when friends are nearest,
And when joys are dearest,
   Oh, then remember me!

When at eve thou rovest
By the star thou lovest,
   Oh, then remember me!
Think, when home returning,
Bright we've seen it burning,
   Oh, thus remember me!

Oft as summer closes,
When thine eye reposes
On its lingering roses,
    Once so loved by thee,
Think of her who wove them,
Her who made thee love them,
    Oh, then remember me!

When, around thee dying,
Autumn leaves are lying,
    Oh, then remember me!
And, at night, when gazing,
On the gay hearth blazing,
    Oh, still remember me!
Then, should music, stealing
All the soul of feeling,
To thy heart appealing,
    Draw one tear from thee;
Then let memory bring thee,
Strains I used to sing thee—
    Oh, then remember me!

                    THOMAS MOORE.

CONSTANCY.

BELIEVE me, if all those endearing young charms,
    Which I gaze on so fondly to-day,
Were to change by to-morrow, and fleet in my arms,
    Like fairy-gifts fading away;
Thou wouldst still be adored, as this moment thou art,
    Let thy loveliness fade as it will,
And around the dear ruin each wish of my heart
    Would entwine itself verdantly still.

It is not while beauty and youth are thine own,
    And thy cheeks unprofaned by a tear,
That the fervour and faith of a soul can be known,
    To which time will but make thee more dear.
No; the heart that has truly loved never forgets,
    But as truly loves on to the close,
As the sun-flower turns on her god, when he sets,
    The same look which she turn'd when he rose.
                      THOMAS MOORE.

INCONSTANCY.

'TIS sweet to think, that where'er we rove,
    We are sure to find something blissful and dear,
And that, when we are far from the lips we love,
    We've but to make love to the lips we are near!
The heart, like a tendril, accustom'd to cling,
    Let it grow where it will cannot flourish alone,
But will lean to the nearest and loveliest thing
    It can twine in itself, and make closely its own;
Then oh! what pleasure, where'er we rove,
    To be sure to find something still that is dear,
And to know, when far from the lips we love,
    We've but to make love to the lips we are near.

'Twere a shame, when flowers around us rise,
    To make light of the rest, if the rose isn't there;
And the world's so rich in resplendent eyes,
    'Twere a pity to limit one's love to a pair.
Love's wing and the peacock's are nearly alike,
    They are both of them bright, but they're changeable too,
And wherever a new beam of beauty can strike,
    It will tincture Love's plume with a different hue!

Then oh ! what pleasure, where'er we rove,
  To be sure to find something still that is dear,
And to know, when far from the lips we love,
  We've but to make love to the lips we are near.
                              THOMAS MOORE.

LESBIA *VERSUS* NORA.

LESBIA hath a beaming eye,
  But no one knows for whom it beameth;
Right and left its arrows fly,
  But what they aim at no one dreameth.
Sweeter 'tis to gaze upon
  My Nora's lid that seldom rises;
Few its looks, but every one
  Like unexpected light, surprises.
    O my Nora Creina, dear,
  My gentle, bashful Nora Creina,
      Beauty lies
      In many eyes,
  But love in yours, my Nora Creina !

Lesbia wears a robe of gold,
  But all so close the nymph hath laced it,
Not a charm of beauty's mould
  Presumes to stay where Nature placed it.
Oh, my Nora's gown for me,
  That floats as wild as mountain breezes,
Leaving every beauty free
  To sink or swell as Heaven pleases.
    Yes, my Nora Creina, dear,
  My simple, graceful Nora Creina,
      Nature's dress
      Is loveliness—
  The dress *you* wear, my Nora Creina.

Lesbia hath a wit refined,
  But when its points are gleaming round us,
Who can tell if they're designed
  To dazzle merely, or to wound us?
Pillow'd on my Nora's heart,
  In safer slumber Love reposes—
Bed of peace! whose roughest part
  Is but the crumpling of the roses.
    O my Nora Creina, dear,
    My mild, my artless Nora Creina,
      Wit, though bright,
      Hath no such light
    As warms your eyes, my Nora Creina.
THOMAS MOORE.

THE TIME I'VE LOST IN WOOING.

THE time I've lost in wooing,
In watching and pursuing
    The light that lies
    In woman's eyes,
Has been my heart's undoing.
Though Wisdom oft has sought me,
I scorned the lore she brought me,
    My only books
    Were woman's looks,
And folly's all they've taught me.

Her smile when Beauty granted,
I hung with gaze enchanted,
    Like him the sprite
    Whom maids by night
Oft meet in glen that's haunted.

Like him, too, Beauty won me,
But while her eyes were on me,
   If once their ray
   Was turned away,
Oh! winds could not outrun me.

And are these follies going?
And is my proud heart growing
   Too cold or wise
   For brilliant eyes
Again to set it glowing?
No—vain, alas! th' endeavour
From bonds so sweet to sever;
   Poor Wisdom's chance
   Against a glance
Is now as weak as ever.
                THOMAS MOORE.

LOVE.

How sweet the answer Echo makes
   To music at night,
When, roused by lute or horn, she wakes,
And far away, o'er lawns and lakes,
   Goes answering light.

Yet Love hath echoes truer far,
   And far more sweet,
Than e'er, beneath the moonlight's star,
Of horn, or lute, or soft guitar,
   The songs repeat.

'Tis when the sigh in youth sincere,
    And only then—
The sigh, that's breathed for one to hear,
Is by that one, that only dear,
    Breathed back again!

THOMAS MOORE.

AN ELYSIUM ON EARTH.
SONG FROM 'LALLA ROOKH.'

COME hither, come hither—by night and by day,
  We linger in pleasures that never are gone;
Like the waves of the summer, as one dies away,
  Another as sweet and as shining comes on.
And the love that is o'er, in expiring, gives birth
  To a new one as warm, as unequall'd in bliss;
And oh, if there be an elysium on earth,
    It is this, it is this!

Here maidens are sighing, and fragrant the sigh
  As the flower of the Amra just oped by a bee;
And precious their tears as that rain from the sky,
  Which turns into pearls as it falls in the sea.
Oh, think what the kiss and the smile must be worth,
  When the sigh and the tear are so perfect in bliss;
And own if there be an elysium on earth,
    It is this, it is this!

Here sparkles the nectar that, hallow'd by love,
  Could draw down those angels of old from their sphere,
Who for wine of this earth left the fountains above,
  And forgot heaven's stars for the eyes we have here.
And, bless'd with the odour our goblet gives forth,
  What spirit the sweets of his Eden would miss?
For, oh, if there be an elysium on earth,
    It is this, it is this!

There's a bliss beyond all that the minstrel has told,
   When two, that are link'd in one heavenly tie,
With heart never changing and brow never cold,
   Love on through all ills, and love on till they die;
One hour of a passion so sacred is worth
   Whole ages of heartless and wandering bliss;
And oh, if there *be* an elysium on earth,
          It is this, it is this!

                    THOMAS MOORE.

THE FLOWER OF ALL MAIDENS.

OH, flower of all maidens for beauty,
   Fair-bosomed, and rose-lipped, and meek,
My heart is your slave and your booty,
   And droops, overpowered and weak.
Your clustering raven-black tresses
   Curl richly and glossily round,
Blest he who shall win your caresses,
   Sweet Blossom all down to the ground!

I have loved you, O mildest and fairest,
   With love that could scarce be more warm—
I have loved you, O brightest and rarest,
   Not less for your mind than your form.
I've adored you since ever I met you,
   O Rose without brier or stain;
And if e'er I forsake or forget you
   Let Love be ne'er trusted again!

My bright one you are till I perish,
   Oh, might I but call you my wife!
My treasure, my bliss, whom I'll cherish
   With love to the close of my life!

THE FLOWER OF ALL MAIDENS.

My secrets shall rest in your bosom,
    And yours in my heart shall remain;
And if e'er they be told, O sweet Blossom,
    May none be e'er whispered again!

Oh, loveliest! do not desert me!
    My earliest love was for you;
And if thousands of woes should begirt me,
    To you would I prove myself true!
Through my life you have been my consoler,
    My comforter—never in vain;
Had you failed to extinguish my dolour,
    I should ever have languished in pain!

O fond one! I pine in dejection;
    My bosom is pierced to the core—
Deny me not, love, your affection,
    And mine shall be yours evermore.
As I chose you from even the beginning,
    Look not on my love with disdain;
If you slight me as hardly worth winning,
    May maid ne'er again have a swain!

Oh, you who have robbed me of pleasure,
    Will *you*, with your mind and your charms,
Scorn one who has wit without measure,
    And take a mere dolt to your arms?
Your beauty, O damsel, believe me,
    Is not for a clown to adore—
Oh, if you desert or deceive me,
    May lover ne'er bow to you more!

Yours am I, my loveliest, wholly—
    Oh, heed not the blind and the base,
Who say that because of my folly
    I'll never have wealth, luck, or grace.

How much the poor creatures mistake me!
I'll yet have green acres and gold;
But oh, if you coldly forsake me,
I'll soon be laid under the mould!

      MANGAIRE SUGACH.

WHITE'S DAUGHTER OF THE DELL.

COME, let us trip away, love;
We must no longer stay, love;
Night soon will yield to day, love,
 We'll bid these haunts farewell.
We'll quit the fields, and rather
New life in cities gather;
And I'll outwit your father,
 The tall White of the Dell!

I am filled with melancholy
For all my bygone folly;
A wild blade and a jolly
 I was, as most can tell.
But woes now throng me thickly,
I droop, all faint and sickly;
I'll die, or win her quickly,
 White's Daughter of the Dell!

There's many a Kate and Sally
Who'd gladly stray and dally
Along with me in valley,
 Or glade, or mossy cell.
Oh, were we in Thurles together,
And each had quaffed a mether,*
We'd sleep as on soft heather,
 My Sweet One of the Dell!

  * *Anglice*, a wine cup.

You bright, you blooming Fair, you!
'Tis next my heart I wear you!
The wondrous love I bear you
    Has bound me like a spell!
Oh, both by land and ocean,
My soul is all commotion,
Yours is my deep devotion,
    Dear Damsel of the Dell!

Oh, were I seated near her,
Where summer woods might cheer her,
While clearer still, and clearer,
    The blackbird's notes would swell;
I'd sing her praise and glory,
And tell some fairy story
Of olden ages hoary,
    To White's Rose of the Dell!
            EOGHAN O'SULLIVAN.

MY CONNOR.

HIS eye is as black as the sloe,
    And his skin is as white as its blossom—
He loves me; but hate to the foe
    Has the innermost place in his bosom.
I forgive him, for sorrow unmixed,
    His child, like himself, should inherit,
If hatred to chains had not fixed
    The strong kernel-stone in his spirit.

The lark never soars but to sing—
    Nor sings but to soar; but my Connor
Surpasses the lark on the wing,
    Though walking the earth without honour!

The fetters—the fetters awake
  Deep passionate songs that betoken
The part and the place he will take,
  When bonds are held up to be broken.

He loves me more dearly than life,
  Yet would he forsake me to-morrow,
And lose both his blood and his wife,
  To free his loved island from sorrow;
And could I survive but to see
  The land without shackle upon her,
I freely a widow would be,
  Though dearly I doat on my Connor.

There is hope for the land where the ties
  'Twixt husband and wife have been reckoned
As virtue the first, in strange eyes,
  Yet are, in *their own*, but the second!
The sun never shines from the sky,
  If the country be long in dishonour—
With women, all braver than I—
  And men, all as brave as my Connor.

J. Fraser.

THE 'DARK GIRL' BY THE 'HOLY WELL.'

'Mother! is that the passing bell?
  Or yet the midnight chime?
Or, rush of angels' golden wings?
  Or is it near *the Time*—
The time when God, *they say*, comes down
  This weary world upon,
With Holy Mary at His right,
  And at His left St. John!

'I'm dumb! my heart forgets to throb;
  My blood forgets to run;
But vain my sighs—in vain I sob—
  God's will must still be done.
I hear but tone of warning bell,
  For holy priest or nun:
On earth, God's face I'll never see!
  Nor Mary, nor St. John!

' Mother! my hopes are gone again;
  My heart is black as ever.
Mother! I say, look forth *once more*,
  And see can you discover
God's glory in the crimson clouds—
  See does He ride upon
That perfumed breeze—or do you see
  The Virgin, or St. John?

Ah, no! ah, no! Well, God of Peace,
  Grant me Thy blessing still;
Oh, make me patient with my doom,
  And happy at Thy will;
And guide my footsteps so on earth,
  That, when I'm dead and gone,
My eyes may catch Thy shining light
  With Mary, and St. John!

' Yet, mother, could I see *thy* smile,
  Before we part below—
Or watch the silver moon or stars
  Where Slaney's ripples flow;
Oh, could I see the sweet sunshine
  My native hills upon,

I'd never love my God the less,
  Nor Mary, nor St. John!

'But no, ah no! it cannot be;
  Yet, mother, do not mourn—
Come, kneel again, and pray to God,
  In peace, let us return;
The Dark Girl's doom must aye be mine—
  But Heaven will light me on,
Until I find my way to God,
  And Mary, and St. John!'

JOHN KEEGAN.

THE LAST REPROACH.

THE charm, the gilded life is over,
  I live to feel I live in vain,
And worlds were worthless to recover
  That dazzling dream of mine again.
The idol I adored is broken,
  And I may weep its overthrow;
Thy lips at length my doom have spoken,
  And all that now remains is woe.

And is it thus indeed we sever,
  And hast thou then forgotten all;
And canst thou cast me off for ever,
  To mourn a dark and hopeless thrall?
Oh! perfidy, in friend or foe,
  In stranger, lover, husband, wife;
Thou art the blackest drop of woe
  That bubbles in the cup of life.

THE LAST REPROACH.

But most of all in woman's breast,
   Triumphant in thy blasting power,
Thou reignest, like a Demon-guest,
   Enthroned in some celestial bower.
Oh, cold and cruel she who, while
   She lavishes all wiles to win
Her lover o'er, can smile and smile,
   Yet be all dark and false within.

Who, when his glances on another
   Too idly, and too long have dwelt,
Will sigh, as if she sought to smother
   The grief her bosom never felt.
Who, versed in every witching art
   That e'er the warmest love would dare,
First having gained her victim's heart,
   Then turns him over to despair.

Alas! and can such treachery be?
   The worm that winds in slime along,
Is nobler, better far than she
   Who revels in such heartless wrong.
Go now, and triumph in thy guilt,
   And weave thy wanton spells anew;
Go, false as fair, and if thou wilt,
   Again betray the fond and true!

Yet this, my last and long farewell,
   Is less in anger than in sorrow;
Mine is the tale which myriads tell,
   Who loathe to-day, and dread to-morrow.
Me, Frances! me thou never knewest
   Nor sawest that, if my speech was cold,
The love is deepest oft and truest,
   That burns within the soul untold.

Farewell! in life's gay giddy whirl
    Soon wilt thou have forgotten me;
But where, oh, most dissembling girl,
    Where shall I from thine image flee?
Farewell! for thee the heavens are bright,
    And flowers along thy pathway lie;
The bolts that strike, the winds that blight,
    Will pass thy bower of beauty by.
But where shall I find rest? Alas!
    Soon as the winter winds shall rave
At midnight, through the long, dark grass,
    Above mine unremembered grave!

J. C. Mangan.

ELLEN BAWN.

Ellen Bawn, O Ellen Bawn, you darling, darling dear, you!
Sit awhile beside me here, I'll die unless I'm near you;
'Tis for you I'd swim the Suir, and breast the Shannon's waters;
For, Ellen dear, you've not your peer in Galway's blooming daughters!

Had I Limerick's gems and gold at will to mete and measure,
Were Loughria's abundance mine, and all Portumna's treasure,
These might lure me, might ensure me, many and many a new love,
But oh, no bribe could pay your tribe for one like you, my true love!

Blessings be on Connaught! that's the place for sport
   and raking!
Blessings too, my love, on you, a-sleeping and a-waking!
I'd have met you, dearest Ellen, when the sun went
   under,
But, woe! the flooding Shannon broke across my path
   in thunder!

Ellen! I'd give all the deer in Limerick's parks and
   arbours,
Ay, and all the ships that rode last year in Munster's
   harbours,
Could I blot from Time the hour I first became your
   lover,
For oh, you've given my heart a wound it never can
   recover!

Would to God that in the sod my corpse to-night were
   lying,
And the wild birds wheeling o'er it, and the winds a-
   sighing,
Since your cruel mother and your kindred choose to
   sever
Two hearts that Love would blend in one for ever and
   for ever!

J. C. MANGAN.
(From the Irish.)

LOVE BALLAD.

LONELY from my home I come,
   To cast myself upon your tomb,
      And to weep.
Lonely from my lonesome home,
   My lonesome house of grief and gloom,
      While I keep

Vigil often all night long,
   For your dear, dear sake,
Praying many a prayer so wrong
   That my heart would break!

Gladly, O my blighted flower,
   Sweet Apple of my bosom's Tree,
     Would I now
Stretch me in your dark death-bower
   Beside your corpse, and lovingly
     Kiss your brow.
But we'll meet ere many a day
   Never more to part,
For ev'n now I feel the clay
   Gathering round my heart.

In my soul doth darkness dwell,
   And through its dreary winding caves
     Ever flows,
Ever flows with moaning swell,
   One ebbless flood of many Waves,
     Which are Woes.
Death, love, has me in his lures,
   But that grieves not me,
So my ghost may meet with yours
   On yon moon-loved lea.

When the neighbours near my cot,
   Believe me sunk in slumber deep
     I arise—
For, oh! 'tis a weary lot
   This watching eye, and wooing sleep
     With hot eyes—

I arise, and seek your grave,
   And pour forth my tears;
While the winds that nightly rave,
   Whistle in mine ears.

Often turns my memory back
   To that dear evening in the dell,
      When we twain,
Sheltered by the sloe-bush black,
   Sat, laughed, and talked, while thick sleet fell,
      And cold rain.
Thanks to God! no guilty leaven
   Dashed our childish mirth:
You rejoice for this in heaven,
   I not less on earth!

Love, the priests feel wroth with me
   To find I shrine your image still
      In my breast.
Since you are gone eternally,
   And your fair fame lies in the chill
      Grave at rest;
But true love outlives the shroud,
   Knows nor check nor change,
And beyond Time's world of cloud
   Still must reign and range.

Well may now your kindred mourn
   The threats, the wiles, the cruel arts
      They long tried
On the child they left forlorn!
   They broke the tenderest heart of hearts,
      And she died.

Curse upon the love of show!
Curse on Pride and Greed!
They would wed you 'high'—and woe!
Here behold their meed!
J. C. MANGAN.
(*From the Irish.*)

GIVE ISAAC THE NYMPH WHO NO BEAUTY CAN BOAST.

GIVE Isaac the nymph who no beauty can boast,
But health and good-humour to make her his toast;
If straight, I don't mind whether slender or fat,
And six feet or four—we'll ne'er quarrel for that.

Whate'er her complexion, I vow I don't care;
If brown, it is lasting—more pleasing, if fair:
And though in her face I no dimples should see,
Let her smile—and each dell is a dimple to me.

Let her locks be the reddest that ever were seen,
And her eyes may be e'en any colour but green;
For in eyes, though so various the lustre and hue,
I swear I've no choice—only let her have two.

'Tis true I'd dispense with a throne on her back,
And white teeth, I own, are genteeler than black;
A little round chin too's a beauty, I've heard;
But I only desire she mayn't have a beard.
RICHARD BRINSLEY SHERIDAN.

OH, HAD MY LOVE NE'ER SMILED ON ME!

Oh, had my love ne'er smiled on me,
  I ne'er had known such anguish!
But think how false, how cruel she
  To bid me cease to languish;
To bid me hope her hand to gain,
  Breathe on a flame half perish'd;
And then with cold and fixed disdain
  To kill the hope she cherish'd.

Not worse his fate, who on a wreck,
  That drove as winds did blow it,
Silent had left the shatter'd deck,
  To find a grave below it.
Then land was cried—no more resign'd,
  He glow'd with joy to hear it;
Not worse his fate, his woe, to find
  The wreck must sink ere near it!

   RICHARD BRINSLEY SHERIDAN.

THOU CANST NOT BOAST OF FORTUNE'S STORE.

Thou canst not boast of Fortune's store,
  My love, while me they wealthy call:
But I was glad to find thee poor,
  For with my heart I'd give thee all.
    And then the grateful youth shall own
    I loved him for himself alone.

But when his worth my hand shall gain,
  No word or look of mine shall show
That I the smallest thought retain
  Of what my bounty did bestow:
    Yet still his grateful heart shall own
    I loved him for himself alone.
RICHARD BRINSLEY SHERIDAN.
(From 'The Duenna.')

AIR.

I NE'ER could lustre see
In eyes that would not look on me;
I ne'er saw nectar on a lip,
But where my own did hope to sip.
Has the maid who seeks my heart
Cheeks of rose, untouch'd by art?
I will own the colour true,
When yielding blushes aid their hue.

Is her hand so soft and pure?
I must press it, to be sure;
Nor can I be certain then,
Till it, grateful, press again.
Must I, with attentive eye,
Watch her heaving bosom sigh?
I will do so, when I see
That heaving bosom sigh for me.
RICHARD BRINSLEY SHERIDAN.
(From 'The Duenna.')

DRY BE THAT TEAR.

Dry be that tear, my gentlest love,
  Be hush'd that struggling sigh,
Nor seasons, day, nor fate shall prove
  More fix'd, more true than I.
Hush'd be that sigh, be dry that tear,
Cease boding doubt, cease anxious fear—
  Dry be that tear.

Ask'st thou how long my love will stay,
  When all that's new is past?
How long? ah, Delia, can I say
  How long my life will last?
Dry be that tear, be hush'd that sigh,
At least I'll love thee till I die—
  Hush'd be that sigh.

And does that thought affect thee too,
  The thought of Sylvio's death,
That he who only breath'd for you,
  Must yield that faithful breath?
Hush'd be that sigh, be dry that tear,
Nor let us lose our heaven here—
  Dry be that tear.
      RICHARD BRINSLEY SHERIDAN.

SOGGARTH AROON.

Am I a slave, they say,
  Soggarth Aroon?
Since you did show the way,
  Soggarth Aroon,
Their slave no more to be,
While they would work with me
Ould Ireland's slavery,
  Soggarth Aroon?

Why not her poorest man,
    Soggarth Aroon,
Try and do all he can,
    Soggarth Aroon,
Her commands to fulfil
Of his own heart and will,
Side by side with you still,
    Soggarth Aroon?

Loyal and brave to you,
    Soggarth Aroon,
Yet be no slave to you,
    Soggarth Aroon—
Nor, out of fear to you—
Stand up so near to you—
Och! out of fear to *you*:
    Soggarth Aroon!

Who, in the winter's night,
    Soggarth Aroon,
When the could blast did bite,
    Soggarth Aroon,
Came to my cabin-door,
And, on my earthen-flure,
Knelt by me, sick and poor,
    Soggarth Aroon?

Who, on the marriage-day,
    Soggarth Aroon,
Made the poor cabin gay,
    . Soggarth Aroon—
And did both laugh and sing
Making our hearts to ring,
At the poor christening,
    Soggarth Aroon?

Who, as friend only met,
    Soggarth Aroon,
Never did flout me yet,
    Soggarth Aroon?
And when my heart was dim,
Gave, while his eye did brim,
What I should give to him,
    Soggarth Aroon?

Och! you, and only you,
    Soggarth Aroon!
And for this I was true to you,
    Soggarth Aroon;
In love they'll never shake,
When for ould Ireland's sake,
We a true part did take,
    Soggarth Aroon!

JOHN BANIM.

THE RECONCILIATION.

THE old man he knelt at the altar,
    His enemy's hand to take,
And at first his weak voice did falter,
    And his feeble limbs did shake;
For his only brave boy, his glory,
    Had been stretched at the old man's feet,
A corpse, all so haggard and gory,
    By the hand which he now must greet.

And soon the old man stopt speaking,
    And rage, which had not gone by,
From under his brows, came breaking
    Up into his enemy's eye;

And now his limbs were not shaking,
  But his clench'd hands his bosom cross'd,
And he looked a fierce wish to be taking
  Revenge for the boy he had lost!

But the old man he looked around him,
  And thought of the place he was in,
And thought of the promise which bound him,
  And thought that revenge was sin—
And then, crying tears, like a woman,
  'Your hand!' he said—'ay, *that* hand!
And I do forgive you, foeman,
  For the sake of our bleeding land!'

JOHN BANIM.

AILLEEN.

'TIS not for love of gold I go,
  'Tis not for love of fame;
Though fortune should her smile bestow,
  And I may win a name,
          Ailleen,
  And I may win a name.

And yet it is for gold I go,
  And yet it is for fame,
That they may deck another brow,
  And bless another name,
          Ailleen,
  And bless another name.

AILLEEN.

For this, but this, I go—for this
  I lose thy love awhile;
And all the soft and quiet bliss
  Of thy young, faithful smile,
          Ailleen,
Of thy young, faithful smile.

And I go to brave a world I hate,
  And woo it o'er and o'er,
And tempt a wave, and try a fate
  Upon a stranger shore,
          Ailleen,
Upon a stranger shore.

Oh, when the bays are all my own,
  I know a heart will care!
Oh, when the gold is wooed and won,
  I know a brow shall wear,
          Ailleen,
I know a brow shall wear!

And when with both returned again,
  My native land to see,
I know a smile will meet me there,
  And a hand will welcome me,
          Ailleen,
And a hand will welcome me!

                JOHN BANIM.

INDEX.

Drinking Songs.

		PAGE
Come, send round the wine, and leave points of belief	*Moore*	131
Fill the bumper fair!	*Moore*	133
Had I the tun which Bacchus used	*Millikin*	125
Here's to the maiden of bashful fifteen	*Sheridan*	124
If Horatius Flaccus made jolly old Bacchus	*Maginn*	127
I filled to thee, to thee I drank	*Moore*	129
If sadly thinking, with spirits sinking	*Curran*	125
I sell the best brandy and sherry	*Magrath*	114
Maggy Laidir	*O'Neachtan*	115
October ale	*Concanen*	119
Oh! think not my spirits are always so light	*Moore*	130
Oh, the days when I was young	*Sheridan*	134
One bumper at parting! though many	*Moore*	131
O'Rourke's noble fare	*MacGauran*	110
Sweet Chloe advised me, in accents divine	*Lysaght*	123
When bickerings hot	*O'Hara*	123
When Fame brought the news of Great Britain's success	*Cunningham*	120
When once I to the tavern go	*Magrath*	113
When St. Patrick this order established	*Curran*	126
Why, liquor of life, do I love you so?	*Carolan*	117

INDEX.

PATRIOTIC SONGS.

		PAGE
Adieu !—The snowy sail	*Williams*	206
Am I remembered in Erin?	*M'Gee*	204
Arise ! my slumbering soul, arise !	*Mangan*	186
As vanquished Erin wept beside	*Moore*	214
Blithe the bright dawn found me	*Furlong*	165
Come, Kathleen, pure and soft as dew	*Williams*	227
Come, pledge again thy heart and hand	*Fraser*	198
Dear Erin, how sweetly thy green bosom rises !	*Curran*	162
Erin ! the tear and the smile in thine eyes	*Moore*	208
Far away from my friends	*Mangan*	173
Feagh M'Hugh of the mountain	*M Gee*	222
For the sake of the dear little Isle where I send you	*Keating*	138
God of this Irish Isle	*M'Gee*	215
How dimm'd is the glory that circled the Gael	*Callanan*	195
I'd rather be the bird that sings	*M'Gee*	224
I lay in unrest—old thoughts of pain	*MacDonnell*	154
In Ireland 'tis evening—from toil my friends hie all	*Orr*	164
In the time of my boyhood I had a strange feeling	*Griffin*	188
I rambled away, on a festival day	*Williams*	225
I walked entranced	*Mangan*	175
Let Erin remember the days of old	*Moore*	210
May God, in Whose hand	*Lysaght*	158
My spirit o'er an early tomb	*Fraser*	189
O Bay of Dublin ! my heart you're troublin'	*Lady Dufferin*	200
Oh, for the swords of former time !	*Moore*	213
Oh, my dark Rosaleen	*Mangan*	170
Oh, my land ! oh, my love !	*Mangan*	177
On Cleada's hill the moon is bright	*Callanan*	168
On the deck of Patrick Lynch's boat I sat in a woeful plight	*Fox*	185
O Patrick, my friend, have you heard the commotion	*Heffernan*	184
O say, my brown Drimin, thou silk of the kine	*Callanan*	194
O Spirit of Song, awake ! arise !	*O'Tuomy*	182

O sweet Adare! O lovely vale!	*Griffin* 197
O Woman of the Piercing Wail	*Ward* 141
Paler and thinner the morning moon grew	*M'Gee* 221
Rich and rare were the gems she wore	*Moore* 209
Take a blessing from my heart to the land of my birth	*MacCon-mara* 180
The brightest of the bright met me on my path so lonely	*Egan O'Reilly* 179
The evening star rose beauteous above the fading day	*Callanan* 192
The gen'rous sons of Erin, in manly virtue bold	*Lysaght* 160
The harp that once through Tara's halls	*Moore* 208
The minstrel boy to the war is gone	*Moore* 212
The night was falling dreary	*Griffin* 216
The savage loves his native shore	*Orr* 163
The tears are ever in my wasted eye	*MacDonnell* 148
There's a dear little plant that grows in our isle	*Cherry* 161
There is an empty seat by many a board	*M'Gee* 205
There is a green island in lone Gougane Barra	*Callanan* 191
There is not in the wide world a valley so sweet	*Moore* 209
Through Erin's Isle	*Moore* 211
Through the long drear night I lie awake, for the sorrows of Innisfail	*Keating* 136
Too long have the churls in dark bondage oppressed me	*Magrath* 157
Twice have I sailed the Atlantic o'er	*M'Gee* 215
Up the sea-sadden'd valley, at evening's decline	*Translated by De Vere* 203
What sorrow wrings my bleeding heart	*Nugent* 139
Who sitteth cold, a beggar old	*MacDonnell* 150
With deep affection	*'Father Prout'* 201

LOVE SONGS.

Ah me! and must I like the tenant lie	*Dermody* 252
Am I a slave, they say	*Banim* 325
And must we part? then fare thee well	*Callanan* 261
As beautiful Kitty one morning was tripping	*Lysaght* 255
A sage once to a maiden sung	*Kenney* 263
As through the woods Panthea stray'd	*Concanen* 242
As when the softly blushing rose	*Carolan* 239
Away, away—you're all the same	*Moore* 301
Believe me, if all those endearing young charms	*Moore* 304
By Cœlia's arbour, all the night	*Sheridan* 255

		PAGE
Come all you pale lovers that sigh and complain	*Duffet*	233
Come buy my nice fresh Ivy, and my Holly-sprigs so green	*Keegan*	276
Come hither, come hither—by night and by day	*Moore*	309
Come, let us trip away, love	*Eoghan O'Sullivan*	312
Come, Patrick, clear up the storms on your brow	*Mrs. Norton*	291
Come, piper, play the '*Shaskan Reel*'	*Keegan Casey*	299
Dry be that tear, my gentlest love	*Sheridan*	325
Ellen Bawn, O Ellen Bawn, you darling, darling dear, you!		
	Mangan	318
Fond Love with all his winning wiles	*Elizabeth Ryves*	247
From a Munster vale they brought her	*Williams*	292
Gille ma chree	*Griffin*	266
Give Isaac the nymph who no beauty can boast	*Sheridan*	322
Go where glory waits thee	*Moore*	303
Had I a heart for falsehood framed	*Sheridan*	256
Had you seen my sweet Coolin at the day's early dawn	*O'Dugan*	231
Have you been at Garnavilla?	*Lysaght*	253
He came from the North, and his words were few	*M'Gee*	289
Here in this fragrant bower I dwell	*Elizabeth Ryves*	248
Her sheep had in clusters crept close by the grove	*Cunningham*	246
His eye is as black as the sloe	*Fraser*	313
How sweet the answer Echo makes	*Moore*	308
I am a wand'ring minstrel man	*Walsh*	278
If I had thought thou could'st have died	*Wolfe*	256
If will had wings, how fast I'd flee	*M'Gee*	288
I love my love in the morning	*Griffin*	268
I love thee, by Heaven!—I cannot say more	*Concanen*	242
I'm sitting on the stile, Mary	*Lady Dufferin*	281
In holiday gown and my new-fangled hat	*Cunningham*	245
I ne'er could lustre see	*Sheridan*	324
In valleys lone I pluck'd the flowers	*Keegan Casey*	301
I was the boy for bewitching them	*Kenney*	263
I was working in the fields near fair Boston city	*Lady Dufferin*	284
I would not give my Irish wife	*M'Gee*	287
Lesbia hath a beaming eye	*Moore*	306
Lonely from my home I come	*Mangan*	319

		PAGE
'Mother, is that the passing bell?'	*Keegan*	314
My fairy girl, my darling girl	*Keegan Casey*	298
My fond social linnet, to thee	*Dermody*	251
My heart is far from Liffey's tide	*Walsh*	280
My Kathleen dearest! in truth or seeming	*Williams*	294
My life is like the summer rose	*R. H. Wilde*	265
My Mary of the curling hair	*Griffin*	270
None remember thee! thou whose heart	*Mrs. Norton*	290
O gentle, fair maiden, thou hast left me in sadness	*Carolan*	235
O God! it is a dreadful night—how fierce the dark winds blow!	*Keegan*	275
O! had my love ne'er smiled on me	*Sheridan*	323
Oh, dark—sweetest girl—are my days doomed to be	*Carolan*	234
Oh, flower of all maidens for beauty	*Mangaire Sugach*	310
Oh! love is the soul of a neat Irishman	*Lysaght*	254
Oh, Mary dear! bright peerless flower	*Furlong*	259
Oh that my love and I	*Furlong*	258
Oh, turn thee to me, my only love!	*Carolan*	236
Once I bloom'd a maiden young	*Walsh*	279
One winter's day, long, long ago	*Keegan*	272
O tender songs!	*Dermody*	249
Since Cœlia's my foe	*Duffet*	232
Sister of Charity, gentle and dutiful	*Williams*	296
Sleep, my child, for the rustling trees	*Callanan*	260
So, my Kathleen, you're going to leave me	*Lady Dufferin*	283
The charm, the gilded life is over	*Mangan*	316
The lass that would know how to manage a man	*Concanen*	241
The old man he knelt at the altar	*Banim*	327
The tie is broke, my Irish girl	*Griffin*	269
The time I've lost in wooing	*Moore*	307
The wreath you wove, the wreath you wove	*Moore*	301
Thou canst not boast of Fortune's store	*Sheridan*	323
Though love and each harmonious maid	*Elizabeth Ryves*	248
'Tis not for love of gold I go	*Banim*	328
'Tis sweet to think, that where'er we rove	*Moore*	305
Were mine the choice of intellectual fame	*Carolan*	237
When first, beloved, in vanished hours	*Mrs. Norton*	286
When I sat by my fair, and she tremblingly told	*Dermody*	250
'Why are you wandering here, I pray?'	*Kenney*	262

www.ingramcontent.com/pod-product-compliance
Lightning Source LLC
Chambersburg PA
CBHW030000240426
43672CB00007B/764